Politics, Fat-Cats & Honey-Money Boys

Press photograph taken during the 1940 campaign for governor.

Politics, Fat-Cats & Honey-Money Boys

The Mem-Wars of

JERRY SADLER

with James Neyland

ROUNDTABLE PUBLISHING, INC
SANTA MONICA / CALIFORNIA

ROUNDTABLE PUBLISHING, INC.
933 Pico Boulevard
Santa Monica, CA 90405

First Printing, 1984
Library of Congress Catalog Card Number—83-063199

Distributed by
HIPPOCRENE BOOKS
171 Madison Avenue
New York, NY 10016

PRINTED IN THE UNITED STATES OF AMERICA

To Laura Sadler
and to Bill and Sam

ACKNOWLEDGMENTS

I wish to express my gratitude to the following people for helping to make the completion of this work possible — to Ernest Jones, lifetime friend of Jerry's and newspaper columnist; to Bill and Sam Sadler for checking material for accuracy; to Jim Holman, editor-in-chief of the *Palestine Herald Press* for reading the manuscript and offering suggestions; to Larry Mayo, of the *Palestine Herald Press* for photo assistance; to Warren Bayless for editing the manuscript with such care; and to Mrs. Laura Sadler, without whom it could not have been completed at all.

CONTENTS

Part IV—SUPPLY LINES

LIST OF ILLUSTRATIONS

FOREWORD
by James Neyland

These memoirs are not being published as Jerry Sadler originally intended them to be. When they were begun, I was hired merely to assist him editorially, and I was to receive no writing credit. That was entirely acceptable to me, because Jerry had some incredible and outrageous things to say about history and about people in history. While he was willing, even eager, to stand behind his statements, I am not the kind of fighter he was. He wanted the truth, the whole truth, and nothing but the truth to be told.

Unfortunately, Jerry died in February of 1982, before the memoirs were completed. There was enough material available concerning the first half of his life to complete one volume of his story, with only a little more work. Jerry's family—Laura Sadler and Bill and Sam—and I agreed that it was important to bring this volume to publication.

However, we were faced with one serious problem—we could not substantiate everything Jerry had claimed as the truth. Jerry knew where all the skeletons were buried; we did not. For this reason, where we could not substantiate the facts given by Jerry, we have deleted anecdotes or names.

We do not feel the story has been harmed by these deletions. There are still numerous stories the reader will find fascinating, even incredible. His view of history, as he lived it, is far different from the usually published view, even in an edited version.

When I met Jerry Sadler in 1981, I confess that I doubted much of what he had to say. Not that I thought he was lying, but I considered it possible that age had taken its toll on his memory. I had been involved in publishing for a great many years, and had come across quite a few people who have sought to make startling revelations, many of them of dubious integrity. I began to check Jerry's stories, where possible, and then I would question him on various specific points.

I never found him to be in error. In the process, I learned a lot of history that was recorded in the newspapers, but never in history books.

If there are errors in the published book—and there may be a few—it is because Jerry was not alive at its completion to correct mistakes that I may have made in trying to fit his material together.

Jerry Sadler was a phenomenal man. He was difficult to work with; he was exasperating and infuriating at times; but despite it all, I liked him and admired him. I also think he liked me, though there were times he was just as furious with me as I was with him. It took me awhile to understand him, but I think I finally did achieve that. I say "achieve," because it is quite an accomplishment to understand Jerry. He did not go out of his way to explain himself or his actions, because he did not believe they needed explaining. I had the impression that this highly complex man had one very simple rule in his dealings with others—the Golden Rule: do unto others as you would have them do unto you. With anyone who broke that rule, he rightly assumed there were no rules at all, and he acted accordingly—an approach that would not occur to most people, but one that actually makes sense, if you think about it.

I hope that something of his special quality of character manages to come through in these pages. Jerry was special, a real, genuine Texas original, and as such, an American original. The world could use a few more like him.

I am grateful to have known Jerry Sadler, and I hope through his memoirs others may get to know him.

Politics, Fat-Cats & Honey-Money Boys

Introduction
Letter to Posterity

When my great-grandpa William Turner Sadler died in February of 1884, he left a letter instructing that "the world not be notified of my death, because there are too many people claiming credit for things they didn't do." It was a strange request, but it was honored by his family. The first the public knew of his passing came several months afterward when a reporter for the *Galveston News* learned of the event and printed the story.

As a child, I heard about this letter to posterity from my grandpa Nat Sadler, the oldest son of W.T. Sadler. I was puzzled over the reasons for such a request. I had studied history in school, including Texas history, and my teachers had taught it as absolute irrefutable fact. As a result, I was constantly asking Grandpa to tell me about his father, and I tried to understand why he wanted to die in such privacy.

The facts I gleaned about Captain W.T. Sadler indicated that he was a man of some importance in Texas history. He was a close associate of others whose names are better known today—Sam Houston, Mirabeau Lamar, Thomas Rusk, and John H. Reagan, to name only a few—yet his name appears in very few history books. He first came to Texas as a young man in the 1820s, then returned to his home in Putman County, Georgia, to make a deal with his father concerning slaves, before moving permanently to Texas. On his return trip, he rode in company with Mirabeau Lamar, who remained his friend for years afterward. William Turner Sadler fought at the Battle of San Jacinto, and later in the Indian wars in Texas, including the Battle of Kickapoo. His first wife and child were killed in the Edens-Madden Massacre, and in a letter to Lamar concerning this tragic event (now in the Texas State Archives) he reported:

> Sir many have been the visisitudes through which
> I have pas'd since I saw you not having saw you
> since soon after the battle of San Jacinto. I

1

> returned to this neighborhood and commenced
> farming and married in March following and was
> doing well until the 18th of October last at which
> time my wife was murdered by the Indians being
> at the time in the army myself in the command of
> Major E. Clapp having left my companion in the
> care of her father. . . .

He lost his second wife and one of their nine children in 1866, when a tornado destroyed the second floor of his two-story log plantation home in Anderson County, Texas.

In 1844 and 1845, he served in the legislature of the Republic of Texas, and with Daniel Parker introduced the bill that created Anderson County from part of Houston County. After Texas joined the United States, he served in the state legislature from 1846 to 1848. In 1849, he joined the Gold Rush to California, but returned to Texas in 1851 with only a small buckskin poke containing a few ounces of gold dust, not much for two years effort.

According to the *Biographical Directory of the Texan Conventions and Congresses, 1832-1845:*

> Returning to Texas, he resumed his occupation of
> farming, lived quietly, and deprecated all
> attempts to honor him for his military service
> under the Republic, protesting that he had done
> only what was his duty.

Grandpa filled me in on some of the unwritten history of his father. My favorite of all his stories was one in which he recounted his own memories of accompanying W.T. Sadler on a visit to Huntsville to see the aged and ailing Sam Houston. Grandpa was 14 years old at the time, and the reason for the visit was W.T. Sadler's imminent departure as a soldier in the Civil War.

Sam Houston was 68 years old, and he had depleted his energy stumping the state, attempting to persuade the people not to let Texas secede from the Union. He was too weak to get out of bed, and so he received great-grandpa Sadler and his son at his bedside.

As grandpa recalled the scene, it was a dramatic one. The two men were almost the same age, Houston being only four years older than W.T. Sadler, yet the great leader of Texas was a broken and defeated old man while great-grandpa remained strong and vigorous.

Grandpa expected a show of warmth and sympathy from his father, yet his manner toward the pale, white-haired figure was stern, even harsh. And he did most of the talking.

"I'm going off to war," W.T. Sadler told him. "And I wanted to say goodbye, because by the time I get back you'll be dead."

There seemed to be a glimmer of defiance from Houston's eyes, but his voice was frail and hoarse as he challenged, "You're sure of that, are you?"

W.T. Sadler nodded. "I've disagreed with you a great many times over the years," he continued. "I disagreed with you at San Jacinto when you were drunk, sitting under a tree and got hit in a foot with a ball. I never said anything when other people wanted to make you a hero by claiming you were riding in command of the troops. You had your reasons, and they had theirs. I just want you to know that I don't intend to contradict that when you're gone, because—despite our differences—there's one thing I can say for you: you do love Texas. You love Texas because it's the last place on earth that will let you be."

Houston's jaws stiffened with anger. "You go ahead and go to the war, Sadler," he said, his voice suddenly strong and firm. "I'll be here when you get back. I've just got a touch of the cold. I'll be back in the campaign in '63."

"No," great-grandpa shook his head. "You couldn't stand to be rejected again. Texas is too important to you. You're going to be gone; and as you go, I'd be willing to bet the last word on your lips will be 'Texas.'"

As it turned out, great-grandpa was wrong. "Texas" was the next to the last word. The last word was the name of Houston's other great love, "Margaret."

It astonished me that W.T. Sadler's version of the battle of San Jacinto differed so drastically from the history books, but grandpa told me other things that didn't match the record, as well. According to the history books, John H. Reagan was responsible for the victory at the Battle of Kickapoo and for the surrender of Chief Bowles, but according to W.T. Sadler, John H. Reagan was at Ft. Houston the entire time. Sam Houston has been praised for the decision to keep the public lands of Texas within the power of the state in return for the state paying its own debt when entering the Union; in fact, it was W.T. Sadler who proposed the idea to Houston.

As a child, it bothered me a great deal that there was this extreme variance. It seemed impossible that the written history could be wrong, yet I did not want to believe that my great-grandpa or my grandpa would lie.

Now, after a lifetime devoted to public service, I feel I understand, not only how and why the recorded history can be inaccurate, but why W.T. Sadler would leave such a curious request.

It has taken a great many years of deliberation to decide to recount my involvement with history. I do not wish to leave a letter to posterity as enigmatic as W.T. Sadler's, nor do I want to alter or disguise the truth. There is much that has not been told, and may never be told unless I tell it. Certainly my dedication to the Jacksonian principles of democracy and respect for the plain people encourages me to believe the public has a right to know the whole truth.

However, since sitting down to write, I have realized that it is virtually impossible to tell the whole truth. Much of what I have experienced is so incredible that it would have to be substantiated in order to be believed. Other things might needlessly hurt innocent people or not-so-innocent people who can no longer fight back. And finally, to tell the whole truth would take too long, and few readers would be able to endure the reading.

Therefore I have chosen to publish only selections from my memoirs, which I call "mem-wars" for reasons that will become obvious to readers. And I have decided to publish the first half of the story, now, covering the years 1908 to 1945. However, I have also decided not to conceal anything I consider to be of great importance.

If what I have to say causes dispute or controversy, then so be it. I was never one to run from a fight.

Part I
BLOOD LINES

The Sadler Home at Hickory Grove, in southeast Anderson County, Texas.

Jerry Sadler, age 13, outside the Hickory Grove School.

The two-room Hickory Grove School.

1

Beginnings

My life, as I remember it, did not begin until July 13, 1910, a date that is still known among the black population of Anderson County, Texas, as "Bad Saturday." My earliest memories are of that Saturday evening. They are impressed indelibly upon my mind's eye, though 71 years have passed.

They are memories that have shaped my entire life.

Of course, not quite three years old at the time—I was born on September 8, 1907—I did not fully understand all of what was happening, but I recognized fear in the faces of the black people who came to see my father that night. I heard the terror in their excited but hushed voices as they told him what was happening. The image that stands out most clearly in my mind is of bare black feet, scratched and cut, below trousers and skirts that were torn and soiled from their fourteen-mile flight across fields and through woods to seek papa's help.

I think, in my childlike way, I perceived from that moment I would devote my life doing what I could to help the good, ordinary, but powerless people of this world.

The details of that Bad Saturday Massacre were filled in for me in later years. Whatever I did not hear from papa or my brothers, I learned from Deaf-and-Dumb Gus, who was there that night and who lost two members of his family in the massacre. He told me the story many times, in the sign language with which we communicated. His two fists would fling out at me in unison four times, conveying that there were forty white men who had come riding that night into the southeast Anderson County river-bottom farmland occupied by the negroes. Then he would pause and extend two fingers, indicating that there were two men who stood up to them and turned them back.

Forty white men from prominent and powerful families murdered ten black men, women, and children in cold blood, and would have murdered more if papa had not come to their defense. Years afterward, the whites proudly claimed three times the number of victims, but the record shows ten: two members of the Sam Baker family, two from the Ed Barnett family, one in the Jim Wilson family, Clem and Ned Larkin, Dick Wilson, and a woman named Rae with her infant child.

There are all kinds of stories of why and how the trouble started. The truth is simply that the whites wanted the land that the blacks owned, and they had decided finally that there was only one way to get it.

The blacks had some of the most desirable farmland in the county, and for that my great-grandpa W.T. Sadler can be blamed. When the Civil War freed his slaves, he gave them some of the best land he owned, and he did everything he could to help the other freed slaves of the area to obtain good land.

This may seem odd considering W.T. Sadler favored secession and fought in the Civil War, but the Civil War was not fought entirely over the issue of slavery, and he was a man who believed in the law. When the South lost, he abided by the defeat, unlike many of his neighbors. The negroes weren't just slaves to him, but people who were part of his extended family, suddenly broken free from home. With little education or training for independence and responsibility, they faced more than enough difficulty surviving without the added burden of trying to make a living farming rocky, lifeless soil. Which was what the blacks in other parts of the county had been given.

For generations, the white Sadlers continued to be friendly toward the black Sadlers and the other black families of the area. Whenever the negro families needed help or protection, they came to my grandpa Nat Sadler or to my papa Claude Sadler.

So when the shooting started on that second Saturday of July in 1910, the blacks knew there was one white man they could trust, my papa.

We lived at Grapeland, in Houston County, at the time, because papa was working at Kennedy's General Merchandise Store, and that was a long way for Deaf-and-Dumb Gus and the other members of the Ed Barnett family to run, but it appeared to be their only means of survival. The whites were hunting down and shooting any black person they could find. (Dick Wilson was shot while sitting on his front porch reading his Bible.)

Papa told Robert, my oldest brother, to see that the Barnetts were fed and given clean clothes and hidden in the hayloft of the barn. Then he hitched two horses to a double buggy, and enlisting the aid of Bob Scarborough who worked with him at Kennedy's, he rode to the store to get guns and ammunition. When they rode to the Neches River bottomland, the two white men took Deaf-and-Dumb Gus with them. Gus had the reputation as the best shot in Anderson County, and the whites had a healthy respect for that reputation. Gus worked hard, hiring himself out to the white farmers. When he wasn't working he wandered the woods with his double-barreled shotgun. He was known rarely to waste a shot.

The three men arrived at the farms of the Sadlers and Roaches 45 minutes ahead of the band of marauders. Papa armed the black men and instructed them to wait in the Sadlers' log farmhouse. He gave Deaf-and-Dumb Gus plenty of ammunition for his double-barreled shotgun and set him in the smokehouse. Then he and Bob Scarborough waited outside in the buggy.

When the marauders arrived, it was two men against forty. Papa gave them warning. "All the negroes here are armed with guns and ammunition," he informed the band. "They're waiting for you in the house. And over in the smokehouse, Deaf-and-Dumb Gus has enough shots to get every one of you if you try anything. So I suggest you turn around and go back to your homes."

That was the end of the massacre, but not the end of papa's trouble with what became, about two years later, a reorganized Ku Klux Klan. The white marauders did not go entirely unpunished. The state authorities came in to enforce the law. A number of the men who participated in the massacre fled the country to escape conviction. Two men were tried and convicted, but a record of their conviction no longer exists. Shortly after the trials, the Anderson County courthouse was burned by an arsonist, and the records were destroyed.

If the experience taught the white leaders anything, it was to be wary of papa and to tread carefully over matters of law. A few years after things had cooled off, one of the leaders of the massacre tried to use the law itself to take the black Sadlers' land from them. Again, Papa came to their aid and hired lawyers who took the case all the way to the state supreme court, which upheld the negroes' right to the land.

By this time, the Klan was an organized movement, hiding behind bedsheets on their night rides. They could not hide their identities from the negroes or from us, because we could always recognize the shoes, but most of the time they succeeded in hiding from the law. Because they couldn't be prosecuted for making threats or issuing warnings, they didn't hesitate to appear in the daytime without their covering. That was the case in 1925 when six prominent men rode up to our house in a shiney new car to warn Papa. "There might be some trouble if you have any niggers living on the place."

One would have thought that these men would've learned eventually that their threats succeeded only in stirring up papa's hot temper, but they never seemed to learn. After I was grown and out on my own, I was called home time after time to help defend the homestead because the Klan was stirring up trouble—as there was more often than not—our family stuck together.

I was the youngest of the five children born to Claude and Maybelle Anthony Sadler. Robert, the oldest child, was nine years my senior, and Loreta—the only girl, whom we called "Sister"—was three years younger than Robert. R.C., whose full name was Roy Claude, was four years older than I was and Nat was two years and seven months older. I was born Gerald Anthony Sadler, but was always called Jerry.

Until I was eight years old, the family moved about a great deal. When I was born, papa was a salesman for Singer sewing machines, and the family was living in Kirbyville, Texas, in Jasper County. Papa's relationship with "John Barleycorn" was a close one, but volatile. After he had imbibed a few drinks, one never knew what to expect from him. Six months after I was born, he accepted a dare from a drinking companion and rode his horse through Dr. Beene's drugstore. He won his ten-dollar wager, but the family found it necessary to move from Kirbyville to San Augustine, Texas. We remained in San Augustine less than a year before the move to Grapeland.

Mama's family lived at Grapeland; her father, S.T. Anthony, had a produce business there. His store was a good-sized one, but his big business was the shipping of eggs and chickens. An article in the Grapeland *Messenger* once added up the volume of shipping he had done that year and concluded that it amounted to an entire trainload.

In Grapeland, Papa went to work at the Kennedy Brothers store, and he kept a small farm south of town. We lasted a full two-and-a-half years in Grapeland before we again moved. I think mama hoped we would be able to settle down at last where we would be close to her family and to papa's, but this was not to be the case. Mama couldn't have changed papa's belief in justice, even if she had wanted to, and it was papa's defense of the downtrodden as much as it was "John Barleycorn" that made our moves inevitable.

Meanwhile I was developing my own sense of justice and learning how to deal with bullies. Aside from Bad Saturday, my earliest memories were of being teased by my older brothers. In those days, little boys wore dresses until they were five or six years old, and I was no exception. They teased me mercilessly about my dress. When teasing grew into a threat, I had to fight back.

The International and Great Northern Railroad passed through Grapeland. Most of the time trains moved at full speed when passing our house. "One of these days," my brothers threatened, "we're going to throw you under the train. If you're run over by a train, nobody will know if you're a boy or a girl." They would grab me and force me up close to the tracks, where the sound of the wheels was deafening.

I grew terrified of the sound of an approaching train, and I would run and hide under a bed so that my brothers couldn't find me. When I was about five years old, I decided I had to do something about the situation. I had a friend who lived about 200 yards down the track from us. His father was a section foreman for the railroad. He had a supply of the torpedoes which, placed under the rails, warned trains of danger. When a torpedo exploded, the trains slowed or stopped.

My friend and I swiped some of his father's torpedoes, and we put them under the rails. Mischievously stopping a train was a serious matter. My friend and I told our parents that my brothers had played the prank, and they were severely punished.

After that, Robert, R.C., and Nat came to me, offering a deal. They would agree never to throw me under a train if my friend and I would confess to the mischief. I considered that a fair deal, and we confessed.

My fear of trains didn't stop immediately, however. Finally I faced the fear by forcing myself to stand on the front porch to watch a train pass. It was an important moment for a five-year-old. Afterwards I was never again afraid of anything.

The teasing from my brothers never stopped entirely, and it caused me one other serious difficulty about this time. I don't recall why they were after me on this particular occasion, but I fought back, and they began chasing me. During the chase, I ran into a barbed-wire fence, which cut deeply into my throat. The severe pain and the large amount of blood put me into a state of shock.

I thought I was dying, and I got up and rushed into the house to hide under my bed where I could die without my brothers watching. I probably would have bled to death if mother hadn't followed my trail and found me in my hiding place. She coaxed me out and got me to a doctor.

Needless to say, I survived, but I did so with only one vocal cord. It requires two vocal cords to speak, and I had to learn to talk all over again, using my throat and my one remaining vocal cord. In normal speech, I managed all right: I simply had a gravelly voice. It was later on, when I entered politics, that I would have some problems. Speaking before large crowds, I had to increase the volume, and that caused my one vocal cord to vibrate twice as fast as it normally would, with the result that my voice would rise six tones higher.

At times, people in the crown would have considerable difficulty understanding me, and I had to be careful to keep that from happening.

Shortly after this, papa decided to move again; this time the move was linked to his decision to break off his relationship with drink. The Kennedy Brothers store was having a big celebration in Grapeland, complete with food and drink. Early in the celebration, in back of the store, papa and another man got into a fight. The ruckus went on all morning, ending when the man got papa's thumb in his mouth. To save his hand, papa got the man's ear in his mouth. The harder one man bit down, the harder the other did the same. Papa saved his hand. The other man lost his ear.

The guilt of what he had done sobered papa. He rode home and called out to me. When I heard him calling, I went onto the back porch. He didn't say a word to me, but he picked me up and put me on the horse with him, and, in silence, we rode all over the farm. When we finally returned, papa announced to mama that he was selling the farm and we would move to Mineral Wells, Texas.

We lived in the Sturdevant community outside Mineral Wells, and during the entire year or more which followed, papa didn't touch alcohol. He drank only Mineral Crazy Crystals, the local mineral water. Before drinking it, he heated it on the stove, and I had my own little pot in which I heated tap water and pretended I'd be drinking the same thing he was. During this time we were close, and I began to pick up some of papa's characteristics. One Sunday, Sturdevant Church had an all-day service, and some older boys pitted me in a fight against a boy my own age. We fought all morning and most of the afternoon. By the time my parents, who had attended the day-long services, came to collect me, most of my clothes had been torn from my back.

In 1915, we moved back to Grapeland. There, papa went into the cash grocery business in partnership with Dave Warren. The Kennedys and Darseys sold their groceries on credit, which meant charging higher prices. Selling goods for cash, papa and Mr. Warren kept their prices low, and business was good.

That year I was seven, then the age for children to begin school. My first day in Grapeland school I was given a whipping for creating a disturbance. When the teacher handed out the Baby Playmate Primers, I announced I had already read it. I was simply telling the truth. Papa had a strict rule about the children doing their lessons before going to bed every night, and I had voluntarily joined my older brothers and sister as they learned to read and write.

The whipping set the pattern of my relationship with my teacher. I averaged three whippings a day; my rear grew so tough that, after awhile, the big wide paddle did nothing more than tickle. Once she had me over her lap paddling me, and I bit her leg. She forced me to sit on the floor beneath her desk, so if I misbehaved, all she had to do was kick me. In the front of the desk, there was a small six-inch space from the bottom of the panel to the floor. It was boring sitting in the confined space with only her legs to look at, but I noticed that she wore low-quarter shoes. I decided to create a bit of fun. Removing one shoe, I tossed it through the space into the middle of the classroom.

That was the last straw, so the teacher took me to the principal and demanded I be expelled from school. The teacher felt I deserved to be sent to a juvenile home, but the principal at Grapeland was a wise man. In the conference called with my father, he pointed out that I had "A's" in all subjects except deportment, and perhaps a better solution might be to promote me to the second grade.

However, it took another promotion—to the third grade—before my deportment improved. Miss Blanche Kennedy taught third and fourth grades; I thought she was the greatest woman in the world. My first day in her class, she seated me at a front desk. While conducting the lessons, she would sit on my desk, occasionally patting me affectionately on the head. Two to three years younger than other students of her class and still making straight "A's," I was treated as special.

When, in the middle of the term, some more students enrolled in school, she ran out of desks in her room. She assigned me her desk and chair in the front of the room.

We were still living in Grapeland when grandpa N.F. Sadler came to live with us. Grandpa, who was always referred to as "Uncle Fletch," loved to argue politics, and although he was an old man, he was still active in the Democratic Party. That year, he was a delegate to the party convention in Galveston. Joseph Weldon Bailey, the elder statesman of Texas politics, came for a visit; our back porch rang with debate. Bailey was noted as a constitutional lawyer, but he was most famous as an opponent to causes ranging from World War I to Women's Suffrage to the Ku Klux Klan. He had resigned from the U.S. Senate in 1913 in protest against the election of Woodrow Wilson.

I can remember grandpa sitting on the back porch with his shoes off, leaning back in his chair, and pointing to a hound dog sleeping in the sun. "You see that old dog out there?" he asked Joe Bailey. "You're just like he is. I think I'm going to name him Joe Bailey."

"Are you trying to say that I'm a son-of-a-bitch?" Joe Bailey asked good-naturedly.

Grandpa grinned, "I'm mighty close to it," he replied.

In truth the two men liked each other, and their bickering was all in fun, but on the special train that had been arranged to take the convention delegates to Galveston, grandpa got into a real fight, and he didn't come out of it with flying colors. He had grown too old for brawling.

That was when papa decided to sell out his interest in the cash grocery business in Grapeland and buy out the other heirs to the Sadler homeplace. In the Anderson County house that had been Grandpa Sadler's home, papa and mama would take care of him until he died. Papa paid $500 down, and the remainder had to be paid off from what he made from farming.

We moved into the homeplace on March 6, 1916, and the following day, I began school at Hickory Grove.

Country boys rarely got into town in those days, and—since I had moved from town—I was naturally looked on with suspicion by my new classmates. And the fact that I was seven years old and already in the third grade made me seem even more strange to them. That morning at recess, a group of boys gathered around me, asking if I knew how to fight.

"Yeah," I told them.

Then they wanted to know if I could wrestle.

"Yeah," I said. "I can wrestle."

They picked out the champion wrestler of my age group, and we spent the recess period wrestling. It was all dog-falls; neither of us won. After that though, I was one of the crowd.

Just as quickly I became a farm boy. We all had to work hard to make the money for papa to pay off the land. There were few luxuries for us, but there was hardly time for us to think of what we were missing. We were lucky if we got into town twice a year.

Papa was always very strict about our attending school and doing lessons, but that was where his involvement in our formal education stopped. He left everything to mama and the school. Whenever we were in the fields, however, he taught us farming. His one lesson was: "Do this right or you'll grow up to be a ditch-digger." That was to be the only incentive and motivation as far as he was concerned.

Papa awakened every morning at four o'clock; and during crop time, that was when he got us up. He had stomach ulcers and couldn't do much of the actual work, so he served as overseer, instructing his sons in the plowing, planting, and harvesting. We would go out into the fields before daylight, and wait in the creek bottom for the sunrise, then go to work. Mama would cook red beans and cornbread and bring them down to us. At noonday, we sat beside the spring to eat our rude country meal.

We could hear mama coming because she would be singing. She was always cheerful, even though her life of constant work must have been difficult for her. It used to worry me that she never got a full eight hours sleep at night; we had been taught at school that people needed eight hours. Mornings, she was up before four o'clock, and she was never able to get to bed until well after eight at night.

Mama was a religious woman, a saintly woman. It was she who instilled me with ambition to make something of my life, and to seek to do good for others, not just to advance myself. She encouraged me to read and to learn everything I could. We had a set of Harvard Classics, and in what spare time I had, I read through all of them. I also read the Horatio Alger stories in the *Youth Companion,* which Mama subscribed to. Papa got the Houston *Chronicle* and *Farm and Ranch,* and I devoured them, as well.

I was particularly interested in one column in *Farm and Ranch—* Aunt Sally's. It was a column in which Sally Buchanan answered letters from kids. I wrote numerous letters, and never got a reply. Mostly my questions were about Texas history and great-grandpa W.T Sadler. The days that *Farm and Ranch* arrived, I would rush to it, turn to Aunt Sally's column, and face my disappointment.

In my work, I took my cue from mama. She never complained about all she had to do, so I dutifully did everything I was asked to do. Plowing was hard work. We didn't have a riding plow, but one pulled by two mules. Some of the bottomland was so heavy that we'd have to put four mules to a middle buster, or breaking plow, to turn the earth. I did my work dutifully, but I did not like it, and I longed to get away from the drudgery and the beans and cornbread. At every opportunity I daydreamed about the things I wanted to do.

Some of the blacks who worked for us helped me in my dreaming. Deaf-and-Dumb Gus was my constant companion, and he told me wonderful stories of Texas history, sitting on a tree-stump with his double-barreled shotgun across his knees, his nimble hands more expressive than any voice could be. And there was Sherm Sadler, one of the blacks who bore our name. His ability to memorize was uncanny; the only man I ever knew who had completely memorized the entire Bible from beginning to end.

Sherm enjoyed going to the Cherokee County courthouse at Rusk to listen to the trials. Memorizing every word that was spoken, he would return and recount the entire proceedings. When the blacks came to chop and hoe cotton, we all knew the time papa would arrive to check up on us; his routine was as regular as clockwork. Sherm and I would reenact the latest court trial from Rusk, getting some of the other hands to play the part of judge and jury.

He gave me the part of a lawyer, instilling the ambition for a legal career from the time I was nine years old. The leading law firm at Rusk at the time was Shook and Norman. Sherm would coach me on what Mr. Shook or Mr. Norman had said or done in court, explaining the reasons, and I would imitate them to the best of my ability, before a jury of field hands.

If ever anyone longed to be a lawyer, I did. There was one big hill on the farm, and standing on it at night, it was possible to see lights far away; lights that were coming from the town of Rusk. There was one light that stood out from all the rest, and I was told that it was on the courthouse. I would stand on that hilltop and gaze at that light, the darkness surrounding me, and I would hope, dream, and pray. "If I can only get to Rusk," my heart would say silently, "I know I can do great and wonderful things." But then, in the light of day, kneeling over the cotton rows, with the hot July sun beating down on my head, it would seem painfully impossible, only a dream. The only reality were my sore knees, my hands chafed and calloused.

Then one day I found a book at school, a book that contained words that were magical. They were from a speech President Wilson had made at the birthplace of Abraham Lincoln, and those words encouraged me to believe that my dreams were possible. I memorized those words, and I have never forgotten them:

> Nature pays no tribute to name or aristocracy, subscribes to no creed or caste, renders fealty to no monarch or master of any kind. There is nowhere in the land any home so remote, so humble, that it may not contain the power of mind, heart, and conscience to which nations yield and history submits its process.

Those words became my Bible, the essence of my faith and confidence in myself, the constant companion of my soul, and the nurture of my yearning. I knew that I was yet a child, that it would be long years before I could begin to do the things I wanted to do. But I was impatient. I endured every day in anticipation of the moment when I would suddenly, magically be a man, able to set off on the adventure of accomplishment.

2

Leaving Home

I doubt anyone respected my father more than I did, although we did have our differences; and they grew as I grew older. In many ways we were alike—strong-willed, determined, and idealistic—and it may have been our similarities that led to our differences. We were probably both too bull-headed and obstinate to live in the same household.

If I were to characterize papa, I think I would say that he was a great man, born into the wrong time and place. He was a man of conscience and justice, who had difficulty dealing with the loneliness of his rectitude. His only flaw was that the only companion in whom he could confide the frustrations of his soul was "John Barleycorn." And with the return to Anderson County, there were considerable frustrations. The Ku Klux Klan was in full operation at this time, and its members had not forgotten papa's sympathies.

If it is difficult to characterize papa with justice, it is impossible to convey in words mama's goodness. She was a saint, all love and understanding and encouragement with patience and endurance beyond simple human understanding. She seemed to have a unity with the earth and with God Himself, an acceptance of life that nourished faith.

I must have been a tribulation to both of them. Bright children are not easy children to rear, and I was too bright for my own good. I was restless to learn everything there was to know, and anxious to grow up and do everything there was to do in a world of limitless possibilities. As a result, most of the trouble my parents had to endure took place at school.

This was complicated even further by the fact that my teacher for my second year at Hickory Grove school was my oldest brother Robert. He was teaching the fourth, fifth, and sixth grades in one room, and he used me to maintain his discipline over the class. By showing the others what he would do to his own brother, he tried to intimidate them. His favorite trick was to walk by my desk and twist my ear painfully, whether I was misbehaving or not.

This procedure succeeded in outraging my sense of justice, and it prompted me to find sneaky ways of giving him trouble, disrupting the classroom. Robert met with papa to complain, and papa punished me. But I simply became more sneaky in my methods of getting even, transferring my efforts from school to home.

Papa had to have ten or twelve cords of wood to burn in the big fireplace, and it was my chore every afternoon after school to saw wood with Robert, using a crosscut saw. I pulled one end of the saw, and Robert pulled the other. When he pulled, I would ride my end of the saw, making him work harder. It took him awhile to realize why it was so difficult. When he did, we discussed the situation and worked out a compromise. I agreed to stop making trouble for him if he would stop using me as his example in class.

My next two years, I had teachers who took a special interest in me, though Mr. Jess Bishop, my fifth grade teacher, wasn't much on discipline. My sixth grade teacher was Mrs. Ernest Day, the wife of the principal, and she would brook no nonsense from me. Until 3:30 in the afternoon, she would give me the dickens, forcing me to sit up and pay attention, no matter how bored I was with going over things I already knew. At 3:30, with half an hour before school's dismissal, she devoted time to what today would be called "show and tell." She asked students to volunteer to tell a story or to stand before the class and talk about things they had done or to speak of particular interests. It was her way of teaching public speaking.

There were never any other volunteers to speak, so that last half-hour of class became my time. I didn't volunteer, but waited until Mrs. Day had called on everyone else in the room. Finally, when she would say, "All right, Jerry, you may come up and talk," I would give the discourse I had prepared the night before.

Usually I picked something from the Harvard Classics, which I read at home. My classmates loved fairy tales, so most of my talks came from Greek mythology or Plutarch's lives. Those half-hour sessions became my grounding in public speaking. With the help of Mrs. Day, I began to learn when I was holding the attention of my audience and when I was not, and I learned why.

Those half-hours were worth the boredom of sitting patiently through the rest of the hours of class, but they did not entirely curb my restlessness to move forward. I was exempt from final examinations in her class because I had all "A's," so I asked for permission to take the exams of the eighth, ninth, and tenth graders. My brother Nat was in the eighth grade, and I had been reading his books along with my own. Mrs. Day's husband taught Nat's class, and he agreed to grant my favor.

I took the eighth grade exam and not only passed it but made the top grade. Nevertheless, Mr. Ernest Day would not allow me to skip any more grades. After all, he explained, I was only ten years old.

I had two reasons for wanting to be in Mr. Day's class. For one thing, it would mean that my public schooling was nearing an end, and I would move on. The other was a child's reason and may seem foolish—I wanted to occupy the classroom seat that had been occupied by my friend Ernest Jones. Ernest, known affectionately as "Bones Jones" (because he was so thin), had been the companion of my soul and my idol when I had first started school at Hickory Grove.

Ernest was considerably older than I was; he was in his last years of school when I was in my first years at Hickory Grove. We were both dreamers, and we became friends, distinguished from the crowd because we were the only two boys in school who wore ties. (We wore overalls, just as the other boys did, but we were considered "dressed up" because of those neckties.) I admired Ernest because he was smart, and because he had a great ambition in life—to be a writer.

When I finally got to that classroom, I claimed possession of Ernest's seat, in the back southeast corner of the room, and I held it until I left that school in the tenth grade. But, by the time I reached the eighth grade, Mr. Ernest Day was no longer the teacher and principal. There was a new man who taught in order to save money to complete his college at Texas A & M. With him my school troubles came to a head.

I didn't realize until I was in his class that politics entered into education. But it was impossible not to notice that he gave preferential treatment to the children of the prominent and powerful families in the community, and that he attempted to squelch the children whose families were poor or unpopular. Because of papa's democratic beliefs, I was on my teacher's blacklist, a position that was intolerable for me.

During that year I first attempted to run away from home.

I was not so brave that I made the attempt alone. My friend, Neal House, felt the same way I did about the situation, and we made our plans together.

When the bell rang one morning, calling the students inside, he and I were down at the edge of the woods. While the others were going inside, we slipped into the woods. We ran all the way to Grapeland, a distance of about fourteen miles. Our object was to catch a train there; it didn't matter to us whether it would be going north or south. We had forty dollars, which I had obtained the night before. I had a bank account in Grapeland containing $65, and I had written a check to my brother R.C. to cover the forty dollars I slipped from his wallet—which he kept in a pair of britches hanging in the wardrobe of the room we shared. It was easy to do, and I didn't think the exchange would be discovered immediately.

Neal and I stayed away from the roads as we ran, keeping to the fields and crawling through the fences. We knew every inch of the territory, so we would make all the shortcuts. However, as we came into Grapeland, we couldn't avoid the road, but were forced to slip through the tall weeds that ran alongside it. We were near our destination when Mr. Jim Hobson's Model T Ford came speeding by, wide open, with my brother R.C. in the passenger seat.

Immediately Neal and I knew that our plan had been discovered. When we reached Grapeland, we hid in the lumberyard and discussed what to do. If we attempted to get on a train, we were certain to be caught. We were still in the lumberyard when the search party came there and cornered us.

Neal and I had eaten nothing all day, and I refused to go home with R.C. unless he bought each of us a dozen oysters at King's cafe. I knew papa would attempt to punish me, and if his punishment was to be sending me to bed without supper, I could avoid an entirely empty stomach. R.C., more annoyed than angry, agreed to the meals.

But papa had more severe punishment in mind. When we got home, he brought out a sawed-off plow-handle to which he had nailed a razor strap.

As he came at me with it, I cried out, "I'm not going to take it, papa."

But he kept coming. "Yes, by God," he said furiously, "you are."

I broke and ran. For the first time in my life, I cleared a three-strand barbed wire fence. I kept running and hid out in the woods.

Some time later, R.C. came to the woods, calling out to me that papa had calmed down. He explained that if I would come home now, there would be no whipping.

It was two years later that I left home, and then it was with papa's blessing. I had finally strained his patience to the breaking point, and so my departure was precipitated by one of the least harmful of my numerous pranks. At the time, I had just returned to Hickory Grove after an unsuccessful attempt to complete my schooling in Palestine, the county seat of Anderson County. The Hickory Grove school ended with the tenth grade, and it was not an accredited system. For anyone who intended to go on to college, it was necessary to complete the eleventh grade in a school with state accreditation.

Mr. Frank Delaney, my ninth grade teacher, persuaded papa that I should attend college. Mr. Delaney, a special teacher, far ahead of his time, believed in allowing his students to progress at their own individual paces. Under his tutelage, I was permitted to go as far as I could as fast as I could, and I completed both the ninth and tenth grades that year.

However, when I went to Palestine and attempted to enroll in the eleventh, the principal refused, insisting I would have to enroll in the tenth. I was bored going over material I had already learned, so I dropped out at mid-term and returned to Hickory Grove. Frank Delaney was no longer teaching there, and I enrolled in Mr. Greenwood's tenth grade. I figured if I were going to waste my time, I might as well do it among my friends at home and have a good time.

Meanwhile, I had developed a very convincing drunk act. Prohibition had come in, so there was now a kind of glamor associated with drinking. I would have a lot of fun fooling my friends into thinking I had acquired some liquor and was blind staggering drunk. Very quickly I was getting a reputation as a hell-raiser.

And just as quickly this reputation reached papa, for whom drinking was a very serious subject. I had gone possum hunting a few times with Mr. Greenwood, and papa assumed that it was my teacher who was leading me astray.

Papa was enraged when he accused me, almost irrational in his determination to think the worst of Mr. Greenwood. No matter what I said, he refused to believe my defense. My sense of justice was offended, and I grew just as angry as he was.

Finally, it appeared that neither obstinate father nor obstinate son was going to back down. Irately, Papa announced, "This house is getting too small for the both of us. One of us is going to have to leave."

And just as irately I agreed. "Well, take your choice," I said, standing my ground.

That night Papa packed up his little bag, got in his Model T Ford, and drove off.

But he was back early the next morning.

It took only one look at him for me to understand. "Well," I said, "I guess you've made your mind up that I'm the one that has to leave."

"That's right," he said simply.

I was fourteen years old. I left home with $43 in my pocket. However, I wasn't cast out into the world entirely on my own; Mama saw to that. I think it would have broken her heart to see me go if I had no destination and no one to turn to when I needed anything. She arranged for me to go to Henderson to stay with her sister and brother-in-law, Aunt Corine and Uncle E.P. Lynch.

In Palestine I caught the train, which took me as far as Overton. The only way to get from Overton to Henderson was by taxi. To me, that sounded like an expensive means of travel, since Overton was a good twenty miles from Henderson. At the Overton station I ran into someone I knew from Grapeland, and for $2.50, we shared the taxi ride to Henderson. On the drive out, the taxi driver asked me if I might be interested in buying some corn whiskey. "I know where you can get some," he said.

The idea appealed to me; starting out in the world, free and independent, I might as well have a bit of corn whiskey to celebrate. Besides, I had been falsely accused of getting drunk—accused, tried, and convicted. I might as well make it true, after the fact.

The driver soon stopped at a farmhouse and informed the farmer what we wanted. The farmer went into his cornfield and dug up some fruit jars, which I bought, and by the time we got to Henderson, I was pretty full of corn whiskey.

It was late when we got to Henderson, and my aunt and uncle were already in bed. I was concerned that they would be upset at being awakened to find me standing on their doorstep in an inebriated state. To my great surprise, they were not upset at all—uncle E.P. Lynch took a drink of my whiskey and thanked me for it.

It seemed my condition was of minor importance compared to the trouble he had been having. He was the only Catholic in town, and the Ku Klux Klan had been after him to leave. Uncle E.P. owned a feed store, and he had promised Mama he would give me a job. It now appeared that my first job was going to involve more than lifting fifty pound sacks of feed in and out of customers' wagons. But I didn't mind; if there was going to be a fight, and it appeared there was, it was the kind of fight I would enjoy.

I gave Uncle E.P. what was left of the whiskey, and he took it down to the store to hide it behind the bales of hay.

The real trouble did not begin immediately. I had been working for him a few weeks the day the Klansmen came by the store to make their final threat. There were six of them, led by one of the town's prominent doctors, and by the owner of the local newspaper.

I knew that Uncle E.P. was upset and would have been grateful for a sip of the corn whiskey behind the hay, but he stood his ground and challenged their threat. "When you get ahold of me," he told them, "you'd better do a good job. Because if you don't kill me, I'm going to kill every one of you sons-of-bitches."

The practice the Klan used to instill fear in its victims was to make direct threats of violence and then to heckle and annoy, leaving its victims to wonder when the real violence would come. Constant apprehension would unnerve even the strongest and bravest man—it was a kind of brainwashing.

The town of Henderson was in the midst of a school trustee election at the time, and the Klan—by intimidating its opponents—tried to get all its candidates elected. Uncle E.P. wasn't their only target. The Klan went after an elderly Jewish man who owned a produce store next door to the Lynch Feed Store. Horace Turner, who owned the furniture store, was on their blacklist as well, simply because he was opposed to the Klan. Also a man named Harvey Nix opposed the Klan.

After the Klan threatened Uncle E.P. in his store, nothing serious happened for awhile. They drove by his house several nights, throwing rocks and yelling. Most nights, he and I took turns standing watch, waiting for the moment they would finally make their big move. As the tension mounted, this small group of store-owners would gather from time to time in one store or another, informing each other of what was happening. No one intended leaving town, and they tried to think of ways to protect themselves.

"I know of a man who could put the fear of God into them," someone suggested. "His name is Jack McWhirter. He's got a niece who lives here in town, but I don't know where he lives."

There were nods of agreement all around the room. Jack McWhirter, something of a living legend in East Texas, was a famous brawler. People told big tales about him, and just about everybody feared him. One celebrated story took place at a carnival at the town of Rusk. Jeff McIver, another famous brawler, and McWhirter decided the games of chance at the carnival were rigged. To get rid of them, they went all through the carnival smashing up the concessions. Then the carnival gang chased them into a tent. They slashed a hole in the side, stepped out on the other side, and as each of the carnies ran through the slit, they hit their heads, knocking them out.

Each of the men agreed Jack McWhirter would know what to do to outwit the Klan. "He lives over in Anderson County, at Slocum. I know him," I offered.

Every man chipped in to pay my way home to Anderson County to ask Jack if he would help them out. I returned to Henderson with Jack one Friday. That night the Klan held its regular meeting upstairs over a store. After talking with Uncle E.P. and the others, Jack decided he wanted to meet the Klansmen face-to-face.

We directed him to their meeting place. He climbed the stairs and knocked on the locked door. When, after several tries, they didn't answer, he kicked in the door and, uninvited walked into their meeting room.

I wish I'd been there to see the shocked reactions of the Klansmen when they faced big, beefy Jack McWhirter. Even the doctor, who was a big man himself, about six feet, six inches tall and weighing about 275 pounds, must have been stunned. Someone, however, had the presence of mind to demand to know what McWhirter wanted.

"I want to join the Klan," he told them, "and I want to join tonight."

Apparently it didn't take much persuasion, because they swore him in then and there. The next morning, Uncle E.P. and other store-owners supplied McWhirter with an old gray mule and two gallon vinegar bottles filled with corn whiskey. He rode that mule bareback up and down the town offering everybody he met a drink on the Klan, naming each of the twenty men he had met the previous night, including their candidates for school trustees.

He was violating his oath as a member of the Klan, but not a single Klansman objected. They all laid low that day. Jack continued his broadcasting until three o'clock that afternoon; then he got on his mule and rode off to spend his last evening in Henderson at his niece's house.

But he wasn't quite through with the Klan yet. On his way to Henderson, he began to be uncomfortable riding bareback on that old, bony mule. Passing a house belonging to one of the Klansmen, he spotted a quilt hanging on the clothesline. He realized it would make his six-mile ride a bit more comfortable.

He got off the mule, walked up into the yard and took the quilt. As he was walking off with it, the lady of the house came running out, screaming, "That's my quilt! You're stealing my quilt!"

Jack turned and replied, "That's all right. Your husband and I are brothers in the Klan. What belongs to one in the Klan belongs to the others." He threw the quilt on the mule's back, got on, and rode off.

After Jack McWhirter left town, things cooled off for awhile. Everybody in town talked about what Jack had done, and Klan members didn't dare go out and do anything that would confirm Jack's claims. As supposedly fine upstanding citizens, they were dependent upon the secrecy of the Klan to achieve their ends. they hoped eventually people would pass Jack's accusations off as the ravings of a drunk.

And most people did.

Things had quieted down enough just before the election to permit the Klansmen to renew their threats against Uncle E.P. and the others. But this time they intended to take no chances; they came armed with guns, and they made it clear they intended to use them.

The violence broke out on election day. I was in Uncle E.P.'s store that day, when I noticed a commotion going on outside in the street. I had a hammer in my hand when I ran outside. I saw the doctor who was in the Klan holding Mr. Fields' head in the crook of one arm while he beat the old man in the head with the jaws of a knife. I was outraged; not only was old man Fields less than half the doctor's size, but he was at least 70 years old.

I didn't hesitate for a moment, but rushed the doctor with the hammer and brought it down fiercely on his head. He slumped to the ground. At first we all thought he was dead, but he was only injured. Nevertheless, the storekeepers insisted that I had to hide out, because word had come through that the Texas Rangers had been called in.

By the time the day was over, two Klansmen had been killed, and two of the store-owners had been arrested for the murders. They would both be acquitted when their cases came to court, but that night things did not look good. It was their lawyer, Will Gray, an anti-Klansman, who suggested to Uncle E.P. that it would be wise for me to leave town.

The decision was made quickly to send me to an aunt and uncle in Houston (bus service to Houston was an old Studebaker car), and

Uncle E.P. put me on the bus that night.

I did a lot of thinking on that long ride down through the Pineywoods and the Big Thicket. I had learned in my first venture away from home, on my own, that it was not so easy to conquer the world as it had seemed back in the classrooms of Hickory Grove. It was sheer luck that I had not killed a man, putting an end to all my hopes and dreams by one rash act. Of course, I had been justified in what I had done, but my great goal was to become a lawyer; and I began to wonder: can I really be lawyer potential if I can't put complete faith in the law to deal with people such as rioting Klansmen and others?

It was a question I was unable to answer for some time, but I prayed about it, long and hard.

3
Deferred Ambitions

Impatience sometimes makes things take longer than they might with patience, but delay has a way of testing hopes and desires. Perhaps it all balances out in the end. At the time I felt that it was taking me longer to get where I wanted to go than it should have done. It was a handicap to be entering the world at age fifteen: although I was sure I knew what I was capable of accomplishing, others looked on me still as too young to know my own mind.

It was fortunate for me, however, that not everyone held a prejudice against youth.

When it came to getting work, I could lie about my age; but I could not lie successfully to college administrators about my lack of a high school diploma, and it was this higher education I needed to get where I wanted to go in life.

When I first arrived in Houston, I stayed with my Uncle J.P. Miller and my Aunt Lee, my mother's sister. They made me feel at home immediately, giving me a bed on their second-floor sleeping porch, and it was my room permanently for years afterward, when I wanted to come and stay. Aunt Lee was as warm and loving and understanding as mama was, and Uncle "Pritchard," as I called him, was as strict as papa, though he loved kids and was probably the most patient man I've ever known.

When I was a little kid living in Grapeland, Uncle Pritchard and Aunt Lee lived in Huntsville, near enough for our two families to visit often. There, he was warden of the state penitentiary during the period of Governor Colquitt's administration. When I arrived in Houston in 1923, he was a detective on the police force.

He helped me get my first job—as a bellboy at the Rice Hotel.

Although I had a minor's release signed by my mother and one of my teachers, I still lied about my age in order to get the job. I claimed I was seventeen; the other bellboys were over eighteen, and most were college students, working to pay for their education while attending Rice University. I was not to continue a formal education, working as a bellboy, but I was to learn much that was invaluable. At the time, the Rice Hotel was the center of finance in Texas and several important, powerful businessmen kept apartments there. Such men as Jesse Jones, Howard Hughes, and Judge Jim Elkins.

Houston was a wide-open town in the 1920s. With the building of the ship channel, it was becoming a boomtown. Compared with today, it was not large, but for me it was an exciting city. The downtown area covered eight paved blocks; other important streets were covered with shell. When the weather was dry, the shell dust would blow about and leave a fine white film over everything.

Prohibition was in full swing, and so was bootlegging. The Rice Hotel was a center for big business and power politics; it was also a center for underworld activities. In fact, it was the center for just about anything that happened in Houston, because it was the only big hotel that was considered respectable. The other hotel in Houston the Windham, managed by Miss Gussie Windham, was a thinly disguised brothel, or call-house.

It was convenient for Uncle Pritchard to have me working at the Rice, because I could keep an undercover eye on what was happening. When I came home at night, I could give him tips on things the police department ought to be aware of. Later on, after I became night bell captain, he would stop in every day to make sure I was all right and to pick up any bits of information I might have gathered.

One case that I actually became involved in directly concerned a series of jewelry robberies that took place in the homes of Houston's high society. A celebrated European prince had come to town and stayed at the Rice Hotel. He was entertained by the bluebloods. Every important society matron in town had to give him a party, and the robberies had taken place at several of these parties.

One day, when Uncle Pritchard came by to see me, he said, "I believe our jewelry thief is the so-called prince. Why don't you see what you can find out about him."

I began by asking questions of the housemaids, prodding them to tell me anything that might be unusual about the man. They all told me the day the Prince had checked in, he had requested a cuspidor for his room—not just a small cuspidor, but a big tall one. In itself, this wasn't particularly odd; quite a few men chewed tobacco. What was unusual was that he had given the housemaids strict instructions: they need not clean the cuspidor because he would clean it himself.

One night when the prince was absent I went to his room with one of the maids to check out the cuspidor. It took one look to know that something was suspicious: the top of the water in the cuspidor was covered with unchewed chewing tobacco.

I notified Uncle Pritchard, and he came to the hotel with a search warrant. Underneath the unchewed tobacco, the cuspidor was filled with diamonds. As Uncle Pritchard had suspected, the celebrated European Prince wasn't a prince at all.

As youngest of the bellboys, I was the favorite of many of the permanent guests, particularly the women. Mrs. Jim Elkins called me "Sonny." and Mrs. Jesse Jones took me under her motherly wing, helping me further my ambitions. She and I had a deal: I would run errands for her; and in return, she would teach me to cook, everything from short-orders to gourmet dishes. "If you can cook," she told me, "you can get a job anywhere." She knew that my goal was to attend college and study law, and that the only way I could do it would be to work my way through.

I learned cooking from her and gained considerable experience in the hotel kitchen. The Rice's coffee shop and the dining room were open 24 hours a day. However, the night chef at the time had a drinking problem. He had installed a cot back in the kitchen supply room, where he would sleep during working hours. When he slept, I took over the kitchen. When I ran into problems with an order or had more than I could handle, I would go to the supply room and rouse him to help me out.

It was a good arrangement for me, and I learned quickly, but it was to be some time before I would be able to put this skill to the use I had intended for it. When I had worked at the hotel for several months, I received a letter asking me to return home for awhile. Papa and I had worked out our differences by this time, and he and mama needed help on the farm.

After about three months at the farm, I returned to the Rice Hotel and was promoted to night bell captain, a position of some responsibility.

In a few months, Uncle Pritchard retired from the Houston police force and accepted a job as superintendent for a dredging company that sold shell for street-paving. I was still familiar with members of the police department, but I was no longer kept abreast of the inner workings of the detective force.

My trouble came when a prohibition agent arrived in town, intending to clean up Houston in a single-handed sweep. The agent was a loner. He had built a reputation for being not only tough but ruthless. He wore a big beaver hat and carried two pistols. From Port Arthur to High Island, he uncovered active liquor stills and went alone to raid and destroy them. He was known to have killed a number of men in the process.

Raiding several stills in Port Arthur, he had learned that their whiskey was being sold in Houston, and he went there intending to finish his job.

The Rice Hotel, the center of everything, was his first stop.

Immediately he discovered two bellboys, both Rice University students, each carrying a five-gallon bottle into the hotel by the back entrance. Before the parking garage was built, there was a brick-paved parking lot and an alley there. As night bell captain, I was on duty, and I felt a responsibility for the two boys.

When I heard that the agent had arrested them and, with guns drawn, was holding them in the alley, I felt I had to do something. It occurred to me that, if the evidence were gone, he would have no case against the bellboys. I slipped out the back door and rushed the agent from behind. I grabbed him and rolled him to the ground, clamping my hands around his wrists to deflect the pistols.

"Break the bottles!" I shouted to the two bellboys. "Smash them on the brick!"

The agent was furious. Struggling with me, he fired both pistols. The bullets ricocheted down the alleyway, as the two boys smashed the whiskey bottles against the brick paving.

The agent arrested me and the two boys, and took us all into the police station. I knew the night chief, a man who later became Frank Hamer's right-hand man.

"Whose whiskey was that?" the night chief asked.

"It belonged to Mr. Jesse Jones," I said. "And he's not going to be very happy about losing it."

He grinned, asking the agent, "Do you want to press charges against Jesse Jones? You don't have any evidence against him."

31

The agent was forced to back down. The chief released us and told us to go back to work. The agent gave us a warning, most of his anger being directed toward me.

I never saw him again. The hotel manager advised me to get out of town; with the agent after me, my life wasn't worth much. I seemed to have a knack for trouble.

Each step toward college seemed to take me further away from achieving my goal, and the thought of moving again, deferring my ambitions further, upset me. I decided to have a long talk with my minister.

I attended St. Luke's Methodist Church, and I'd developed a friendship with the minister, W.C. Martin. Martin possessed a powerful mind, and he was a man who could understand the frustrations caused by my delayed education. He had been forced to drop out of fourth grade and was unable to go back to school until he was 21 years old. In one year, he completed his grades through eleven, and then enrolled at Southern Methodist University. Again his education was interrupted by World War I. When the war was over, he returned to SMU and completed his college education in one year. St. Luke's Methodist was his first church assignment.

He heard me relate my dilemma. "Have you ever thought about going into the ministry?" Martin asked me.

I admitted that the idea had never occurred to me.

"You say you want to help people," Martin continued. "Law isn't the only way, and you seem to have a lot of trouble with the law anyway. The church can sometimes be more powerful as a weapon for the ordinary person."

Martin was very convincing. He told me that he was leaving St. Luke's, the Bishop of Texas having reassigned him to the First Methodist Church of Port Arthur, in danger of closing because attendance and income was low. He was going to try to save First Methodist, and he was to pick his own assistant pastor.

"I don't need the kind of money they're offering me," he told me. "I've told them I'll take a lower salary if they'll give me funds to buy books and train an assistant pastor. They've agreed to it. If you would consider the ministry, you are the young man I'd like to pick."

It was a startling offer, and, honored and flattered that Martin would think so highly of me, I accepted.

Martin would not be making the move to Port Arthur for a few months, but I had to leave town immediately. My brother Robert was living in Port Arthur then, and my brother Nat was preparing to go there to attend business college. I would have a place to stay temporarily, and I was sure I could get some sort of job to tide me over until Martin arrived.

As it turned out, my temporary job only got me into more trouble.

The *Houston Post,* then known as the *Houston Post-Dispatch,* and owned by the *St. Louis Post-Dispatch,* needed a Port Arthur man to be the local circulation manager as well as correspondent, or "stringer." I took the job before I learned about all the requirements.

This was the mid-twenties, and the Ku Klux Klan was at the height of its power in Texas. Soon after I was hired by the *Post-Dispatch,* a man called on me to inform me that all the newspaper's employees were required to join the Klan. If they had known my true age, I wouldn't have been permitted to join, but that wasn't the reason I refused. With my experience with the secret society, I wouldn't have joined under any circumstances.

When I refused, I received a call to come to the newspaper's office in Houston.

On my arrival at Port Arthur, I had managed to learn about the Klan's activities there, much of it from a young man who was Worshipful Master of the Port Arthur Masonic Lodge. Just recently the Klan had killed a man there, and among the details I had gathered, I learned the name of the High Cyclops and all of the men involved in the murder.

On the way to Houston, I put together my first story for the *Post-Dispatch,* a blockbuster of an article about the Ku Klux Klan. I had my article ready when I was asked why I wouldn't join the Klan. "I have a story here I want you to print," I said when I handed it over to the editors.

Promptly, I lost my job. I picked up the article and walked out, straight to their competitor, the *Houston Chronicle.*

The *Chronicle's* editor, N. E. Foster, called "Nefo," was not only a man of principles, but he was a Catholic and had a distinct hatred for the Ku Klux Klan. I explained to him what had happened. "I wrote this for the *Post-Dispatch,* but they refused to print it."

He read the article carefully, his excitement growing with every line. "Hell, if you can substantiate this, I'll take it," he said, when he had finished his reading.

I gave him the names of the people who could verify it, and he bought it. "I've been an editor here a good many years," he told me. "This is the best story I've ever had. How would you like a job with the *Chronicle?*"

It was a tempting offer, but I had already made a promise to W. C. Martin, and his move to Port Arthur was now imminent. "I appreciate the offer," I told Nefo, "but I think this article is going to be the first and last of my writing. If I stay in the newspaper business, I'll only get into trouble."

As it turned out, I doubt if I could have experienced more trouble as a newspaperman that I did as trainee for the ministry in the Methodist Church. Especially since several of the leaders of the Ku Klux Klan were also leaders at First Methodist in Port Arthur.

W.C. Martin began his ministry at First Methodist with a big revival, complete with visiting revival preacher and an evangelistic singer. I was put in charge of the young people's services, which were to be held just prior to the regular services. The young people volunteered their assistance to make the revival a success. One such volunteer was a young lady whose family had just moved to Port Arthur from Oklahoma. She had a fine voice and wanted to sing in the choir.

One morning I sent this pretty young lady to the printer's to pick up the programs for the evening's service. The printer, one of the most important members of First Methodist Church was a choir member and a large contributor to the building fund. "Just tell him that Jerry Sadler will come by later to pay him," I instructed the young lady.

She returned in tears, and I pressed her to tell me why she was crying. "He told me that I had to pay him for the printing, and he didn't want money. He attacked me and wouldn't let me out of the shop."

As her story unfolded, I grew more and more angry. I had heard about the printer before beginning to work for the church, but out of respect for W.C. Martin, I had steered clear of the man. He was one of the leaders of the Ku Klux Klan, and had been involved in the murder I had reported about in the *Houston Chronicle* article. He was also owner of one of Port Arthur's larger brothels.

I knew that I was laying my job on the line, but I was too angry to keep silent now. When I went to the printer's home, the man's son answered my knock and told me his father was having his supper. Probably the son saw how angry I was, because he suggested I return later.

"I'd like to talk to him now," I said loudly. I stuck my foot in the door to keep him from closing it.

Finally the commotion attracted the boy's father. "What's going on, Sadler?" he asked coolly.

"I'd like to talk to you," I said. "Would you come outside?"

"Sure," he smiled confidently. "I'll talk to you anywhere. Just wait a minute."

He went back into the house, and when he returned a moment later, he was carrying a gun. "Why don't we take a little walk?" he suggested.

He led me down a path to a wooded area next to his home. I walked ahead, I didn't know if he intended to talk or if he simply planned to use the weapon to keep me from talking. I couldn't afford to take a chance on waiting to find out.

Suddenly, I wheeled around, knocked him down, and grabbed the gun. I was holding the gun over him, when his wife came running down the path. She knew me from the church, and so she was more astonished than upset. "Jerry," she demanded, "what's happened? What's this all about?"

I handed her the gun and said, "Your husband will have to tell you." And I walked off before he could get up and try to stop me.

The man didn't show up for choir practice that evening. However, the following morning, the Methodist Bishop arrived in Port Arthur. He had received a phone call from the printer, and had taken the first train that morning to come to see W.C. Martin.

"I want you to do whatever you have to," he instructed Martin, "in order to keep this man in the church. We can't afford to lose him. He's given $10,000 to the building fund. He's one of only four big contributors in Port Arthur."

I had told Martin what had happened the night before, and he was prepared to defend me before the Bishop, but I don't think he was prepared for the Bishop's response. He was irritated that the Bishop continued to be more concerned with financial matters than with moral issues.

"Two of our four big contributors," he pointed out, "own brothels. Personally I don't think the church needs their money."

"I'm not asking for much," the Bishop persisted. "Just have the boy apologize to the man."

But Martin stood firm. "You sent me down here to run this church," he replied, "and I intend to run it my way. I won't order the boy to apologize, and I won't apologize for him. In my opinion, he did the right thing. If he wants to quit the church, he can quit and take his money with him."

When Martin told me about this conversation, I was upset. It meant a lot to me that he had stuck up for me, but I disliked creating any trouble for him. He had worked hard to be ordained a minister, and all his work would have been for naught if he alienated his superiors.

I spent a lot of time thinking about what I might do, and those thoughts were an important influence on me in the years that followed. W.C. Martin truly endeavored to perform God's work, a man whose very life was devoted to what was right and good. But he was doing this work in his own quiet way, and to do it he had to exist within what people of today call the "establishment." He would not have dealt with the printer in the manner I had done, but my action had forced him to support me, setting aside any ministerial role of impartial spiritual guide to every one of his parishioners.

I was not really ministerial material. My sense of right and wrong was too easily outraged, and I was not capable of turning the other cheek to an enemy. I wanted to genuinely do good with my life, but my methods and my temperament were more suited to layman's work.

I told W.C. Martin that I was grateful for all he had done for me, but I had decided it would be best for all concerned for me to leave the Port Arthur church.

4

Higher Education

My original goals and ambitions were restored, and I returned to East Texas, stopping briefly at Hickory Grove to see my parents. The year was 1925, I was seventeen years old, and on my way to Stephen F. Austin College in Nacogdoches, Texas. Truthfully I felt myself the adult I wanted to be, but I was still a poor boy; my years of working and struggling, deferring my ambitions, had resulted in no savings.

When I arrived in Nacogdoches, I had $10 in my pocket. I didn't even own a suit of clothes, and my one pair of breeches were hand-me-downs from Nat; my sole sweater was one that Robert had discarded. All I had, aside from that, was faith I could succeed at anything I attempted and my ability to cook.

I had chosen Stephen F. Austin College for two reasons. The first was that it was close to my parent's home, and I would return there if I really got hungry. The second reason was that it was a part of the Texas state college system, and therefore considerably less expensive than private universities. In concept, the state universities and colleges of Texas were intended to be available to everyone, rich and poor alike. Stephen F. Austin, founded in 1923 as a state teacher's college, was one of the newest in the system.

My $10 covered the college registration fee and my first week's lodging in a rooming house. (At the time, the college had no dormitories.) Somehow I had to find a job fairly quickly. As it turned out, I got one without having to look.

The first day of school, I tried out for the football team. This was the first year the college would have football. That day there was a large group of spectators around, and the officials had considerable difficulty keeping them off the field. I was going out for the team's end position, and Coach Bob Shelton had the quarterback—a man named Jesse Summers—throw some passes to me.

I was running back for a pass, and had turned to look for the ball, when I collided with what felt like an elephant. It was one of the spectators, an enormous man over six feet tall, who I judge weighed more than 250 pounds. He landed flat on his back on the ground with me on top of him; his cigar, still clenched in his teeth, was flattened all over his face.

With the help of one of the other players, I pulled him to his feet and helped him to the bleachers. When he caught his breath he introduced himself: H.T. Peritte. He and the other men on the bleachers had a good laugh about the mishap.

When Peritte learned that I was new in town, he asked, "What church do you belong to?"

When I told him "Methodist," he was pleased. He was a Methodist as well, the presiding elder of the Nacogdoches district, a title now called District Superintendent.

"I'll come by your boarding house on Sunday," he offered, "and take a group of you to Sunday School."

I agreed to his offer, and then we were interrupted by a man on the bleachers. "You don't happen to know of any boys who can cook, do you?" he asked.

"Yes, sir," I replied hopefully. "I know one. Why?"

"My name's J.D. Bright," he explained. "I own Bright's Cafe, and I need a cook."

"I'll have you a man tonight," I told him,

That ended my football career. That night I started to work at J.D. Bright's Cafe, working eight hours a day on weekdays and sixteen hours on Saturday. I moved out of my boarding house and into J.D. Bright's house, taking room and board as part of my pay.

Luck—helped along by the good-hearted people of Nacogdoches— was with me in supporting myself, but I had to struggle every step of the way in getting my education. When I tried to register as a freshman, claiming to be 21 years old, I was caught. C.E. Ferguson, the registrar, a man who had taught school in Palestine, knew me. "You're only seventeen," he said, "and you don't have your high school diploma. I'll have to enroll you in the sub-college class until you complete the necessary preparatory work."

I was not happy about the prospect of repeating studies. The college had a rule that permitted students over 21 to take an examination for placement. I considered it merely a technicality that I was under age, so I took my case to the president of the college.

It required all of my powers of persuasion, but President Birdwell gave in and allowed me to take the exam. My scores placed me halfway between a freshman and a sophomore. I began that level, and I had no problem with the academic work until the spring, when I contacted the flu and pneumonia.

I was no longer cooking at Bright's Cafe, but had gone into the cleaning and tailoring business. I had been at school only a short time when H.T. Peritte and H.A. Williamson helped me obtain a bank loan to form the College Tailoring Company, which I set up in a building Williamson built alongside the campus. By offering the students a special club rate, I garnered all the college trade. I arose at four each morning and made the rounds of all the boarding houses, picking up clothes before going to classes.

A bit of luck that helped to make the College Tailoring Company a big success was locating the only graduate tailor in all of Nacogdoches. One day I happened to be talking to a city marshall and learned that there was a black man in jail, who claimed to be a tailor, and he had no one to post his bail.

I arranged to hire him and get him out of jail. He proved to be just what he claimed, capable of cleaning, pressing, or tailoring anything. Because of him I picked up a lot of town business as well.

When I caught the flu and it developed into pneumonia, there was no way I could keep my rugged schedule of work and classes. In the 1920s, medical science didn't have all the wonder drugs, so my recovery took a long time. I was laid up in bed in my boarding house for four weeks, taking creomulsion and home remedies. The tailoring company managed all right without me, but when I went back to class I was far behind in my studies.

At Dr. Birdwell's suggestion, I hired a tutor. Dr. Hazel Floyd, a young woman of 21, had her doctorate. By the end of the semester, my grades were greatly improved, and I passed my classes and enrolled in summer school.

That summer, two graduate students made a cash offer for the College Tailoring Company. I had no intention that cleaning and tailoring were my life's work, so I accepted their good offer. I considered moving back to Port Arthur and transferring to the business college there. My prospects for law school seemed far away, especially with dividing myself between running a business and studying. The flu experience had taught me that one or the other would have to suffer.

There was one significant event during that summer, a lesson taught me by my psychology professor, Dr. I.A. Costen. Psychology was my best subject, and I was making the highest grades in Dr. Costen's class, although I had not purchased the rather expensive textbook that he required. The hour-long class had Dr. Costen lecturing for 55 minutes, then passing out a twenty true-and-false test based on his lecture. We had two minutes to complete the exam.

I was one of two students in the class who had a perfect score of 100 for each exam throughout the summer semester. However, when the final grades were posted, Dr. Costen had given me an "F" for the course.

I was extremely upset, and I went to the Dean to ask the reason. The Dean and the President, Dr. Birdwell, called in Dr. Costen.

"Isn't it true," Dr. Birdwell asked the professor, "that you graded your students every day with a true-false test, and Sadler here had a consistently perfect score the entire semester?"

Dr. Costen nodded. "Yes," he admitted, "that's correct."

"Well, why did you fail him?" the college president asked.

"Because he didn't have a textbook for the course," Dr. Costen replied. "And that was one of the requirements of the course. He knew that."

Then I broke in. "I learned more in your class without a book than the other students learned with one," I said angrily. "Requirement or no requirement, I don't see that I deserve to fail."

At that point, Dr. Costen grinned. "I see that I've accomplished my purpose," he said. He turned to Dr. Birdwell. "I wanted to teach Sadler to fight for what he's entitled to," he announced. "I've accomplished my purpose, and he accomplished his. He's got the 'A'." Then he slapped me heartily on the back.

That was only a day or two before I left Nacogdoches. I had to take one more final exam, trigonometry; not one of my best subjects, although my professor was a good friend. Jack was an upperclassman, student-teaching the lower-level classes. He was a ham radio nut, and his dream after completing college, was to sign on as radio operator on a merchant ship. He intended to accompany me to Port Arthur with the hope of signing aboard a ship there.

The night before my final exam, Jack and I went out together to celebrate our imminent departure from Stephen F. Austin. Jack urged me to test the challenge of a fellow claiming to be the champion wrestler of Texas. He had observed me wrestling and thought I could beat the claimant and put an end to his boasting.

The evening began in a friendly fashion. We bought a quart of corn whiskey and went out to a churchyard in the country to drink and prepare for the wrestling match. When the bottle was finished and wrestling began, the claimant realized I was a bigger challenge than I appeared to be. Not long after that he knew he couldn't handle me; he grew angry, and the wrestling match turned into an outright fight.

As a result I was not in great shape for my trigonometry exam the next day. Sore, bruised, and hung-over, I sat in Jack's class staring blankly at my paper. Finally Jack, not feeling in top form himself, came by my desk. "Just fold up a bunch of papers, put your name on them, and hand them in," he said. "You've passed the course."

The following day, he and I left for Port Arthur. A group of students and teachers were standing on the campus in front of the main building, talking about dreams and aspirations, as young people do. Farewells always seem to bring out contemplation of the future, and conjecture about whether the friends will see or hear from each other again. We went around the group, each saying what we aimed for— teacher, lawyer, scientist, businessman. When it came my turn, I announced, "I intend to become governor of Texas."

It was a strange announcement, because I had given little thought to a political career. I knew only that I intended to join my friends in Port Arthur who were planning to try to clean up the city, electing to local office their own reform candidates.

During my year as a student at Stephen F. Austin—if anyone had asked me—I would not have been able to say that it was one of the happiest times of my life. Now, I look upon that time with great nostalgia. As most people grow older, they have memories of one place that they look back on for spiritual sustenance and moral rejuvenation. For me, that place is Nacogdoches. It doesn't matter how hard that year was or how much I had to struggle. Whenever I get to feeling low or sorry for myself, or lose hope for the future of mankind, if I can direct myself back to that seventeen-year-old boy beneath the towering pines of the Stephen F. Austin Campus, I can be a little happier with what I am and a lot surer that everything I believe in is worth fighting for. The Christian love and unquestioning goodness of people I knew there can always restore my faith in humanity.

The day I left Nacogdoches, I made a promise to myself: if ever I did succeed in my own personal ambitions, I would help others as unselfishly as those people helped me. It's a promise I continue to hold myself to.

Of course, I had to achieve some success before I could do anything about fulfilling that promise. I still had a long way to go.

The first night in Port Arthur, Jack and I stayed with my brother Robert, who was working for the Texas Company. The next day, Jack signed aboard a ship and set off to see the world, while I prepared to enroll in the Port Arthur Business College.

When I started to school, I moved into the college dormitory and got a job as conductor on the streetcars that ran from the boat docks to the oil refineries, and were used generally by the workers going to and from work. However, I was in school only a short time before I found a better job, as a lumber checker in the lumberyards on the Texaco Island. All the Texas Company shipping was done from the island, where they had can and crate factories. They shipped in five-gallon cans, packed ten to a crate. I was soon promoted to can inspector in the factory.

Meanwhile, I contacted some of my old friends by attending church at First Methodist. We formed the Young Men's Voters League, and together made our plans to clean up the town by electing honest, honorable men to public office. I had been aware of politics all my life, and had observed it from the under side during my bellboy time at the Rice Hotel, but this was my first direct involvement. It was a heady exprience for a young man of eighteen who was unable to vote, especially when we succeeded in getting one of our candidates elected Chief of Police. This proved to be the beginning of the end for the powerful Ku Klux Klan leaders.

Within a few years, the Young Men's Voters League was to make a clean sweep of the town, and the printer who had once given me so much trouble would be making his living on the street, selling fried pies his wife had baked.

I had been in Port Arthur a few months, when after a Sunday service I was talking to Dr. A.M. McAfee, a member of the First Methodist Church. "How would you like to come to work at Gulf?" he asked casually. "We've got a couple of openings in the labs."

"I'd like that," I replied eagerly. "What do I do?"

"Just go to the employment office and talk to Andy Dobbs," he said. "I'll tell him to expect you."

I went to see Andy Dobbs the next morning. There was a long line at the employment office, so many applicants I was afraid I would have little chance. But when I got to the window and gave my name, I was taken in to see Mr. Dobbs immediately. Within a few moments I was hired.

The Gulf Laboratories were among the most progressive in the country. The divisions for testing, analysis, and experimentation—during the next two years I worked in all three labs, learning things that would prove indispensable to me—had brilliant men in the chemical sciences. Their association with me, and their work, study, and research during these formative years of the petrochemical business was invaluable to me.

For the first time I began to feel a degree of affluence. My salary was enough to pay for my room, board, and schooling, with some left over to spend on pleasurable pursuits. I had been wanting to learn to fly, and I now signed up for flying lessons with Frank Hawks of Texas Aviation. I had other friends interested in flying, and four of us decided to build our own airplane.

One of our group, a construction engineer, supervised all the work. It was to be the smallest airplane that had ever been built, but the engineer's plan was to double the strength of every structural specification, we used two for one all through the plane and placed a 150 horsepower engine in it. When it was all completed, the Civil Aeronautics Inspectors tried it out. They were impressed and informed us the plane would be approved, but we would have to await official notification before flying it.

During the waiting period, one of the partners decided secretly to take it into the air. He was a man who worked with me at the Gulf Labs. The least experienced flyer in the group, he was still a student flyer with no license. He was in the air, stunting, when the plane went into a nosedive, and without the experience to know how to pull out, he crashed and was killed.

Football was a pleasurable pursuit during this time. Port Arthur had a non-professional independent football team, the Pirates. My football aspirations had to be set aside at Stephen F. Austin because of financial needs, so I now joined the Pirates. Again I played end, but the only notable occurrence during my football career took place off the field.

A dollar-a-year man, working with me in the labs, was on leave from his job as a chemistry professor at the University of Iowa. One evening, he came with me to watch football practice. "You've been saying you want to study law," he said to me after it was over. "Iowa has an excellent law school. Rutledge, the Dean, is one of the best legal minds in the country. If you want to go there to study, I think I could get you a football scholarship."

It was in incredible offer, the kind of thing I had dreamed of, but now that it had happened, I turned it down. "I appreciate the offer," I told him, "but I've already made other plans, and it's too late to back out now. You see, I'm leaving the Gulf Labs."

I didn't tell him what my plans were; they were entirely secret. In the past months, I had acquired a taste for adventure, and an opportunity had come my way promising more excitement than I had ever known.

5

Lower Education

Through an acquaintance I managed to get a job with the Bureau of Investigation, the federal bureau that would become the FBI. At least, I thought I was working for the Bureau and J. Edgar Hoover, its new Chief.

After the Teapot Dome Scandal and the death of President Harding, Calvin Coolidge wanted to begin with a clean slate. To replace Harding's chief crony Harry Daugherty, he selected the eminently respectable Harlan Stone (later to be appointed Chief Justice of the Supreme Court) as Attorney General. During Harry Daugherty's tenure, the Director of the Bureau of Investigation was William J. Burns, former head of the celebrated Burns International Detective Agency. When Stone came into office, Burns submitted his resignation, and was replaced by his former assistant, J. Edgar Hoover. However, Burns did not entirely let go of the power he had held in the governmental agency. For years afterward a number of the Bureau agents maintained allegiance to him, taking his orders and reporting to him. Gradually Hoover weeded these Burns men from the organization.

I was unaware of any of this at the time; I knew only what most of the public knew, that the Bureau of Investigation had managed to maintain its integrity throughout one of the biggest scandals ever to hit the federal government. In my youthful eyes it was unimpeachable because of its recent campaign against the Ku Klux Klan.

I did not question the means by which I was paid—in cash, sent by mail—nor the manner in which I reported—by randomly chosen telephone booths to an agent in Washington.

My first assignment was on the Texas border, and I was to join the United States Cavalry as a part of my cover. As a member of the Twelfth Cavalry, I was stationed at Fort Brown, near Brownsville, where I was to investigate Congressman John Nance Garner and the state Republican Chairman, R.B. Creager. Gus Creager was an oil and land speculator, referred to as "the Red Fox of the Rio Grande" because of his red hair and his shrewdness. He had seconded Warren Harding's nomination at the 1920 Republican Convention, and now was suspected of being involved in a bootleg operation.

I had been in Brownsville about three days when I met Creagar's secretary. We quickly became heavy drinking buddies. I worked it so that our drinking sprees would end up in Creager's office; and, after the secretary passed out, I would quickly read through the Red Fox's files and records, gathering information which then I would pass along to my Washington contact.

It was not a demanding job. Except for obtaining information, I was like other men at Fort Brown, subject to the military duties and regulations. Even my commanding officer did not know my real reason for being there.

For awhile, it actually was boring; all I did was nose around, gathering information that ended up in a file somewhere. I spent my spare time in the Fort Brown library, which was situated next to the service club that doubled as a chapel. For me, the attraction in the library was a complete LaSalle extension course in law, which the chaplain in charge of the library had used to get his own law degree. I had all the questions and all the answers.

Bennett arranged my assignment as his orderly. I became his librarian as well and moved into a small back room. Cavalrymen don't do much reading; there were never more than four of five who came to the library during the two hours it was open. So I studied law, with the chaplain as my tutor.

From time to time, my cavalry friends would create a bit of excitement. The Mexican border was a pretty rough place in those days, with fights and brawls commonplace in the saloons and bordellos that catered to the men at Fort Brown. The cavalry was a bit like the French Foreign Legion: it attracted a good many young men who didn't wish to talk of their pasts. It was understood you didn't ask many questions about each other. If a man offered information about himself, that was fine, but one never repeated what he said.

For a time, two good friends were Frank Mellas and Clarence Vanesley, and both of them confided some of their pasts to me. Mellas had formerly been secretary to Frank Hague, the political boss of Jersey City and an important power in the national Democratic Party. Mellas received a cashier's check for $250 every two weeks from Frank

Hague, and he needed someone to cash it for him. He didn't wish to be seen in the bank, so he gave me ten percent to go to a Brownsville bank and cash his check.

He always carried a lot of money with him when he left Fort Brown, and that inevitably attracted trouble. One night he went into Rio Grande City to a place called the Green Chimney, a brothel and gambling house—no sign to name it, only a chimney painted green for identity. Later that evening, a man told us Mellas was in a fight at the Green Chimney and was outnumbered. Cavalrymen, always prepared to aid their buddies, went over to Rio Grande City in full force.

By the time we got there Mellas had been beaten, and he was being held prisoner. We slipped around the house, looking in the windows at the back, and saw him sitting in a chair surrounded by other men. There was only one light in the room, a kerosene lantern hanging from the ceiling.

With my pistol, I took aim at the lantern and fired. When the light went out, all bedlam broke loose inside the Green Chimney. We managed to get Mellas out of there, and all returned safely to Fort Brown.

The next morning, however, we learned the Green Chimney had burned to the ground. All that was left was ashes, charred iron bedframes, and the chimney, now black instead of green.

Vanesley was not Clarence's real name, and he was not—as he claimed to be—a plumber's helper from Denver, Colorado. He confessed that much to me at the time, but I did not learn until years later, when Eisenhower attempted unsuccessfully to appoint him to his presidential staff, that his real name was Vandenburg, a member of the prominent Michigan family.

When Clarence decided to desert the military, he confided in me. "Do you know where I can catch a ship going up the East Coast?" he asked.

I gave him the name of a man in the Seaman Church Institute in Port Arthur who could help him get a job aboard a merchant ship. Before he left, he sold me his expensive tailor-made uniform for $2.00.

I had two other friends, Cain and Dawson. Cain was from Kentucky, and Dawson came from Richmond, Texas. One day, I went across the border with them to Matamoros. We were in the Palace Saloon, minding our own business, when we noticed some trouble starting a few tables away, centering around an American tourist family. A group of Mexicans were trying to pick up the tourists' two daughters. He was ready to fight.

Cain, Dawson, and I went to the rescue. In the brawl that followed, somebody threw a *Salinas* beer bottle, and it hit the big mirror behind the bar, shattering it. Naturally we *gringos* were being blamed when the police arrived. We scattered, trying to get the tourists out of the place. Cain didn't make it; the police arrested him, and prepared to take him to jail.

We couldn't let that happen to our buddy. Dawson suggested, "Let's go into the wholesale house and get a couple of stone wine bottles, slip behind the policemen, and hit them over the heads."

When we came out of the shop with our weapons, the police were dragging Cain down the street. He struggled and cursed the two policemen holding onto each side of him. Dawson and I slipped up behind and whacked the wine bottles onto their heads, and down they went.

We had to get across the border to safety, and we knew it was risky to cross the international bridge. As soon as the policemen got their wits about them, the authorities at the bridge would be notified, and we would be arrested. Our only chance was to try the river. We cut out across the woods toward the Rio Grande.

When we arrived, we discovered the river waters were high, full to the banks, and running swiftly. There seemed no way to swim the current, but we jumped in hoping the curve of the river itself would guide us. We drifted with the water for a mile or so before the current deposited us on the opposite side, in the U.S.A. We had to conceal our clothes, so we found a small hole up in the attic of the barracks and stuffed them inside.

The next morning at reveille, Mexican authorities were on hand to pick us out of the line-up. Luckily Cain was in another troop, because the two policemen we had fought were there, with heads bandaged. They would have recognized him, but Dawson and I were safe because they had never seen our faces.

After the Mexican authorities left, we were dismissed from reveille, but the troop commander approached me. "Sadler, what did you do with your wet clothes? You'd better do something about them," he said.

Eventually the Bureau of Investigation found more for me than to poke in other people's file drawers. There was a question of voter fraud in Hidalgo County, and a group of angry citizens had sent a petition to President Coolidge requesting federal intervention and supervision of the upcoming election.

Sheriff A.Y. Baker was political boss of Edinburg and Hidalgo County, and he ruled with an iron hand. There was a story told that when Baker was elected he made the former sheriff get down on his knees so that he could urinate in his mouth. And it was suspected that the murder of Ed Couch, committed for political reasons, had been ordered by Baker. Couch, big citrus farmer and rancher in the area; didn't like taking orders from anyone. He and his wife were found murdered near Edinburg, but no one was ever brought to trial.

When ordered to go to Edinburg to investigate the political situation, I was told there was one man I could confide in. Texas Ranger Captain Bill Sterling was supposed to know as much about what was going on there as anybody, but after what happened I realized that wasn't much.

I told Bill Sterling I needed a safe place to hang out in town, and I asked him to advise me. "If you were taking care of this," I asked him, "where would you go?"

"I would say the safest place would be the office of the Justice of the Peace," he told me. "It's down in the basement of the courthouse. The Justice of the Peace is a good man. His name is Pat Haley. His father was an Irishman, and his mother was Mexican. He's a great big fellow, and he wears a big white hat. You can't mistake him at all."

I went to Pat Haley's office, not knowing that it was A.Y. Baker's machine headquarters. Bill Sterling had sent me straight into the lion's den. It certainly enabled me to gather the information I was seeking, but when I continued to hang around there, people began to be suspicious.

About two o'clock in the afternoon, Haley came right out and asked me what I was doing.

Thinking quickly, I replied, "Well, I'm going to get married, and I want you to perform the ceremony."

Somehow I had to get myself a bride, and I didn't have much time to do it. I went to Bill Sterling and arranged to have his sister go to Brownsville to get a young woman who would marry me, with the understanding that the marriage would never be consummated and that it would later be annulled.

When Bill's sister returned with an attractive, dark-haired young woman, we went to the County Clerk and took out a marriage license. At five o'clock, we were married. That cleared the suspicion, and I managed to obtain the needed information.

Based on my report to Washington, indictments were issued against A.Y. Baker, Pat Haley, Cam E. Hill, and several others.

Soon I received instructions to buy my way out of the Cavalry and prepare for an assignment involving travel. (In those days a military resignation was acquired for $120.) Trouble was brewing in Mexico, and it appeared to be developing into a full-scale revolution.

In 1917, Mexico adopted a new constitution, one that was socially advanced and economically radical. It granted universal suffrage, provided for arbitration of labor disputes, specified an eight-hour workday and set minimum wages, broke up large estates and granted land to the peasants. It placed restrictions on foreign ownership of lands, mines, and oilfields, and restricted the property of the Church. Naturally, this was opposed by a great many factions within Mexico, particularly by the Catholic Church.

The United States supported this constitution and the President, Plutarco Calles, who was trying to make it work.

I had had a brief assignment related to the political trouble in Mexico. In February, 1927, President Calles began to enact the constitutional provisions concerning Church property, closing Church schools and nationalizing lands belonging to the Catholic Church that were not directly related to religious worship. The Church resisted, repudiating the Constitution. Calles began arresting priests, monks, and nuns of foreign birth and deporting them from the country.

One of the most important leaders of the Church opposition was a nephew of Calles himself, a priest in Matamoros. His church was the largest on the North American continent, and he wielded considerable power. The young priest, at 24 years, seemed intent on martyrdom by his defiance of his uncle.

In that crisis, my assignment was to slip across the border, "rescue" the young priest, and keep him secreted away in my bunkhouse behind the Fort Brown library until the situation cooled down.

Now the situation had grown much more serious. The opposition was well-organized, and armed revolts were planned throughout Mexico. The success of the revolution depended upon secretly purchasing arms in the United States. The deal had been arranged, but the exchange of money and weapons had not taken place.

I was to help prevent that transaction.

I flew from Brownsville to El Paso in an old crate of an airplane. When I arrived at Fort Bliss, I met with the commanding General. The situation was already so serious that his office was set up in an old steel-reinforced railroad engine cab as a protection against bullets, and the United States army under his command was alerted to be ready at any moment to move across the border and take Juarez, if it became necessary to save the constitutional government.

I learned that the arms transaction was to be accomplished by the former mayor of Juarez. My assignment was to take a good look at this man, and then fly to Kansas City, Missouri, to be prepared to identify him when he got off the train there.

I flew in another old crate to Kansas City and reported to Union Station when the train was scheduled to arrive. I pointed the man out to the other agents there. He was arrested, and when he was searched, he was found to have $300,000 sewed into the lining of his topcoat. With the guns and ammunition it would buy, the revolution might have had a chance at success. However, by the end of December, 1928, Calles managed to defeat the revolutionaries.

With this misssion accomplished, I was ordered to stay on in Kansas City. From this center, my assignment was to travel around the Middle West gathering information about the underworld and its bootlegging operations. For a cover, I got a job as a salesman, selling automobile parts to garages.

I spent time settling into Kansas City, getting to know my way. The biggest dope peddler and bootlegger there was Frank DeMayo, and I had to work my way into his circle, and just keep my ears open for any useful information. I began hanging out at dance halls, mingling until I got to know a few people on the lower level of society. Before long I was into DeMayo's headquarters.

The first important piece of information was that one of Al Capone's men was coming to Kansas City, to take flying lessons at Art Goebbels' flying school to become the gangster's private pilot. Art Goebbels was known to be one of the great flying teachers in America. To my delight, I was ordered to take flying lessons and to come to know Capone's man.

As with many flyers in those early days, Art Goebbels was a wild, unpredictable man. He possessed a large ego, and liked all his publicity. (Later, in World War II, he thought he should have General "Hap"

Arnold's job, and raised a stink until he was made a Major and placed in charge of the Midland, Texas, bombardier's school.) Once, I thought he was going to get me killed. He stormed onto the field, mad as hell, and told me to get in the back seat of a single-engine airplane. I got in and found that the safety straps were broken; all I had was stubs. He flew the craziest that day of any flyer I'd ever seen, stunting all over Kansas City—flying upside down and swooping under telephone wires. I had to hold onto those two little stub-ends of straps to keep from falling out of the plane. My hands became numb, and by the time he landed, his temper had cooled down. I never learned why he was so angry.

Getting to know Martin, Capone's man, was easy. He was a well-educated and cultivated gentleman. Most of the men taking flying lessons from Goebbels weren't high-school graduates. He gravitated toward me because I talked his language.

When we had become friendly enough, I asked Martin if he knew of a room to rent.

"Sure," he told me. "They have two or three vacancies where I'm staying on 15th Street. It's clean, and comfortable."

He took me to the place, a large brick house, owned by an elderly man and his wife. "Why don't you just move into my room with me," Martin suggested. "There are two beds."

It would be an ideal arrangement for me. Living in close quarters, we became close friends. He owned a shiny Chrysler automobile, and frequently we drove to Chicago for weekends.

He took me to one special function, a birthday party for Al Capone, a big blow-out, in a large open pavilion behind a Chicago restaurant. It was a banquet, with some of the finest pastries I'd ever tasted, lots of drinks, and fine entertainment.

When Martin obtained his pilot's license, we parted company, and he returned to Chicago.

My last assignment for the Bureau involved the feud between the Sheltons and the Burgers. The underworld divided into territories in order to function effectively. When gangs couldn't agree on territorial rights, they spent their time killing each other off. Al Capone controlled northern Illinois, but two underworld families were quarreling over control of southern Illinois, from Springfield to Cairo.

Most people think they were bootleggers, and the gangs were involved in bootleg business, but their income was dependent on the sugar sold, at exhorbitant prices, to the bootleggers.

At the time I arrived on the scene, the Sheltons and the Burgers had had several shoot-outs.

I rented myself a cottage at Jiggs and Maggie's Place in Centralia, Illinois, and went about my business selling automobile parts. I received news that a truck had been hijacked near Edwardsville, and the driver and another man were killed. I went calling on the garages there and learned the truck was supposed to have carried shoes, but I learned that it was loaded with sugar.

I went to Cairo, Illinois, stopping there at an Italian restaurant for dinner, a big place, nicely decorated, with crisp white cloths on all the tables. But the restaurant was empty, so I selected a table at the back, near the kitchen. I sat down with my back to the wall.

I hadn't had time to order dinner before two men entered and walked straight to my table. Without invitation they pulled out chairs and sat down, one on either side of me.

"How long you going to be in town?" one asked me.

"Well," I said, trying to sound casual, "I have two or three places to call on here, and when I call on them . . . ."

"No," the other guy interrupted. "You're going to leave now."

I shook my head. "I'm sorry," I said, "but I have to call on these other garages before I leave."

I ordered my food, and sat there and ate it, while they continued to try to persuade me to leave. I had no idea who they were, whether they were Burgers or Sheltons, but I knew I couldn't turn and run, because that would be a sign that I had a reason to. I had to proceed with business as if their threats meant nothing to me.

That night, when I got back to my cottage at Jiggs and Maggie's Place, I found that Earl Shelton had rented four cottages there and, with several of his men, moved in. Jiggs and Maggie's Place was well-known for its barbecue. Not long after I had begun staying there, Jiggs had asked me about Texas barbecue. I helped him dig a pit and taught him the style of Texas pit barbecue. People drove for miles to eat there.

Earl Shelton claimed to have come to Jiggs and Maggie's Place because of the barbecue.

I became acquainted with Shelton, and one night I received a message that he wanted to see me at his cottage. Although I had spent time with him in the bar or restaurant, and had stood talking with him in front of the cottages, I had not been asked to come to him. I knew something was up.

Shelton was quite friendly, asking me to sit. He offered me a drink, then spoke seriously. "I know what you're doing here," he said. "I don't want you to confirm or deny it. I know that you call your report every night at midnight, and I know everything that you report. I don't expect you to believe me, so I want to prove it to you. Tonight, after you make your report, I want you to come back here to see me. You can go anywhere in the world to make your call, but an hour later I'll know everything you said."

I admitted nothing, but it was probably obvious to Shelton that he had taken me by surprise. "Do you have anything more to say?" I asked him.

"No," he said genially. "But will you come back here to see me between one and two o'clock?"

I hesitated a moment, and then agreed.

I took a lot of care that night to see that I wasn't followed. I drove to East St. Louis, crossing the Mississippi river, and taking a circuitous route. I looked continually into my rear-view mirror, and when I was absolutely sure no car was following, I crossed the river again to the Missouri side and found an isolated phone booth.

That night my report concerned a new nightspot and gambling joint that Earl Shelton's brother was opening just south of Springifield. My Washington contact seemed to find the information interesting.

It was almost two o'clock in the morning when I got back to Jiggs and Maggie's Place, but the light was still on in Earl Shelton's cottage. He welcomed my knock, still quite friendly.

When I had sat, he repeated to me word-for-word my report to Washington. I was stunned. I was certain I had not been followed, and there was no way someone could tap all the telephones in the area.

"I guess you realize you're working for a bunch of crooks," he said.

"Why are you telling me this?" I asked.

"Like I said, son," he smiled. "I like you, and I like your barbecue. I have never harmed anyone that I like, but it might get to the point where I couldn't protect you, even from my own men. And you could get killed." He deliberated for a moment.

"For example," he continued, "that report you gave tonight is going to make a lot of trouble for my brother. It's not going into files of the Bureau of Investigation. It's going to William J. Burns, and he's going to be mad at my brother. Because my brother hasn't paid him the money for that new club."

I felt like a callow, naive child, a complete fool.

"Don't feel bad about this," Shelton said, obviously reading the expression on my face. "There are older and wiser men than you who have been tricked the same way." He grinned. "Oh, yes, I know how old you are. The Bureau thinks you're 23, but I know you aren't even 21 yet. I also know you have four different sets of license plates for your car, from four different states, and I know what they are. In my business, a man has to know everything, because what he doesn't know can kill him. That's why I think you ought to get out now, before it's too late."

Part II
PIPE LINES

Jerry Sadler, age 17.

The note Tom Clark left after the near fatal auto accident in 1934.

6

Back to Basics

To take the Bureau of Investigation job, I gave up an opportunity for law school. Two years had passed since I had been offered a football scholarship to the University of Iowa. I was not sure if that offer remained a possibility. Before resigning the Bureau, I decided to find if the Iowa option was open to me. The state was in my investigative (and sales) territory.

Earlier I had made a trip into Iowa, and had learned then to be careful about fitting in with local people. One thing I did to meet townspeople was to attend church. In Texas men wore white linen suits to church in the summertime, and it never occurred to me that Iowa custom would be different. I made my first summertime stop in Sioux City, and naturally I wore my white linen suit to church.

It was the first time the people there had ever seen a white linen suit. I attracted so much attention that I packed the suit away and never wore it again until I returned to Texas.

When I arrived in Iowa City, I arranged to see Wiley Rutledge, Dean of the law school. I found him a peculiar fellow—probably the most unmaterialistic man I had met—but we hit it off very well. He cared deeply about only two things—the law and fishing. He claimed his great aim in life was to be a hobo, but it was an aim he fulfilled only on vacations. The practice of the law required a degree of stability. He died in 1949, a Justice of the United States Supreme Court. In his will he left a set of law books, an old Buick automobile, and a bank account of a few hundred dollars.

Dean Rutledge invited me to stay with him while I was in Iowa City. We went fishing together, talking about the law, my prospects, and the future. He offered me advice without speaking outright what I should do. Rather we weighed the pros and cons of my prospects in such a way that I could set the best course for myself.

This was late summer, 1929, several months before the Wall Street crash. But he predicted the crash accurately. "When that happens," he told me, "lawyers will be a dime a dozen. The only people working will be those providing the basic services in life—food, clothing, housing. You'd be better off working in the oil company laboratories, because people will still need heat and fuel for transportation. It will certainly be rough trying to work your way through law school."

He praised my desire to help the little guy. "For awhile," he predicted, "the little guy is going to need to survive more than he's going to need a lawyer."

During the fishing trip, I thought a lot about his advice and his views of all the economic indicators. I decided to return to Texas. I was back into my old job at the Gulf Laboratories when the depression hit. Rutledge's prediction proved correct for awhile. Businesses were going under all over the country, but the oil companies kept going. Skilled employees kept their jobs. However, I doubt even Rutledge realized how deep the depression would go.

About two years later, Gulf's management began to lay off employees. The first time the executive vice-president, Pete Burger, attempted the layoffs, the general manager, Walter Pyron, refused. He knew the company was economically sound, that cutbacks were not necessary. He told Burger that the men had mouths and they had rectums, and they had to use both. "I won't lay off a man. And if you try to force me to, I'll resign and set myself up in competition to the Gulf Oil Corporation; I have enough Gulf stock to do just that."

"How did you get it?" the VP demanded. "Did you steal it?"

"That's none of your damned business," Pyron replied.

He did resign, thereby postponing the layoffs until the company could hire a new general manager. Pyron made good on his threat. He moved to Pittsburgh and opened up a brokerage office directly across the street from the Gulf Building.

I had worked at Gulf long enough to know some strange dealings that involved management, but the layoffs were shoddy, taking advantage of ordinary workers who lacked power to fight on their own terms. Gulf was doing all right, making a profit at a time when many businesses were closing. Layoffs were not necessary.

Many fired employees had homes financed by a building-and-loan company owned by the Mellon family, which also owned Gulf. When these men were laid off, they were unable to keep up mortgage payments, and the loan company repossessed their homes.

Gulf laid off over 6,000 workers. It was a long, painful process: one week a couple of thousand would go; then more the next week. I understood the psychology of the layoffs—if all workers were let go at once, the entire group might protest. But men who missed the axe the first or second time wouldn't stand up for their associates. With wives and children at home, they kept silent, hoping they would go unnoticed the next time the axe fell.

I knew most of the men in the laboratories by name—my job involved sampling and testing throughout the plant. The day the first 2,000 were given notice, I sat on a wooden box outside the gate, watching the workers leave, misery and fear evident on their faces. I counted the men I knew whose homes were mortgaged to the Mellon's loan company. The percentage was a disproportionate one, I felt. Some were men who had only a short time before retirement.

Finally, after they had all come through the gate, I was in a rage. I picked up my wooden box, and smashed it against the wall of the commissary, then stormed to the main office building. The new General Manager, Charlie Stephenson, had offices on the top floor. Employees needed permission to go there, but I walked into Charlie Stephenson's office unannounced.

Unlike most of the men, I had little to lose by endangering my job. I had no family depending on me for support and no outstanding debt, such as a mortgage.

Before I could say anything at all, Stephenson stood up from his desk. "I know," he said. "I have it coming. But I couldn't help it. I had to do it."

"You could have done the same thing Walter Pyron did," I told him angrily. "You could have stuck by the men."

Stephenson appeared genuinely distressed. "I would have lost my job," he said, "and eventually they would have gotten someone who would do what they want. And I'm not like Pyron. I don't have anything to fall back on."

"It didn't have to be layoffs," I argued. "You know as well as I do that every man in this plant would accept a cutback to two or three days a week just to keep everybody on the payroll."

"I'm sorry," he apologized. "I'm just following orders."

Leaving Stephenson, I went to see the plant superintendent. I asked him if there wasn't something he could do about the situation. With tears in his eyes, he told me there had been nothing he could have done.

He turned away from me, concealing the tears. "It's the worst thing I've ever had to be a party to," he said staring out the window.

I knew then my Gulf Laboratories days were numbered. I was not a favorite of top management. On one occasion Pete Burger had been forced to come down from Pittsburgh to try to get me in line. It concerned the efforts to put into effect the group life insurance plan. Supposedly for the welfare of the workers, management wanted to withdraw a dollar a month per thousand dollars of insurance from each employee's paycheck. For the 10,000 employees, the total would be an enormous sum, and I was convinced they were trying to rook the workers. At the time, there was a state law that 100 percent of a company's employees had to sign before a company could have group insurance. I was holding out, and I continued to hold out despite Burger's attempts at persuasion.

There was also the matter of my political activities. When I returned to Port Arthur, I also returned to my interest in local politics, and in 1930 expanded to activities on behalf of one of the candidates for state office. Gulf management had posted notices on the bulletin boards "recommending" that all employees vote for Slim Calhoun for Attorney General of Texas. Within the company, I was the campaign manager for Jimmy Allred, who beat Calhoun in the election. Gulf management was unhappy about that.

The thing that surprised me was they waited several weeks to lay me off; the apparent reason for the delay was that several of my superiors had gone to bat for me. They insisted they could not get along without me and several other "renegades."

When I got the axe, I approached Charlie Stephenson, this time without anger. "There's one thing I want to know," I said. "Did my layoff order come from Pittsburgh?"

"It did," he told me. "But I've got an idea. I'd like you to stay with the Gulf Oil Corporation where they can't get to you. O.H. Carlisle, the General Sales Manager, needs a lab man in Houston. You've got just the requirements he's looking for. You've tested stuff at different places, under different state laws. I'd like to give you a letter to him."

"I'll take the letter," I said, "but I'm doing it just so I can go by and tell Mr. Carlisle personally what I think of the Mellon family."

When I went to see Carlisle in Houston, he listened to everything I had to say. "Despite your feelings, I'd like you to come to work for me," the sales manager said. "I can't guarantee that you wouldn't get laid off here as well, but I need someone like you."

"I'm sorry," I told him. "But the way I feel about the Mellon family, I don't think I could continue to work for Gulf in any capacity."

"I'm sorry, too," he said. "You don't know how badly I need a good lab man right now." Then he surprised me. He told me he knew of another job. He said the State Comptroller's office needed someone with lab experience.

I told him I was interested and thanked him for the reference. I did not admit to him that I had thought of applying there. I wanted to be in a position where I could examine the Gulf Oil Corporation and its activities. Working in the tax department of the State Comptroller's office would be a way to accomplish this. I had my own way of applying for the position, however. I intended to go to see the Attorney General, Jimmy Allred.

I was not sure Carlisle would give me the reference he promised. I considered him an honrable man, but I guessed when he reflected upon it, he would realize Gulf would not wish me working in the Comptroller's office. I knew far too much.

Then I went to Austin, the Texas capitol, to see Jimmy Allred. He was aware of me, and he knew a little of my background. I expanded on this, then mentioned my interest in the lab job with the Comptroller's office.

He asked his secretary to take me to meet George H. Shepherd in the Comptroller's office. "Mr. Allred would appreciate anything you can do for Mr. Sadler," she told him. To my surprise, I was told Carlisle had called, as promised, and recommended me.

I was immediately hired, and was assigned to Tyler headquarters, the area of the East Texas oilfields.

The State Comptroller's office needed a lab man because a number of the oil companies were illegally billing gasoline as kerosene to avoid paying taxes. Kerosene was not a taxable commodity, but gasoline was. The practice was rampant, some companies sending out the illegal "kerosene" by the shipload. The state was losing a great deal of money, and the oil companies were increasing profits. The only way to prove the lawless practice was to have a laboratory chemist test shipments to determine precisely what was being shipped.

7

The East Texas Oilfields

In 1933, the nation was in the depths of the depression, and I joined the ranks of the unemployed. In one of my disputes with Pete Burger at the Gulf labs, I had boasted that, if a deep depression ever hit, I could always return to papa's farm, where I would have more to eat than Andrew Mellon did. Now I didn't have much choice but to make true that boast.

Like most people, mama and papa had little money, but unlike most others, they did have food. They had their land and the ability to grow what they needed. I was not happy about having to return to Hickory Grove, but I did not consider it a permanent move—it was not a defeat, merely a temporary setback.

That spring I helped papa start a tomato crop in the hope of making at least some money. We put the plants in the cold frame, and prepared the ground for planting.

Mama observed I wasn't a happy farmer. One evening she consoled me, encouraging me to have faith that the depression wouldn't last long. "Mr. Roosevelt's right," she told me. "As soon as people have confidence in their country again, there'll be jobs."

"I don't know, Mama," I replied. "It seems to me that people just have to have confidence in themselves first. Nothing's going to happen until some people at least go out and try."

Mama was sympathetic. "But what can anybody do?" she asked. "What can you do?"

"I've still got my knowledge and my skills," I replied. "There ought to be plenty of things I could do. Just what I know about oil refining should be enough."

Until that moment, I hadn't thought about the situation seriously. I had accepted as something inevitable the fact that I was jobless. If jobs were to be had, I felt there were others who needed them more than I did. I didn't want to take a job away from a man who had to support a wife and kids. But I realized there was another way to look at the situation. I didn't need a job belonging to another; I could go out and make a job for myself. In truth, that was the only way the country would get out of the depression—individuals had to put all their effort into starting over.

The situation was not unlike all those Horatio Alger stories I had read as a kid.

"Mama," I said suddenly, "I want to make a deal with you. I think I can make money, but I have to have a partner. I've got ability, but I don't have a cent to live on until I can start making money."

She smiled. "But your papa and I don't have anything either."

"No," I agreed, "you don't have any money. But you do have eight old yard hens you don't need. I'm sure we could get something for them. We would be equal partners. I'll send you half of whatever I make."

"You don't have to do that," she told me. "Take the hens as a gift. If you do make more money than you need, use it to help others get back on their feet. Your papa and I can manage on our own."

I received a total of $4.35 for the eight chickens from D.S. Lively's store in Elkhart—my funding to travel to Gladewater to look for work in the East Texas oilfields. I made that $4.35 last as long as I could. I slept under a boiler at a refinery where I could keep warm, and I made the rounds of the oil companies during the day. I ate as little as possible, and tried to convince my stomach to stop grumbling, promising it would have all the food it needed in a few days.

As days passed, it appeared my venture would be a failure. My efforts at selling myself were not well received by the businessmen I talked to. Some men looked at me as if I were crazy to talk so positively about the profits I could gather for them. "Don't you know we're in a depression?" they asked.

Finally, down to seventy cents, my stomach wouldn't trust me any longer. I blew my whole bankroll on some bread and bologna. Then, before giving up I made one last try.

At the Cherokee Chief Refining Company in Jacksonville, I asked to see L.B. Haberle the president. As soon as I met him, I liked him, and I felt his instant liking of me. We discussed refining operations; he admitted he was merely topping the crude oil, producing only high octane gasoline. It was a perfect opening for me.

"You know," I said, "you could increase your profits considerably by branching out to make kerosene and heating oil as well. Why don't you?"

"I've talked about doing that," he admitted, "with my plant superintendent. But we just don't have the equipment or the ability, and we can't afford to get them."

"Well," I said, "I've got the ability, and I can get you the equipment for next to nothing, if you're willing to hire me."

He hesitated. "I couldn't afford to pay you much."

"Until I get this idea operating," I offered, "all you have to give me is my room and board. Once it's working, you can afford my salary."

"You believe in yourself so much," he said "that I believe in you. It's a deal. What's first?"

We shook hands on it. I could not quite believe I had actually created a job. "We take a trip over to Shreveport," I told him, "to check out the junkyards and find out what sort of equipment the major oil companies have disposed of."

At one of the junkyards we found what we needed—an old bubble tower that Magnolia (the company that is now Mobil) had sold as scrap-metal. It was about a hundred feet tall and still had all its trays. A bubble tower works like a still, vaporizing crude oil. The top trays pull off the lighter stuff, and the bottom trays take the heavier fuel oil.

That bubble tower cost $75.00, but we still had a problem. As big as it was, and weighing in at 300,000 pounds, it would be extremely difficult to transport to Gladewater. In those days, we did not have heavy moving equipment. We rigged two trucks and were granted a special right-of-way highway permit. Once we moved it to the refinery, we constructed a special concrete foundation and set it up.

It took quite a bit of work to get it in operation. Haberle had to return to his Jacksonville office, so he left me in charge at Gladewater. To assist me, Haberle assigned an employee, Bill Parks, one of the strongest men I've seen, before or since. He had been in and out of prisons most of his life; he possessed an array of scars over his body from being knifed, shot, and beaten. But he could lift and carry anything. He would pick up a Worthington pump—normally it took four men to carry—cart it single-handedly where I needed it, and set it down.

With his help we had everything ready in less than a week. On a Sunday morning, I called Haberle and told him we were ready to process. He came from Jacksonville, and we placed the bubble tower in operation—that pile of scrap metal worked perfectly.

Haberle was pleased and impressed. For a minimal investment he had doubled his production potential. He was able to ship kerosene, heating oil, and high-octane gasoline, just like the major oil companies. He named me superintendent of the refinery and gave me a salary of $250 a month and use of an automobile, a Chrysler, once his wife's car.

I was as pleased as Haberle. With the backing of yard hens worth $4.35, I had gotten myself back on my feet.

However, it was impossible for my life to remain peaceful for long; working as superintendent for only a short time, I discovered two of Haberle's production men were stealing oil. It wasn't petty pilfering either; they were taking oil by the trainload. My problem was that the robbers were two men that Haberle trusted. One was a man who was a neighbor of Haberle's in Jacksonville, the other man a geologist.

I tried to tell Haberle what was going on, but he wouldn't listen. He considered these men his friends, and there was never a man more loyal and trusting than Haberle. So I went to see Judge Gibson, one of Haberle's partners. He and Steve Barber were part owners of the company, but Haberle ran it. Judge Gibson listened to me. "Haberle will never believe it unless you can show him the proof," he said. "You'll have to catch them in the act. If you can find out when they next intend to make a shipment, we'll take him to the railroad siding and show him."

I expressed my concern to Gibson that Haberle's trust in me seemed to have fallen. "One of these men has been talking to him about you," Judge Gibson informed me. "He claims you're a troublemaker. He's investigated you, and says you made trouble at Gulf."

This revelation angered me. "I didn't make trouble," I said. "The trouble was already there. I just found it."

I should have realized that an underhanded man would not have stopped at investigating my past. I learned too late that he had been having me watched to determine just how much I knew and what I intended to do about it.

We all had sleeping quarters at the refinery, and that made matters more difficult. On the night I discovered that they were going to be loading about forty tankers of stolen oil, I was preparing to alert Judge Gibson and again talk to Haberle.

However, as I was about to leave, one of the men stopped me.

"Where are you going?"

"I have a date tonight," I replied.

"You have to cancel it," he said threateningly. "You're not going to leave the premises tonight." He had been drinking pretty heavily, and had had a dice game going with the geologist and Haberle's lawyer, Fred Upchurch. He backed me into my room and began to rave. "You think you run things around here," he went on almost incoherently. "But you're going to find out you don't. You know, I was in France in the war, and I've killed plenty of men. It doesn't mean a thing to me to see a man die. I've seen them get blown to bits; I could watch you die and not feel a thing. You wouldn't like it very much, would you?"

Backed against a wall, I refused to cower. I decided to try to placate him. "No," I admitted, "I wouldn't like that."

"Then you'll stay in your room tonight, won't you?" he pursued.

"Sure," I said. "My date's not that important."

Instead of pacifying, my attitude seemed to reinforce his belligerence. "Of course it's not important, because I say it's not. And you're going to do what I say from now on. Isn't that so?"

"I don't know about that," I said, standing my ground. "I'll stay here tonight, but I'm my own boss. I do only what I want to do. And right now I want to stay in my room, and I want you to get your ass out."

The situation was quiet after that, until September 8, when I planned a celebration for my birthday. I didn't invite the two men, but they came anyway. One spiked my drinks with pure alcohol, and I was soon drunk. With my guard down, I was hit over the head and knocked unconscious. Luckily, one of the fellows I had invited to my party called Haberle in Jacksonville.

When I came to, I was in the bathtub, and Haberle was washing the blood off a cut on my head. Soon after that, a doctor arrived, called by Haberle, and I got my wound sewed up.

Haberle was mad as hell at the two men he had trusted so loyally, and he finally believed what I had been trying to tell him.

He wanted to do his own housecleaning; and to accomplish his objectives he wanted me out of the picture. "I want you to go up to Dallas to see a doctor and make sure your injuries aren't more serious than they appear. After you're all right, I want you to go over to see Jesse McKee at the Tyler Refining Company. He's got some problems you can solve for him, and I think he can offer you a better deal than what you have with me."

As a bonus, Haberle gave me his Chrysler and a thousand dollars in cash.

When I had recovered from the head injury, and my face had healed, I left Dallas and went to Arp, Texas, to meet with Jesse McKee, president of the Tyler Refining Company, which owned two refineries— Tyreco Number 1 in Arp and Tyreco Number 2 in Overton. His problem was similar to L.B. Haberle's, but his business was in bad shape and in danger of going under completely.

McKee and his board of directors knew about me, and they seemed ready to make a deal immediately. But I was cautious. "First," I told the board members, "I want to look at your books."

McKee agreed.

From the account books, I learned the company was in poorer shape than I had suspected. Tyreco owed everybody; bills remained unpaid for months.

I met with mcKee and other board members. "All right, I'll make a deal," I told them. But if I get you out of trouble, I want a part of the company."

"We can't do that," McKee protested. "We're in too bad a circumstance to give anything away."

"I don't want it now," I explained. "While I'm getting you out of this, I'll take a salary—say $250 a month. But the day I get this company into the black, I want one-third of the company. That's fair, isn't it? Without me, you've got nothing but debts."

Finally, they gave in, and we shook hands on the deal.

In the beginning, the biggest problem was dealing with the company's creditors. Almost every day, several of them would come to the office—always, they were angry. I explained I had to have time to pull the company back on its feet. If they kept bugging, I wouldn't be able to do that, and the company would be forced to bankruptcy, leaving them with nothing. If they would be patient, they would get their money, every cent of it.

Most accepted that without too much complaint.

I had pulled Cherokee out of the hole by buying a discarded piece of junk and putting it into shape. This time I wasn't as lucky in the junkyards. However, in Wichita Falls, I found some good used cracking equipment, which breaks up the molecules of fuel oil to make gasoline. It had belonged to American Refining Company, which had gone broke, American had owned most of the best equipment available.

I made a deal to buy the cracking equipment for a price of $25,000.

Since Tyreco had no cash on hand, I had to persuade the sellers to accept payment in gasoline. And I had to make a similar deal to get the equipment moved to East Texas, though for awhile I thought my $25,000 worth of cracking machinery was going to have to stay where it was.

I talked to several hauling companies, and their rates were all in the range of $3,000 to make the move. None were willing to take payment in gasoline; they all wanted cash up front. Then Ed Loving, the father of a young lady I had been courting, came to the rescue. He had a gasoline trucking business, and he knew the economic potential behind what I was doing.

He came in to see me one day, wearing a blue work-suit. "I hear you're having some trouble getting some equipment moved," he said. "I thought you might welcome a loan."

"How did you know that?" I asked.

"My daughter told me," he explained. "And she seems to think pretty highly of you. She says you're a gentleman."

I was embarrassed about taking a loan from a potential father-in-law, but I wasn't going to turn down the answer to my prayers. When he took a wad of money out of the pocket of his blue work-suit, I knew he was in earnest about his offer.

"Here's the $3,000 you need," he said as he handed it to me. "And I'll take my repayment in gasoline."

We moved the equipment, set it up, and put it into operation. We were now able to make everything—gasoline, kerosene, heating oil, lube oil. Gradually, I began to pay off the creditors, a few at a time.

In took awhile, but in time the Tyler Refining Company was in the black. But meanwhile, I had gotten myself into some big trouble with the federal government, and I had a tough fight on my hands to keep from going to the penitentiary.

8

Oil and Politics

By the time I reached the age of 26, I had learned a great many lessons on how the system worked. The big guys with the money had the power, and they used that power to keep the little guys from rising to being big guys (a lesson Horatio Alger never revealed). Nowhere was this more true than in the oil business, and at no time was the practice more ruthless than in the 1930s.

There was big money in oil, and big oil companies wanted it all for themselves, legally or otherwise. Most of the big companies were not native Texas companies, but they were managed from Wall Street, and they wielded their power to keep the small, new independent companies in Texas—and elsewhere—from establishing any foothold in the business. I witnessed the action during the period I worked at Cherokee and at Tyreco.

The oil companies controlled the Texas Railroad Commission, which in turn controlled the state's flow of oil, and they controlled the Federal Tender Board, recently established as a part of Franklin Roosevelt's NRA—National Recovery Administration.

I'm not sure which situation galled me more. It certainly made me angry that native Texans, elected to public office by Texas voters, would sell out to the Wall Street boys; that was simple greed. I believe the NRA upset me more, at least at the time. Roosevelt had set himself as the defender of the little guy, and the NRA was undemocratically working against the little guy.

While I was endeavoring to bail out Jesse McKee and Tyler Refining Company, a group of owners and managers of independent refineries met in Gladewater to find a solution to the problem. Most of the men were from East Texas, some were from other parts of the state, and from Louisiana, Arkansas, and Oklahoma as well. Attendance included R.J. McMurrey, of McMurrey Refining Company, Haberle of Haberle Refining Company, Freeman Burford of Greggton Refining and Grogan and Crittenden of Grogan Refinery at Shreveport. I believe the owners of Gladewater Refining, and Sabine Refining were represented as well.

We formed the Independent Refiners Association of America, hoping that, united as a group, we could successfully fight the power of the big oil companies.

Before that meeting, I had called on my friend Dean Wiley Rutledge, of the Iowa Law School, for advice. I felt the National Industrial Recovery Act was unconstitutional.

He confirmed this, giving me the legal reasons.

The specific clause (Section 9-C) of the National Industrial Recovery Act that affected oil production was authored by Texas Senator Tom Connally. It stipulated that the federal government would prohibit the shipment of interstate commerce of oil produced in defiance of the laws of the separate states (known as "Hot Oil"). Section 9-C gave the President, or the executive branch of the federal government, the power to dictate to oil businessmen how they would run their businesses. More significantly, it gave power to determine which businessmen would get the business, entirely negating the free-enterprise system.

The concept of the law was a good one; it was intended as a means of conservation. However, in effect, it set up a monopoly.

The National Industrial Recovery Act (NIRA), which set up the National Recovery Administration, established boards (of business-men) to enforce the act—in effect, running businesses, large and small, within their own industry. The Federal Tender Board, supervising the oil business, was controlled entirely by the larger oil companies—the Wall Street crowd. Independent oil companies didn't have a chance of survival.

Fortified by the legal arguments of Wiley Rutledge, I proposed to the Gladewater meeting of independent refiners that we test the legality of Section 9-C of the NIRA. The discussion was heated! The only way to test the law was to break it, to produce hot oil knowingly and blatantly, subjecting ourselves to: criminal prosecution. If the courts failed to overturn the NIRA, we would all go to prison.

I argued that only one person—a person chosen as a sacrificial lamb—would have to face this prospect. My idea: to have one person sign daily reports for all independent refiners. These daily reports represented the real tangible inequity in the law. Large oil companies were not required to file them, but independents had to file reports on oil produced each day, swearing that their production was not in excess of federal regulations. There was so much paperwork involved, I doubted those reports were really read by the Railroad Commissioners.

As a result, I was selected as the sacrificial lamb and elected Chairman of the newly formed Independent Refiners Association of America. R.J. McMurrey was elected President. The refiners' daily reports passed through my hands, and I took responsibility for filing (and signing) them. There were 128 members of our association; that's a mountain of reports. Some of the refiners would produce in excess of their proration—"hot oil"—so as to break the law, and I took full responsibility for it. Since I assumed the big risk, I would be paid a small fee for each barrel of "hot oil" I signed for.

We settled privately on a fee of 25 cents a barrel; the amount, when added in thousands of barrels, could make me a rich man. I liked this idea, being rich, but not so much that I was willing to go to prison. What a man sows, he reaps, and I had no intention of using that "ill-gotten gain" entirely for myself. I had made a promise to my mother when she contributed eight old hens to my future. I'd use that money to help the needy.

Of course an easy way of disposing of my promise would have been to give the entire amount to an organized charity and allow them to see to the needy. However, a serious problem with organized charities is their defining "needy," proscribing limitations and boundaries for their grants. Too, a large percentage of money given to a charity is spent on the organization itself, so that it may perpetuate itself.

I wished my "charity" to be as direct and simple as my mother's gift of chickens, and I wanted the gift to be anonymous. I organized a volunteer group of women to be responsible for finding the needy and giving funds according to invididual needs. Once in operation, money was going out to the needy at a rate of $1,000 to $1,600 a day. The largest amounts went for food to hungry families. Large amounts went to pay medical expenses for the sick. There was room also for outright gifts of money to help individuals get back on their feet, out from under the burden of public charity.

Always the source remained anonymous. Many years later, women who were operating the grants program did talk about it, and the City of Arp named me honorary mayor and honorary president of the Chamber of Commerce for life.

I did not worry that I might need some of it for myself. The Tyler Refining Company would soon be going fluid, and I would receive a third of the company stock—or, so I expected. As it turned out, Jesse McKee reneged on our deal. It was easy to do because, by the time the company was in the black, I was in the thick soup of the Federal Tender Board's inquiry into the hot oil violations.

I continued filing daily reports in a form of my own devising. Rather than declare that the oil produced was *not* in excess of proration orders, I declared that it *was* in excess; thereby making it clear I challenged the legality of the Federal Tender Board. I did not attempt to cheat and lie. R.J. McMurrey, in the FTB soup with me, had chosen to sign his own reports rather than let me suffer the brunt alone.

When I appeared before the board of Tyler Refining Company, I anticipated indictment by a federal prosecutor for violation of the National Industrial Recovery Act. I was referred to in the courts and in newspapers as the "owner" of the Tyreco Refining Company Number 2. Now that I had pulled the company in the black, I approached the board to make that true in fact as well as in public references.

The entire board was present for the meeting. I showed them the company's books as proof that it was finally showing a profit. "Now I would like to have one-third of the company's stock as promised when I undertook this job," I announced.

Jesse McKee, the president, looked grim. "We're not going to do it," he said. "We don't have to. There's nothing in writing."

I was furious. "But we had a handshake!"

"We can't help that," McKee shrugged. "Things have changed. We've discussed the situation among ourselves, and we agree. The company can't afford the publicity you're giving it right now. We want you to resign."

The Sadler temper exploded. I was ready to face Jesse McKee and demanded that he step outside with me, so that I could have the satisfaction of beating him to a pulp. But as I lunged at him, the other board members grabbed me and held me back. McKee cowered, protesting that he had a bad heart and couldn't fight.

The other board members calmed me, and we continued to talk; I saw their reasoning, but I was not happy about it. It would do no good to force our dispute into the law courts at this point. Doing so would serve merely to weaken my already shaky public image.

By way of apology, McKee told me he realized the salary of $250 a month had not been satisfactory for the work performed for Tyreco. "Therefore we're willing to pay you $25,000 for your interest in the company," he said.

I was still fuming. "My third share is worth close to half-a-million dollars," I protested.

McKee actually smiled. "You can't cry poverty," he said. "Your association with us has been quite profitable. I don't know what you're getting for signing the reports for the other refineries, but I'm sure it's a good sum."

I couldn't reveal that money was going out to others as quickly as it was coming in. Finally, I agreed to accept the $25,000 and resign.

I made no attempt to find another job; my hands were full with the court cases, and my severance money from Tyreco would keep me for awhile.

I was also active in politics, realizing that the only way the independent refiners could compete effectively with the majors would be to have influence with the state's lawmakers.

For awhile, we tried playing the game the same way the majors did, by lobbying and offering payoffs. However, our most notable effort—an attempt to pay off Governor Ma Ferguson—backfired on us. (Ma Ferguson was never called by her name, Miriam. It was always "Ma" or "Mrs." Ferguson.)

We hired John Punt to do our lobbying. He was an independent oil man, and he had opposed Lon Smith for Railroad Commissioner. He and Ma Ferguson's husband, the impeached ex-governor Jim Ferguson, were said to be good friends. At least, Ferguson had supported John Punt in his effort to be on the Railroad Commission.

The major companies had managed to get a bill introduced in the legislature that would place further restrictions on the independent refiners and would, in the long run, put some of our number entirely out of business. The big oil companies put a lot of money into getting the bill passed, both in the Senate and the House. One representative, we found out, had been paid $50,000 for his vote, though several legislators collected considerably less than that.

After the restrictions bill had passed the Senate and had gone to the House, Punt notified me that we were going to have to fight fire with fire. There was no way our organization could afford to go in and pay off the representatives; we didn't have that kind of money. However, Punt proposed, we could pay off the Governor to veto the bill. He had already sounded Jim Ferguson out on the idea, and he had indicated that Governor Ma Ferguson would accept a $25,000 contribution to her last campaign expenses.

Furthermore, Jim suggested, we would have to provide Ma an

obvious public reason for her veto. If we could provide a public demonstration against the bill in the House gallery when it was scheduled for debate, he would see that Ma showed up to witness it. When vetoing the bill, she would be able to defend her reason, that it would be bad for the economy of East Texas.

We chartered a special train to take our group of public-spirited citizens to Austin, some of whom would be testifying before the House, while others would lend their physical and moral support in the gallery. The hearing that day in the house chamber lasted about three hours, and Ma Ferguson with Jim at her side, sat through all of it, listening attentively.

After it was over, Mrs. Ferguson thanked everyone for their presentations and assured them she would consider the merits of the bill carefully. Frank Adams, who was Secretary of the Independent Refiners Association, had been handling the presentations. In closing, he presented Mrs. Ferguson with an apple, telling her, "You're our teacher, and a good student always brings the teacher an apple."

Throughout the day, I had remained in the back of the House chamber, keeping quiet. My part in the plan was giving the $25,000 to Jim Ferguson and waiting for word that Ma had decided to agree to our request and veto the bill.

That night I was in my room at the hotel when John Punt knocked on my door. He said we were requested at the Governor's Mansion. We arrived there, but we did not see Mrs. Ferguson—Jim was waiting for us, and he was upset. Word of our transaction had been leaked. Jim had received a call from Carl Estes, the lobbyist for Sun Oil Company, and owner of a newspaper in Longview. Estes had learned from an independent refiner all the details of our pay-off. He asked for confirmation or denial of the facts for publication in his newspaper in the event Ma Ferguson vetoed the bill.

The Governor now had no choice but to sign the bill, and she did so the next morning. Only the largest and the hardiest of the independent refiners survived.

It was an uphill fight all the way for the little guys, and we took it inch-by-inch. The big oil boys had the Railroad Commission and the state legislature so well under control that we small refinery boys had a hard time keeping up with all the rules and regulations. It was so bad that an independent could hardly turn without breaking some law or other, while the majors breezed along unhindered.

At the same time, the independent refiners in East Texas had been suffering from a siege of robberies and burglaries. Sometimes it was difficult to keep from being paranoid about this double-edged attack and feeling that both things were a part of the same concerted effort to get rid of us.

One event gave me more suspicion.

To comply with a rule of the State Comptroller's office, I had to take $25,000 in World War I bonds to Austin as a gasoline deposit for one of the refineries. The old World War I bonds were as good as money, because they were transferrable. (Anybody could cash them. We had ordered them from the Republic National Bank in Dallas and were to pick them up at the Arp State Bank one morning.) That afternoon I was to drive to Austin.

In Arp, only a few days before, I had witnessed a bank robbery, but I was not nervous about carrying such a large amount in negotiable bonds. That day, I had been next door at the hardware store, talking with Mr. Allen, the proprietor. We saw the robbers run from the bank with two hostages, a man and a lady, a teller. No one attempted to stop them.

Old Mr. Allen grabbed a rifle from behind the counter. "I don't even know if this thing will fire," he said. "Hasn't been used in 35 years."

He got to the door of the hardware store before the robbers had even backed their car from the parking space, and peering nearsightedly through his Ben Franklin bifocals, took aim.

The sound from that old rifle was ear-shattering, but he had a direct hit, severing the driver's arm at the shoulder. Despite his injury, however, the driver managed to back the car out of the parking space and drive about a hundred yards before passing out. Dr. Tubbs was called, but he couldn't save the man; the other bank robbers were arrested and jailed.

The day I drove alone to Austin, the only protection I had was the pistol I had been carrying more and more often since I had started working in the East Texas oilfields. I couldn't drive faster than 45 miles an hour, because I had had a governor put on the car to keep me from wearing it out as fast as I had done with my previous cars.

Just outside of Kilgore, at Pitner's Junction, the road was blocked. Two trucks had pulled up and stopped as if waiting for someone. The road at that place was built on an embankment, with a steep drop of 75 feet down to fields below.

I sensed that those trucks were waiting for me. I didn't dare stop. I pushed the gas pedal to the floorboard and reached my top speed of 45 miles an hour, and prayed. My one chance was to try to make it around their roadblock.

The embankment was just too steep to make it at that speed, and the car rolled over. I didn't let go of the steering wheel. The rest of my body tumbled all over the front seat as the car flipped over and over down the embankment. I counted each time it turned over—one, two, three, four, five, five and a half.

The engine was still running when the car came to rest. Quickly, I cut the motor off and looked through my open window to see several men begin to scramble down the embankment toward me. It was clear that they were not coming down to see if they could help me, because they were carrying guns.

I was badly shaken up, but I grabbed my pistol and took a shot right into the middle of the group moving toward me, more to frighten them than to kill or injure.

A man used to firing guns can usually tell if the bullet hits target. I felt the thud when that one shot hit. Those men turned around, scrambled up the embankment to their vehicles, and drove off in haste.

A gasoline truck had been stopped on the south side of the junction, the other side of the roadblock. As soon as the blocking trucks pulled away, he drove up, stopped, and called out to ask if I was all right. Within moments, other cars had stopped.

I was bruised and shaken, but otherwise I was uninjured. The all-steel body on my new Dodge had saved me. The roof of the car was flattened out like somebody had spent several hours working with a sledgehammer, but the roof supports weren't even bent: the doors opened and closed as smoothly as before. The engine ran perfectly, and after a tire that had been blown had been replaced with the spare, I was able to drive away.

I was certain the men who had stopped me were the same thugs who had been robbing the refineries; their descriptions matched perfectly. The driver of the gasoline truck told me afterward, confirming my suspicions, that he had stopped well back of the roadblock. He was carrying a good sum of money—around $800—to pay for a load of gasoline. He had waited and watched for some time, and it was clear the roadblockers weren't waiting for just anyone. They were watching for someone who would come from the north, the direction I was on.

Two days later a man with a gunshot wound showed up at a tourist court outside Overton; the tourist court was known to be a hang-out for thugs.

The more I thought about the occurrence, the more I knew it was linked to the big oil companies. Only one man could have leaked the information about the bonds I carried and the time I would leave for Austin; a man of some importance in East Texas. I had trusted this man; he had been my friend. But I began to learn that even good friends can't be trusted when large amounts of money and power are involved.

The year 1934 must have been my year for automobile accidents. I survived this first one all right; I almost didn't survive the next one at all. A few weeks after the first incident, on July 19, I had another one-car accident.

As a part of our efforts to have the independent refiners compete favorably with the major oil companies, I was more active in supporting candidates for state office, physically and financially. The most important candidate I worked for during 1934 was William McCraw, who ran for Texas Attorney General. I contributed money and time to his campaign, traveling around the state, talking, organizing, and enlisting support.

The man managing his campaign was Tom Clark, whom I met at the Independent Refiners Association organizational meeting, and he was responsible for enlisting my support for McCraw. Years later, Clark would be appointed United States Attorney General by President Harry Truman. Then, I was placed in the position of giving him a reference for that post, when a congressional committee checked his credentials, approving him. (More years later, his son, Ramsey Clark, would reach a position of equal prominence in the federal government.)

On a hot July day, Tom Clark and I were returning by auto to Tyler from a campaign trip in Brownsville. The trip was about 650 miles, but it took longer than it might have because I insisted on stopping in San Antonio for a short visit with a girl friend.

It was my car; I was at the wheel. Several times Tom offered to take over the driving, but I insisted I was all right. It was a long, tiring drive for both of us; we were exhausted from the campaign work before we had even set out. Between Austin and Jacksonville, Tom slept off and on in the passenger seat.

About four o'clock in the morning, just outside Jacksonville, with only a short distance yet to go, I stopped the car to put some mentholatum in my eyes. The sharp tingling of the mentholatum could help me stay awake awhile longer.

Tom roused from his sleep and said, "Don't do that. Let me drive.

I've been sleeping all night."

"Are you sure you're awake enough?" I asked.

"Of course I am," Tom replied.

I was so groggy I was grateful to turn the wheel over to him and close my eyes. We switched places and set off again. Having fought sleep so long, I drifted in and out, dozing and then opening my eyes to check the road ahead.

We hadn't traveled very far, only about nineteen miles, when it happened. It was near Bullard.

I felt the car lurching, and my eyes opened. I managed to perceive that the car had left the road before it flipped over and I was pinned in the mass of wreckage.

Somehow Tom had been thrown clear, and he was able to go for help. However, he did not stick around to see if I would regain consciousness. He left a note for me, scrawled on a telegraph form, which stated:

> Jerry:—I can't tell you how sorry I am—it just couldn't be helped—I know you will pull thru—I'm OK and will carry on—Don't worry—Good luck—Tom

I kept that note as a souvenir of a friendship that soon proved to be over.

I was taken to the hospital at Jacksonville. I was lucky that a young doctor there was somewhat knowledgeable of new techniques in surgery. Otherwise I might not have survived, or at the very least would have been confined to a wheelchair for life. My back was broken, and my right hip had been completely torn away from my body. In a series of operations, I was given a new plastic hip.

It was a long, slow, and painful process. The most painful part for me was learning patience. I was accustomed to being active, doing things constantly, but I was stuck in a hospital bed unable to move, day after day, while the world went on without me. There were court cases coming up, and I was concerned that I could do nothing about them. With each operation, I could see my remaining money dwindle. I could not bear the thought that, after it was all over, I might yet be an invalid, a burden for my parents.

The doctor could guarantee nothing. I counted the days—52 of them.

9

Knocking out the NRA

A few days before my release from the Jacksonville hospital, I had two visitors. Duncan and Holt had recently bought the two Tyreco refineries and another, the Constantine Refining Company, located at Overton. I was able, by this time, to move about the hospital, and I'd learned to walk again. Duncan and Holt observed my efforts with some satisfaction, behaving as if their visit were merely a friendly one.

They had seen that I was surviving as a whole man, and then they got down to business. They offered me work. "We need somebody to manage the two refineries at Overton, someone who knows how to produce heating oil. Nobody knows that better than you."

I could not relate how much I valued their offer, how much it meant to be able to work. I tried to respond as if I were not a man who had still to struggle with crutches. "What are you willing to offer?" I asked.

"We'll give you a one-third interest," they told me, "and you can draw $500 a month for expenses. It's a better deal than you had with Tyreco before, but it's fair, since you'll be managing two refineries."

I had to smile. Once, I had been promised one-third of Tyreco. "When would you turn over to me the one-third share in the company?" I asked.

"As soon as you start to work," I was told.

"How about next Monday?" I suggested. "I get out of here on Friday, and I'll have the weekend to see what the world is like now."

On Monday, I appeared on time, and I was given my share certificates as promised. I set to work making the Overton refineries the best in East Texas, and soon we produced the best heating oil in the world. We rented railroad tank cars from General American Tank Car Company and shipped heating oil all over the country.

Everything went well for me, but I still faced court cases. FDR was determined to keep the NRA and its symbolic Blue Eagle as the heart of his New Deal, and he had sent Charlie Francis down to see that we lost our cases. Francis, as Chief Prosecutor, vowed to send R.J. McMurrey and me to Leavenworth for life. McMurrey and I weren't sure that he wouldn't succeed.

Due to my accident and hospitalization, we had little opportunity to plan our defense. Now we had to act quickly.

McMurrey and I met one afternoon to make plans, with the help of a couple of pints of New Orleans brandy. For awhile, we discussed what we were up against. In effect, we were having to match wits with FDR and his entire Brain Trust. In addition to Charlie Francis, Roosevelt had sent two of the top oil company lawyers, one a cousin of Eleanor Roosevelt.

Finally, after several hours of commiserating with each other—and with the brandy—we faced the impossible situation. "So what do we do?" McMurrey sighed.

"We need two good lawyers," I said. "Two who are as smart and as tough as FDR's team."

"Who do you suggest?" McMurrey asked.

"I know of two," I told him, "but they're both U.S. senators. Huey P. Long, of Louisiana, and William E. Borah, of Idaho."

"So why don't we call them?" McMurrey asked. "All they can do is say no."

We tossed a coin to determine which of us would call which lawyer. (Neither of us wanted the task of calling Borah, known as the "Great Opposer," with a reputation for being an unpredictable maverick.) I lost the toss, so McMurrey called Long, and I called Borah. We were able to make appointments in Washington, D.C., for the next afternoon. Quickly, we drove to Dallas and chartered an airplane to fly us to the Capitol.

We met with Long and Borah and received favorable responses to our proposition. Borah believed the NRA was unconstitutional, and Long said he *knew* it was. Borah asked a fee of $20,000, paid in advance in $20 bills. It would take a great deal of preparation; he had not practiced law for 28 years, since he had first been elected to the U.S. Senate. Long told us he would represent us free of charge, and he could give us his brief within 24 hours, before we left Washington to return to Texas.

I went to a Washington bank and obtained Senator Borah's $20,000 (in twenties). That night, Huey P. Long began dictating a petition against the President of the United States, the National Industrial Recovery Act, and General Hugh Johnson, the NRA administrator. It was the most amazing legal feat I had ever witnessed. He never sat down all night, just paced back and forth. He didn't have law books at hand, yet he cited cases and page numbers without hesitation. His only pauses were to stop his pacing to take a sip of beer.

As soon as he finished dictating the petition, he proceeded to dictate the brief to his secretary. He finished dictating about 4:00 a.m. (also finishing off eight bottles of beer). Later that afternoon his secretary had the documents typed up and ready for us to read and use.

That was the beginning of the famous *Panama et al* case, known in the history books as *Panama Refining Company vs. Ryan*. (Panama Refining Company was one of the many independent refiners involved.)

When McMurrey and I returned to Texas, we presented the petition to Judge Randolph Bryant in the federal court in Tyler. When he had read the petition and brief, Judge Bryant looked at us with astonishment. "This is a thing of beauty!" he exclaimed. "A beautiful piece of work! Who prepared it?"

"Huey P. Long," I told him.

He smiled and nodded with understanding. "He's the smartest constitutional lawyer the world has ever had," he said. "Who do you intend to have present this petition to the court?"

"We hoped you would recommend someone," I suggested.

"You need someone who can do justice to it," he said. "Why don't you go down and get Big Fish, but don't pay him more than $500. He'd be too damned egotistical if he got more. He won't know what's in it, but he'll do justice to the fine language."

F.W. Fisher, nicknamed "Big Fish," was six feet, seven inches tall, with the bulk and girth to go with his height.

We made a deal with Big Fish, who then presented Huey Long's petition and brief to Judge Bryant, who then issued an injuction against the President of the United States, the National Recovery Administration and General Hugh Johnson, enjoining them from interfering with the normal business of independent oil refiners until the Panama case was resolved.

Of course Bryant's favorable decision was appealed by the government. It was reversed by the Fiftieth Court of Appeals, and we then had to take the case to the Supreme Court of the United States.

For his appearance in the hallowed court halls in Washington, D.C., we bought Big Fish the largest robe we could find. It was so long it dragged the floor, making him a more ridiculous sight than he was normally. The Chief Justice of the Supreme Court at the time was the dignified Charles Evans Hughes, one-time candidate for president, appointed to the court in 1930 by Herbert Hoover. He was then 72 years old, a strong opponent of Roosevelt's New Deal, and the main object of FDR's later attack on the "nine old men" of the Supreme Court.

The astonishment shown on the faces of the nine justices when Big Fish arose to address the court was worth all the trouble we endured to bring the legal case this far. Several of them found it difficult to keep smiles from creeping over their mouths.

We had a problem in obtaining a copy of an order issued by the Federal Tender Board; a problem that had been resolved only when we had managed to catch one of the board members outside his office. Big Fish explained this situation.

He spoke in his natural but nasal voice. "Yer Honor, we couldn't get a copy of the 'ahrder' at first," he told the court. "We didn't know what the 'ahrder' was." After he had gone on about this for awhile, Chief Justice Hughes finally asked, "Counsellor, did you get a copy of the order?"

"Oh, yes," Big Fish replied, "we've got a copy of the 'ahrder' now."

"Well, where did you get it?" Hughes asked.

"We caught one of them thar Carpetbagger agents of Roosevelt's coming down the road," Big Fish replied earnestly. "We shuck him down, and got it out of his back pocket."

If it had been difficult for Hughes to restrain himself before, it was now impossible. He began laughing and couldn't stop. The fact that Big Fish stood before the bench in his tent-sized robe unable to understand what was so funny made it funnier. The entire Court was laughing, but Hughes was hysterical, so much so that—before he could do anything to save his dignity—his false teeth fell from his mouth and landed before him on the bench.

Finally, dignity was restored, and the case was presented. However, the next morning, the newspaper headline criticized "The Decorum of the Court."

When the opinion was handed down by Chief Justice Hughes, it was in our favor. In effect, the NRA Blue Eagle had been shot down.

That was January, 1935, but it would take one more shot to kill it. In May of that year, the Supreme Court heard the case of the Schechter Poultry Company and gave the NRA the death blow. The constitutional issue was quite clear: the Congress could not assign legislative powers to the Executive, the President.

It was a great victory for independent refiners, but I had one legal hurdle remaining before I personally would be in the clear: the matter of 178,000 barrels of hot oil I owned personally. If the courts decided that it was indeed hot oil, Charlie Francis would be able to make good his threat to see me behind bars. But I was depending upon a small loophole in the law to free that oil from its illegal status.

On the last day of January, I again appeared in Federal Court before Judge Randolph Bryant, this time seeking an injunction to prevent the Railroad Commission from interfering with the sale and movement of the 178,000 barrels of crude oil.

Both Attorney General William McCraw and Railroad Commissioner Ernest O. Thompson appeared in court to testify against me. It was galling for me to find myself opposed by the man I had given so much aid to be elected, the man who promised to help the independent refiners. After the auto accident, however, McCraw and Clark made it quite clear that I was no longer of any use to them. As soon as Tom Clark had seen that I was safely in the hands of doctors, he had left and never bothered to come back to see me. McCraw did not even call to express concerns for my injury.

By the time of the election, McCraw seemed firmly in the pockets of the major oil companies, along with his old college roommate, Railroad Commissioner Thompson.

This court case was to be my first direct confrontation in opposition to the two men, but not my last. The Independent Refiners Association and the success of its campaign against the NRA had made me a threat to their seat of power. However, they were confident that this was an open-and-shut case against me, and after it was over they would be rid of me.

They failed to realize that I was holding a trump card.

I was prepared to prove that the 178,000 barrels of oil that had been impounded by the Railroad Commission was not technically hot oil. The technicality that freed it from that category was that the Railroad Commission had failed to publish the orders as required by law.

When I dropped that little piece of information, Judge Bryant put

Ernest Thompson on the stand and asked: "Is it true that you did not publish those orders?"

Thompson began to stutter, attempting to avoid the issue, but Judge Bryant interrupted him sternly. "I just want to know if this is true or not! Yes or no!" the Judge demanded.

Thompson sighed and nodded in resignation. "Yeah, it's true," he admitted.

"Then I have no choice but to issue the injunction," the Judge announced.

I was free, and I had 178,000 barrels of legal oil I could sell at a considerable profit. I had bought it at 25 cents a barrel, the hot oil rate, and I could receive $1.10 a barrel for it as legal oil. But all I could think of at the moment was to take a vacation, go home to Hickory Grove to rest. I would take a few days off from the refinery, and do nothing but sit and think; take peaceful walks in the woods, maybe even go fishing.

At least, I thought I could. I had forgotten that the telephone had now invaded Hickory Grove. Papa had not had one installed, but there was one a mile down the road from Papa's house.

One evening, I was sitting in the kitchen with my parents when a neighbor knocked on our door. "There's a phone call for Jerry," she told us. "It's from the White House. From President Roosevelt."

"Sure it is," I replied, cynically. "It's probably just one of my friends playing a joke. Take a number and tell him I'll call back tomorrow."

She left, disappointed, but a short while later she returned. "It really was the President," she told me. "He left his number and said you could call him back tomorrow. He said he had a hard time tracking you down. But he laughed when I told him what you said."

Only when I called back the next day did I really believe that it was FDR. He wanted me to come to Washington immediately to talk. "You knocked out my hot oil plan," he told me. "Now I expect you to help me come up with a new one, one that your people will accept."

Roosevelt and I hit it off very well as soon as we met. For a man with his family status, their money, and his New York upper-class breeding, he surprised me by the earthiness of his language. I had expected the profundity of his thoughts, but not the profanity of his speech. I was greatly impressed by the manner in which he had adjusted to his wheelchair. Having so recently escaped a similar imprisonment myself, I understood the frustrations a man of his power and energy must have felt.

There was one other facet of his personality that surprised me. He loved mystery and detection, and he considered himself the world's greatest detective. He had authored a detective story that had been published in a national magazine. He delighted in uncovering motivations of the people surrounding him and surprising them by revealing aspects of their lives they would not expect him to know. As far as I know there was only one thing that was beyond his powers of detection: knowing where Eleanor was at any given moment.

I had played a significant role in defeating the cornerstone of his New Deal, and I expected him to treat me with a degree of coolness. But his attitude was more like that of a good sportsman who had just been bested at a game of tennis. He joked with me about the fact that I dipped stuff, and promptly gave me the nickname of "Snuffy," which he continued to use during our long friendship.

He had not really intended to be unfair to the small businessman when he created the NRA. He still believed firmly that his concept had been a good one, and that it would yet work when all the wrinkles had been ironed out. Even as good a detective as he was, there was no way he could know the internecine problems of all the businesses in the country. He had depended upon experts—business leaders and congressmen—to work out the details of his programs. For Section 9-C of the National Industrial Recovery Act, he had depended on Texas Senator Tom Connally.

I briefed FDR on what was happening in Texas between independent refiners and major oil companies, showing him transcripts of hearings before the Railroad Commission proving that Sinclair, Gulf, and Humble—all the big companies—were taking products from the hot oil refineries and making them legal simply because they were not subject to the same regulations as the independents. Further, I explained that the big oil lobby could get the state laws written any way they chose.

Roosevelt listened to everything I said. Then he told me he still believed we must endeavor to regulate the oil business, for the sake of both conservation and economic recovery. "We cannot have hot oil depleting our resources and fostering cutthroat competition," he said. With a gesture of his hands, he threw the problem into my lap. "Now, what's the answer?"

"You write a new bill," I said and smiled. "One that's constitutional."

He returned the grin. He hoped I would say that, "because I want you to tell me how we do it." For obvious reasons, he didn't want Senator Connally to do the actual preparation and writing of a new law. But for political reasons he wished Connally to sponsor the bill in the Senate.

"I can't write the bill myself," I told him. "I'm not a lawyer. But I can recommend a committee that will write a law that will be fair to the independents as well as to the majors, and I'll be glad to testify before that committee as Chairman of the Board of the Independent Refiners Association."

Roosevelt appointed three of the lawyers I recommended to that committee—Rex Baker and Hines Baker, who represented Humble Oil, but were, nevertheless, fair-minded men, and Malcolm McCorquedale, an attorney with the Department of the Interior in Texas. Roosevelt wanted me to do more than testify before the committee; he asked me to sit with the committee and participate in the planning.

We met in the Federal Building in Tyler, Texas, to draw up what was to become the Connally Hot Oil Act. We spent long tedious hours writing, rewriting, and checking phrases for loopholes and questions of constitutionality. When it was all done, we read it through and took an opportunity to comment. McCorquedale turned to me and asked: "What do you think, Jerry?" I replied with a scowl, "It ain't legal."

McCorquedale turned pale, and there were nervous, uncomfortable movements all around the table. "Why?" McCorquedale asked.

I replied seriously. "There aren't enough 'whereases.' "

There was relieved laughter all around the table.

The Connally Hot Oil Act was passed by Congress, and we now had a law that was entirely fair, that worked, and was constitutional. My experiences in aiding to draft the bill renewed my desire to be a lawyer. Year after year, I had deferred my goals and ambitions, continuing to believe that one day I could accomplish them, rationalizing that, after all, I was still young. However, I was now 27 years old, and it seemed a bit late to think of going to law school. I also had the responsibilities of a business, of which I was part owner. I wasn't sure what a sudden break would do to my career.

I had done a lot of studying on my own. I had read the LaSalle extension course while I had been with the Cavalry, and during the previous year, while fighting the NRA, I had paid Wiley Rutledge to travel from Iowa for several visits. It occurred to me that I might get him to come to Texas for an extended visit and tutor me in law. Perhaps during his vacation. Then I might be able to get closer to a law degree by attending one of the night schools in Texas.

Dean Rutledge agreed to my proposal.

At the refineries, no one had any idea who Rutledge was. He looked like a bum, and they assumed that was what he was. The fact that he was living with me didn't alter that opinion in the least. During days, I worked at the refineries, and that gave him an opportunity to fish and pass the time of day with other town loafers. In the evenings, he would conduct law school for one student, a perfect arrangement for both of us. I paid him more than he wanted, but much less than the worth of his vast knowledge.

He was fascinated by local Texas dialects; he picked it up quickly, making himself at home with farmers, roughnecks, and oilfield workers. Secretly he would make notes for future reference. But the moment we would get in the car alone, his fine speech patterns returned, and he would propound the law or quiz me on the knowledge he had imparted.

My life moved along peacefully, though busily, for awhile, falling into the routine of work and study. Then suddenly I was thrust into a crisis at the refineries.

One morning, Duncan and Holt came to my office and announced: "We've been talking it over, and we've decided we ought to go into hot oil."

I was stunned that, after all we had experienced, they would make such a suggestion. "Nope," I said, shaking my head firmly. "Never again. The laws we've got now are good ones. If we go to hot oil and are caught, there are no loopholes in the law to pull us out."

"Some of the other refineries are doing it," they said. "And we can certainly improve our profits."

I stood my ground. "I won't agree to it."

They had obviously not expected this response. "We own the majority stock," they challenged angrily. "We can outvote you. We'll do it anyway."

"If you do, I'll send you to Huntsville or Leavenworth!" I replied, equally angry.

We were at an impasse, neither side giving in. Finally we decided the solution would be for one or the other to leave the partnership. "Either the two of you will buy me out at book value," I suggested, "or I will buy you out."

"How do we decide which buys and which sells?" they asked.

"We'll roll high dice," I said. "Whoever rolls high will sell, and low will buy."

They agreed.

I sent Ed Berg, a bookkeeper, down to the drugstore to buy a sack of dice. I let Duncan and Holt pick out the pair of dice we would use.

Dick Duncan rolled for them, and the dice came up with eleven.

There was only a slim chance I would top that throw—I felt it a foregone conclusion that I would be buying them out. I picked up the dice. "Well," I said, "I might as well go in to R.C. Bowen and have him draw up the check."

I moved to leave the room, the dice in my hand.

"You've got to throw anyway," Duncan protested.

I bent, tossing the dice through my legs, causing them to bounce off the wall on the other side of the room. Reaching for the doorknob, ready to go to see the accountant about figuring book value on the company stock, I felt the total silence of the room.

I turned around; Duncan and Holt stared in astonishment at the dice. I walked back and looked at the dice; I had rolled twelve, two sixes. I was as astonished as they were.

R.C. Bowen soon wrote a check for $75,000, and I sent him to the bank to get me a cashier's check for the buyout.

Again I was out of a job.

10

Partners

During the period of the various court cases, I made the acquaintance of a man known as Captain Stanley—E.N. Stanley, chief engineer for the Railroad Commission in East Texas. (I had appeared before him in the efforts to clear the 178,000 barrels of hot oil.) We became good friends. He was among the most honest men ever to work for the Railroad Commission, and I respected him.

When Stanley began working for the Commission, supervising the proration enforcement program in East Texas, he had just left Gulf Laboratories. He intended to serve the Commission only two weeks, until he could get his own business going. Within the two years he served, he attempted to leave office numerous times. Always there seemed some crisis, and he would agree to stay on until it was settled.

He finally resigned on February 1, 1935. A week later, we announced the formation of a partnership—Stanley-Sadler, Inc., a management engineering company specializing in property management, pipeline management, and appraisal work, complete with our own oilfield laboratory. We would work primarily with the independent oil companies, supplying services they could not afford to perform for themselves. We also obtained a license to buy, sell, and store oil.

It was a good partnership, and we had high hopes for success. As Chairman of the Independent Refiners' Association, I formed many business friendships and I could attract companies needing our services. In his years with the Railroad Commission, Stanley had established a reputation for honesty and integrity in the federal courts, so he could attract business from judges needing independent appraisals during court cases. I was a petroleum engineer, and he was a civil and construction engineer.

We set up the finest and most elaborately furnished offices in Gregg County, buying our furnishings from the recently bankrupt Peacock Military Academy.

We thought we would be in business for a great many years. As it turned out, our partnership lasted only nine months to the day. It wasn't for lack of success that we called it quits.

Stanley and I operated respective divisions of our company without a great deal of consultation. We wanted no conflict of interest charges in the event a company I tested for was brought to court on a case for which he might be hired to do other testing. I had more than enough business from independent refiners, and he did an equal amount of work for the federal courts. His fees were set by the court, and I set my own.

One of our engineering projects was to build the municipal swimming pool for the city of Kilgore. Mayor Roy Laird came to us and asked us to design and engineer it. At the time, it was the largest swimming pool in East Texas (still in use). We also did some work for the library building at the request of Mayor Laird.

On those projects, we worked together, and we were a team on another job, a sort of moonlighting occupation. In the evenings we played bridge. Until then I had never played bridge, but Stanley was a wizard at it. We worked out a system, not one with signs, but one that was silent. I was always the dummy, and we never lost. We played against other men in the oil business, and we made a great deal of money at it.

One opponent, determined to beat us, was Harry Miles, who had replaced Stanley at the Railroad Commission. He was so determined that, one night, he brought in a professional gambler.

He started off playing with $100 bills. I was suspicious. An honest man couldn't possibly make that kind of money working for the Railroad Commission, supervising the East Texas office. His salary couldn't have been more than $400 to $450 a month.

He lost $10,000 to us that night, and it didn't seem to bother him a great deal.

It did bother me. I had no proof, but I suspected Miles must be taking payoffs.

The next morning I took the train to Austin and made an appointment to see Railroad Commissioner Ernest O. Thompson. I didn't care for what I felt had to be done. It would make my partner and best friend sore at me, and it might mean the end of our partnership.

Miles' activities were not unusual in the oil business. The big oil companies hired "scouts," men with unlimited expense accounts who nosed around the independents, spying on them, and coming up with ways of obstructing plans. The oil companies didn't want to know what their scouts were up to; they just allowed them carte blanche. The scouts formed an association and hired a lawyer. The lawyer sat in on hearings of the Tender Board, raising objections to applications from the independents.

When possible, the scouts used their unlimited expense accounts to obtain favors from the Railroad Commission office. They were especially good at getting many exceptions to spacing regulations for their employers, while getting them denied to the independents.

When I got in to see Thompson, I hold him, "I think there's some trouble brewing in East Texas. If it goes any further, you're the one who's going to suffer."

Thompson valued Stanley, frequently taking credit for Stanley's acts of honesty and integrity. Because of E.N. Stanley, Ernest Thompson had an excellent public image.

"I suspect that Harry Miles is taking payoffs," I told Thompson. "And I don't think he's being very discreet about it. Someone's bound to start asking questions soon, and that will be embarrassing for you."

Thompson studied me for a moment. "What do you think I ought to do about it?" he asked.

"I think you ought to get rid of him," I said, "and persuade Captain Stanley to go back to the Commission."

"I didn't want to lose him in the first place," he told me. "Do you think he'll come back?"

"I don't know. All you have to do is ask him."

While I sat in his office, Thompson called Stanley, but he did not reveal I was present. He asked Stanley if he would be willing to return to the Railroad Commission for awhile.

I knew Stanley was wondering why.

"Because I think Harry Miles is crooked," Thompson said. I could hear Stanley's sardonic laugh crackle over the phone. "I don't think he is," he said loudly. "I *know* he is."

Thompson played on Stanley's sense of altruism and managed to persuade him. Stanley insisted he would stay no longer than six weeks. "Just long enough to straighten out the situation and give you time to find somebody else," he told Thompson. "I just don't know how I'm going to tell Jerry about this, though," he added.

Thompson laughed. "Don't worry about Jerry," he explained. "He's sitting right here in my office, and he understands."

Stanley was still furious when I returned to Kilgore. "You're supposed to be my friend," he accused. "For the first time in my life, I'm able to make a decent living, and you have to go and interfere."

I grinned. "You didn't have to take the job," I said.

"You knew damned well I couldn't say no," he cut back. "Of course, you realize I can't take a cent out of the company after I go."

"I realize that," I said. "and I don't intend to pay you anything. I wouldn't want you to be compromised in any way."

The big oil companies were not happy about this development, and they were determined to get revenge. Not long after Captain Stanley set about cleaning up the East Texas office of the Railroad Commission, the State Senate appointed a committee to investigate the East Texas oil fields—and that committee, under the chairmanship of Joe Hill of Henderson, chose to investigate only one company, Stanley-Sadler, Inc.

I was managing the company on my own at this point; Stanley no longer had any connection. I had given up the tutors and was attending Jefferson Law School in Dallas two days a week. With some private counseling from Andrew Priest, the president of the law school, my long-awaited goal seemed in sight. Within months, I would have my law degree and would take my bar exam.

Senator Joe Hill, by virtue of his state office, managed to obtain my bank records and those of the engineering firm. He was determined to go over every deposit and withdrawal with a fine tooth comb, hoping to find even the slightest irregularity to latch onto. He was not satisfied to go over the records just once, but found it necessary to call me, and Stanley, a second and third time to review the same material.

In the beginning, I accepted the probe without protest, confident that, in the end, the five-man investigating committee could come to only one conclusion—that there was nothing amiss in the Stanley-Sadler financial records. In addition to Chairman Joe Hill, the senators on the committee were W.R. Poage, of Waco, Tom De Berry, of Bogota, Tom Holbrook, of Galveston, and Wilburn Colly, of Eastland.

However, a few days before Christmas, 1935, Joe Hill came to Kilgore alone, a committee of one, calling for another round of hearings. Through my lawyer, I refused to appear, insisting that I would decline to answer any questions before a committee of one.

Joe Hill left Kilgore, swearing he would be back in a few days with a quorum.

He returned the day after New Years, and this time he had Poage and De Berry with him. He did not have the full committee, but he had a quorum, as I had requested. I had the company lawyer present to advise me. I had almost completed my own study of law, but I had not yet passed the bar exam.

Very early in the hearings, it was clear that Joe Hill was attempting to crucify Stanley and me. He had acquired all of the Stanley-Sadler bank records, and he went over every deposit and expenditure, questioning each detail. Most of the questions were the same as ones he had asked in earlier hearings.

Finally he hit upon the 178,000 barrels of oil I had purchased while at the Overton refinery—the oil I had freed by a technicality in Federal Court. Though Stanley and I had known each other at this time, we had not even discussed the possibility of going into business together; yet Joe Hill considered this extremely suspicious. He picked and prodded, needling me to excess.

Finally he managed to arouse my hot temper. "Are you inferring there was collusion involved?" I asked angrily.

"No," Hill replied, satisfied with himself. "I'm saying there was collusion."

"Then you're making a very serious charge," I said. "Because, if there was collusion, it was with Federal Judge Randolph Bryant." And I turned my back to return to my seat, feeling I had bested him at his argument.

Hill refused to be bested. "There *was* collusion," he, repeated.

I saw red. In a fury, I grabbed a chair, and turned to advance toward the committee chairman. Hill turned and fled from me down the aisle, until I was restrained by lawyers.

The next day the incident made major headlines in newspapers all over the state. Judge Bryant had the federal marshalls pick up Joe Hill and deliver him to his court. Bryant recessed to have a private conference with the state senator, and the investigation wound down with no charges made against me, Stanley, or Judge Bryant.

For awhile I continued to operate as G.A. Sadler, Engineer. But that was only until I could change the sign on my door to read, "G.A. Sadler, Attorney at Law."

When I passed the bar exam, I made no big announcement. I made plans to go into partnership with one of the best criminal lawyers in the State. That announcement was to take place January 1, 1937.

While still operating as an engineer, a problem came my way that involved both the law and the oil business.

A man named Alex Pope came by my office, introducing himself. "I'm in trouble," he announced, "and I'm told you're the only man in the country who might be able to help me out of my situation."

"What's the trouble?" I asked.

"I'm a cotton farmer down in Nueces county," he told me. "I guess it's the biggest cotton farm in that area. Well, I owe the federal government about $650,000 in back income taxes, and I don't have the money to pay it. The Internal Revenue Service is threatening to take my farm to satisfy the debt."

At first, I wasn't sure the man was on the level, especially since he seemed reluctant to divulge the name of the person who had referred him. "I can't help you," I told him, "unless you can be entirely open with me. You'll have to tell me who referred you."

After he had given me the name of our mutual friend, I was satisfied. I asked him to put what money he had at my disposal, and he did. Then I set to work, calling various refineries in the East Texas oilfields.

Alex Pope had come into my office at four o'clock in the afternoon. By six o'clock, I had managed to buy over a million barrels of hot oil in Pope's name at fifteen to twenty cents a barrel. It was more than enough to be worth $650,000 on the open market.

The next day, after I had all the bills of lading on my desk, I called the deputy director of the Internal Revenue Service in Austin.

"I understand you are attempting to collect back taxes on Alex Pope," I queried.

The deputy director acknowleded that to be the case.

"You might be interested," I suggested, "in the fact that he has purchased over a million barrels of hot oil. I have the bills of sale on my desk right now."

"I'll catch the train tonight," he told me. "I'll be in your office in the morning."

I met the director at the railroad station, and took him to my office. Whereupon he seized the hot oil to satisfy the lien against Alex Pope. He knew, as I knew, the oil, when auctioned from the courthouse steps in Longview, would bring much more than $650,000. What he did not realize was that we were putting the federal government into the hot oil business. Once the oil was auctioned, it would become legal oil, and the federal government would have to issue tenders on it and allow it into interstate commerce.

That auction set off a furor in Austin and in Washington. The Texas Attorney General sent Tom Clark to Washington to try to halt the sale. As a result, I received a call from FDR asking me to come to Washington to see him.

"Do you realize what you've done?" he asked me. "You've put me in the hot oil business."

I acknowledged that I had realized fully what I was doing. "If you recall," I said, "when we got through with the *Panama et al* case, I told you I would pee on your leg one more time. Well, this is it. You don't have to worry about trouble from me again." Then I explained. "I've just passed the bar, and I'm about to go into the practice of law. From now on I intend to stay clearly on the right side of the law."

Roosevelt laughed. "In your case, that gives you plenty of latitude," he said. "You haven't violated any law with this."

"No," I admitted, "but it was a narrow lane that I traveled."

The president was a good sport. He was able to enjoy it when he was beaten at a game fair and square, and he chuckled about this a good deal. "How did you ever think of this?" he asked.

"It didn't take much thinking," I told him: "Any dumb cluck could have done it—and would have, sooner or later, if I hadn't done it first."

As I left, he admonished, "Don't do it again, please."

"Don't worry," I assured him. "It'll only work once."

The story of how I had dealt with the IRS did get around, and the next week I was requested to repeat the trick. Arthur Temple, Sr., explained that he owed the IRS $800,000. "Can you buy me some hot oil?" He told me that the Temple Lumber Company was land poor and timber poor. They had no way to pay the exhorbitant income tax.

"Sure, I could buy more hot oil," I had to tell him. But that wouldn't get you out of your problem. The federal government is onto the trick. They won't fall for it again."

I was sincere in my promise to Roosevelt. I was on the brink of achieving my childhood ambition. I was to commence the practice of law, defending and helping the weak and helpless. I had studied the law; I knew it, and I understood it. I intended to stay safely on the right side of it. Then I would use it to benefit others.

97

11

Jerry Sadler, Attorney at Law

My legal career began with a case that had national attention.

It was just before Christmas of 1936. I changed my sign to read "G.A. Sadler, Attorney at Law." Soon, that sign would read "Shead and Sadler." Our partnership was to begin January 1, 1937. As a new lawyer, I had no reputation, but I had some money saved. Harvey Shead had a good reputation as a criminal lawyer, but not a great deal of money. (Business for lawyers had not been profitable during the depression; not more than ten criminal lawyers made money in the late 1930s.) With my savings, I set up the offices in Longview and guaranteed Harvey Shead $250 a month. Due to his reputation, he worked constantly, but few of his clients had the money to pay him for his efforts. The partnership would be a good deal for both of us: he would bring the clients, I would supply the money.

I did not expect to have clients until he arrived on the first of January, but I went to the office every day, enjoying the sense of accomplishment of having finally become a lawyer.

A day in late December I sat at my desk reading the newspaper. I had just read a news item about a young man who had been arrested in California for threatening to kidnap movie actress Ginger Rogers. Moments later, a woman came in, extremely distraught.

She introduced herself. "My son is in trouble in California, and he needs a good lawyer. I know lawyers charge a lot, and I make only $40 a month working in a beauty shop, but if you could help him, I would find some way to pay you."

"What is your son charged with?" I asked.

"He wrote some threatening letters to a movie actress," she said, "and he's already pleaded guilty to kidnapping under the Lindbergh Kidnapping Act. I'm afraid it may be too late to do any good, but I will never be able to forgive myself if I don't try to help him."

I was surprised; the woman seemed to be talking about the case I had just been reading about in the newspaper. "Is your son's name Hall?" I asked.

The woman nodded. "We don't have the same name," she explained, "because his father and I were separated some years ago. My ex-husband and I had two children. I took care of one son, and the father took the other."

"How old is your son?" I asked.

"Eighteen," she told me.

"Did you or your former husband agree to let your son plead guilty?" I asked.

She shook her head. "I haven't been able to contact him," she explained, "and his father has refused to speak to him since this came out in all the papers." She began to cry.

"Don't worry," I said. "I'll do whatever I can."

I picked up the telephone and called Judge Albert Lee Stephens, the federal judge in California who was hearing Hall's case. I introduced myself and informed him that I had just been retained by Hall's mother to represent the boy.

"You're too late," Judge Stephens told me. "Hall has already pleaded guilty. Except for sentencing, the case is over."

"Judge Stephens," I said as diplomatically as I could, "there is something you may not have taken into consideration. This boy is under 21, and he has pleaded guilty without consent of parent or guardian."

"How do you know that?" the Judge asked.

"Because the boy's mother has told me so," I explained. "She's sitting here in my office now."

There was a pensive silence at the other end of the telephone line, so I pursued the issue. "I think, in all fairness," I said, "you ought to give the boy a chance to talk to his mother and hold another hearing."

"All right," Judge Stephens agreed. "I'll set the judgment aside and schedule the case for trial on the second of January. Can you be here by then?"

I'll be there," I said, not at all sure I could make it that quickly. I was somewhat disappointed I would be absent at the time the Shead-Sadler partnership was to be announced in the newspapers.

Hall's mother was less certain about making the trip to California. "I don't have the money," she told me. "I can't even afford to pay your train fare."

"Don't worry about it," I said. "We'll come up with the money."

Unfortunately, at that time, I was low on funds myself, having just laid out a large amount of cash to set up the office. But I borrowed $2,500 from one of my friends, John T. Crim, to cover expenses.

Ginger Rogers was at the height of her popularity as a movie star. The Hall case attracted the attention of not only the press but the FBI as well. I knew this would be a sensational start for my law career, but I also knew that I would have to be careful. Many eyes were watching me. I paid the train fare and hotel accommodations for Hall's mother, but arranged that she take a different train from mine and stay at a different hotel. I did not know what I would be able to do for Hall, but once in California I intended to look for every loophole in the law.

Until we appeared in court, I believed I would have the assistance of the experienced Harvey Shead, who accompanied me to Los Angeles; he gave me the impression he could practice law in California. The judge for the Hall case informed me that this was incorrect. Some earlier misconduct barred Shead from practicing before Judge Stephens, not an auspicious beginning for our partnership. The only aid I would have was the court-appointed attorney, Ames Peterson.

There was no doubt that young Hall had written the letters to the film star; he had already admitted it. However, celebrities attract cranks and crackpots just as they do ordinary fans. Some cranks are dangerous, others are not. After meeting with Hall, I sensed that he was emotionally immature but otherwise relatively harmless, the kind of boy who gets into trouble more for the attention than to cause harm. His letters showed his ardent crush on the beautiful and talented Miss Rogers and that he became hurt and angry when she had not responded to his written expressions of love.

When I took the deposition of Ginger Rogers, I sensed that her view of the situation agreed with mine, though she hesitated to admit it outright. She is not only a beautiful and talented actress, she is a sensitive human being. She was upset by the trial and the attention it brought, but it was more embarrassment than fear for her own safety.

Then I took a deposition from Ginger's mother, Leila Rogers, and I understood fully. Ginger Rogers would have preferred to ignore the crank letters, but it was Mrs. Rogers who created the fuss and enjoyed the attention.

My objective was not to get young Hall off scot-free; he was, after all, guilty of criminal acts. However, conviction under the Lindbergh

Kidnapping Act carried a severe punishment. The best Hall could hope for with a guilty plea was a sentence of forty years in prison. I set my sights on persuading Miss Rogers to drop the charges.

This proved to be the best solution. Miss Rogers could see that Hall had learned his lesson. As long as he did not threaten her again, she was willing to drop the charges and allow him to go back to the military services.

I returned to Longview with the pride of accomplishment. However, I returned to problems. I was not pleased with Shead and his management of the office in my absence. We had started off on the wrong foot together, and we continued out-of-step with each other. It seemed the only thing we could agree upon was to part company.

There was another lawyer who had an office down the hall. Fred Erisman and I got along quite well, and we decided to become partners. Shead left, and almost immediately I was hired for one of the biggest cases I would ever handle.

But before I could get started on the Pacific Mutual Case, there was a terrible disaster near Kilgore, and I was occupied—along with other citizens—in its aftermath. On March 18, 1937, the school at New London, Texas, exploded, killing 494 children and teachers. It was a disaster that should not have occurred. Natural gas had accumulated in the basement of the school, which was built in the middle of the huge East Texas oil and gas field, and there were no safety regulations concerning seepage of natural gas.

That Friday, there was total chaos in the small town of New London, with sightseers driving in from all over East Texas. Virtually no family was untouched by the tragedy, and the town had no facilities to take care of a problem of this magnitude. Led by Mayor Roy Laird, a group of Kilgore citizens met to try to be of help. We raised about $35,000 to aid the families. Mayor Laird was placed in charge of the funds, and he appointed me as his representative on the scene in New London.

The most serious problem was the disposition of the bodies. In the pandemonium, ambulances were coming from as far away as Texarkana to pick up the bodies and take them back to their funeral homes. One child might be at one funeral home, while a brother or sister or mother might be at another, 60 or 70 miles away.

As it later turned out, not all of these funeral directors were operating from benevolent motives. When families attempted to get bodies released, some demanded exorbitant fees before they would turn them over for burial—as high as $2,500.

However, the greedy were in the minority. Most people genuinely tried to help, and there were numerous unsung heroes of that terrible weekend. The most notable one was A.S. "Spot" Robertson, who operated the radio from our command post in Kilgore. At that time, our only means of instant communication was the local commercial radio station, and it was turned over to Spot for use around the clock all weekend. All the rest of us kept our car radios on for instructions from him. Spot stayed on from Friday night to Sunday night, without sleeping and without flagging.

On Saturday morning, I received instructions from Spot to go to the Crim Funeral Home in Henderson, to attend a meeting of funeral home directors. The subject of the meeting was to be the setting of a standard price for all the bodies, and it was already under discussion by the time I arrived. The funeral directors were considering fees ranging between $1,500 and $2,500 for each victim. Those were outrageous prices for that time.

I was about to open my big mouth, when Mr. Crim, owner of the Crim Funeral Home, spoke up, saying what was on my mind, but stating it more politely than I would have done, He pointed out that the caskets they were using cost only about $37.00 each, and that there was to be only one massive ceremony for all the victims. He spoke about civic spirit and helping one's neighbor, and finally he stated, "Any funeral director who attempts to make a huge profit from this suffering deserves to be put out of business."

The majority were shamed into going along with a price of $250 a body, though a few greedy ones still tried to get their originally proposed amounts.

The massive funeral was set for Sunday, and that day we had the biggest crowds of all. Not only had relatives and friends of the 494 victims come for the service, but thousands of sightseers filled the highways. Traffic was stalled for miles on all the roads around New London.

The Red Cross had come in from Dallas and Houston to help with the crowds, providing meals and any medical attention that might be needed. On Sunday morning, word came to me over my car radio that the Director of the American Red Cross, Basil O'Connor, had also come to New London, and he wanted to see me urgently. O'Connor was at the headquarters the Red Cross had set up at the Humble casing head gasoline plant, about five miles outside New London.

Cars were bumper-to-bumper on that road, but my car had a siren and a Red Cross flag, and I managed to get through, however slowly.

The urgent matter that O'Connor wanted to discuss with me was the $35,000 we had raised to help the victims' families. He insisted that it be turned over to the American Red Cross, stating that they would decide who would or would not receive assistance.

"No," I told him, "that money was raised specifically to pay bills for the victims' families—funeral bills, medical expenses, whatever they need to get through this difficult time."

O'Connor informed me that he was the former law partner of President Roosevelt, and that—if necessary—he would call the President to have him settle the matter.

If the Director thought he could intimidate me by dropping names, he was mistaken. I had already peed on the President's leg a couple of times, and I wasn't afraid to do it again, especially when I was right. "Go ahead and call him," I said, "but it won't do you any good."

O'Connor called Roosevelt at Warm Springs, Georgia, and informed him of the situation. I stood listening, getting a degree of satisfaction from seeing the expression on the Director's face after he mentioned my name, when he extended the telephone receiver to me, stating, "The President wants to speak to you."

Again, we were like a couple of bulls butting our heads together. The President tried to tell me that the money had been raised for the Red Cross. I asked him how he could be so sure of that, from so far away. "I ought to know who it was raised for," I said, "because Mayor Roy Laird and I did the raising."

Roosevelt tried another tack. "The Red Cross is more accustomed than you are to handling this kind of situation," he said. "They know how to allocate the funds wisely."

I almost lost my temper at that, but I restrained myself and said, "Maybe so, but the people donated this money with an understanding of how it was to be allocated, and we're not going to change that. If there's any money left over, we'll give it to the Red Cross."

When Roosevelt hung up, he was clearly not happy. As it turned out, there was nothing left from the $35,000, once all the bills were paid. In fact Mayor Laird and I had to go back to the people and raise more to take care of all the expenses.

An interesting footnote to this long unhappy weekend concerns one of the numerous radio reporters who came to New London. To me he stood out from the rest because of his gentle nature and his desire to be of help when he could, attributes one would not expect to contribute to success in such a tough hard-bitten career. In the middle of one of the long nights, we drank coffee together and talked. He was genuinely touched by the tragedy and moved by the generosity of people who tried to help. The name of that young man was Walter Cronkite.

12

Erisman & Sadler

Not too long after my return to Longview, I received a telephone call from a California man who had been impressed by the manner in which I had handled the Hall case. His name was Asa B. Call, president of the Pacific Mutual Life Insurance Company. He had held that position for about six months, and he had a serious problem. He was appointed president because the former officer and founder of Pacific Mutual was under indictment, accused of stealing $15 million of the policy-holders' money.

Despite that, Call explained, the company was still sound. Pacific Mutual Life had plenty of money to take care of the policy-holders. The problem was the government. Thirty-six states had forced Pacific Mutual into receivership. "We're up against a bunch of attorney generals and politicians who don't care whether the company survives," he said. He believed the politicians saw dollar signs and wanted to grab as much of it as they could for themselves and their friends.

"Sounds like you need a good lawyer," I replied.

"I've already got more lawyers than I need," he told me. "Some of the most capable lawyers in the country."

"Then why are you calling me?" I asked. "Do you think I have more ability than the lawyers you have?"

"No," he replied. "But you've got guts, and that's what it's going to take to go up against the attorney generals of these states."

I laughed. "I charge more for my guts than I do my ability," I told him.

"How much, then," he asked, "just to meet me in Houston and talk to me?"

"Five-thousand dollars," I replied, aiming high. "But if your company is in receivership, it'll have to be a cashier's check."

I met Asa B. Call in Houston a few days later. He handed me a cashier's check. "Who represents your company in the State of Texas?" I asked him.

He named the three biggest and most important law firms in the state, one in Houston, one in Dallas, and one in Austin. It was clear that he wanted me for my guts.

"Under the lawyer's canon of ethics," I told him, "I can't take your case unless all your lawyers agree to it, and are willing to cooperate with me."

"Don't worry," he told me. "I'll notify them that you're hired, and I'll make sure they cooperate."

Asa Call was short, bald, and at least 99 percent honest. He was not a fast-talker or a fast-thinker, but he was as intelligent as he was quiet, the kind of man who isn't impressed with fast-talkers and fast-thinkers. He had married well, a daughter of the cement king of California.

With Pacific Mutual, he had a serious problem on his hands. He was in the midst of widespread panic. As a Mutual Fund, the company was owned by its policy-holders, and most were extremely upset by the loss of $15 million. In any time that's a lot of money; in the Thirties, it was considerably more than most companies or banks had on hand. Asa Call assured me, however, that the amount was just a small drop in the bucket to Pacific Mutual. The company could easily pay off all current claims, and if given time to reorganize the company, it would continue to thrive. During the Great Depression, Pacific Mutual's money had been invested wisely and well, with loans to companies such as MGM and Disney Studios. It held liens on buildings all over California, businesses, apartment buildings, even homes in Beverly Hills.

"I've explained all this to the state attorneys," Call told me. "I've given them proof we're financially sound, but it doesn't seem to matter, In certain key states, we're a political football." He felt attorneys saw an opportunity to bring money into the state treasuries, make a little for their lawyer friends, and advance themselves up the political ladder. It was the only explanation, he said.

"Can you prove it?" I asked.

"No," he replied, "but I would swear it's what's happening."

"Well," I said, "I guess it'll be up to me to find the proof."

I agreed to take on the case for a very high fee, more than I thought I was worth at the time, but less than some of the big law firms were getting. To begin with, I intended to concentrate on three major states—Texas, Louisiana, and Minnesota—in the hope that once they were cracked the other 33 states would follow like a line of dominoes. I wanted to take another trip to California; I was beginning to like the sun, the palm trees, and high-living.

In Los Angeles my big break on the case came along. Asa B. Call heard from a lawyer representing the receivership in Texas. A group of lawyers wanted to go to Los Angeles for a conference with Call, hinting—but not saying outright—that they wanted to propose some kind of deal with him. Call made an appointment for the following week. There were four of them—the lawyer appointed as receiver, the attorney for the receiver, also Tom C. Clark, and W.W. Heath, all big guns in the State of Texas.

Immediately I formulated my plan. "You've got plenty of pull at MGM Studios, haven't you?" I asked Call.

"What have you got in mind?"

"Could you get the use of one of their recording technicians for a day?" I asked.

"I suppose so," he said. "Why?"

I told him my plan.

"Isn't that a bit unethical?" he asked.

I smiled. "You hired me for my guts, remember?"

The two MGM sound technicians set up a dummy telephone in Call's office. Inside the telephone was the best microphone money could buy, which was wired into another office where I sat with the two technicians, who disc-recorded the "conference."

The legal eagles from my home state incriminated themselves beyond my wildest expectations. They propositioned Asa Call blatantly, offering him a good percentage of the $28-million in receivership in Texas if he would not fight their efforts. At the conclusion of the meeting, Call told them he would think about the offer.

The disc record the technicians cut was of excellent quality. Played back on any standard phonograph at 78 rpm, all the voices were easily recognizable. With this in my hands I returned to Texas, accompanied by Lyman P. Robertson, whom Call had hired to assist me.

At Austin I made an appointment with Judge J.D. Moore, who was to hear the Pacific Mutual Case in Texas. Armed with a phonograph, I stopped by the offices of Hart and Hart and picked up the insurance company's chief of counsel for the state. I did not tell him my plan.

In Judge Moore's office, I set up my phonograph and played the record; the judge was greatly entertained. At one point, recognizing Tom Clark's voice, he quipped, "You know, if we had Tom in here this afternoon, we'd have hot Tom and Jerry."

But chief counsel Hart was not amused. "I won't be a party to anything like this," he said, jumping from his seat. Then he stormed from the room. That left me as general counsel for Pacific Mutual in the State of Texas.

We knew the recording could not be entered as evidence in court. I told Judge Moore that my object was not to create a public scandal, merely to see that justice was done. "Pacific Mutual is willing and able to pay all legitimate claims," I explained." But it would be unfair to the policy holders to have the company go bankrupt just to feed a bunch of greedy and hungry lawyers."

"Leave it to me," Judge Moore told me. He said he would be fair, to tell him the time needed to determine legitimate claims. Then he set a date for the hearing.

The hearing lasted a full week. Judge Moore's courtroom was packed, not so much with spectators as with lawyers. The Texas Attorney General, Bill McCraw, was not present, but he was well-represented by several assistants. The receiver and his crowd of lawyers was there, and over 100 attorneys representing claimants.

Judge Moore listened to the claims all week, I sat quietly listening in the jury box, where I could watch the activities of all the lawyers. It was an enjoyable spectacle, and anticipating the presentation of my case, I was prepared to take each of the more than 200 claims case by case, showing why each was either valid or invalid.

When Judge Moore had heard each of the claims, he called on me. "Have you made a thorough investigation of all these claims?" he asked.

"Very thorough," I replied.

"Are you prepared to settle all the valid claims?" he asked.

"Yes, your honor," I said. "I have the investigators and the actuary here to . . ."

"What do the valid claims amount to?" he asked. "In total dollars?"

I was somewhat taken aback. "I believe it is approximately $168,000," I said.

"Are you prepared to prove these claims?" he asked.

"We are, your Honor," I replied. "First I would like to put the actuary on the stand. And then, if necessary, the investigators can . . ."

"That won't be necessary," Judge Moore said simply. "This court instructs you to pay the approximately $168,000 in valid claims, plus a $1,000 fee for the receiver and $500 for the lawyer for the receiver."

That statement was not unlike the throwing of a bomb into the courtroom. The more than 100 lawyers leaped to their feet to protest. The lawyers from the Attorney General's office, Archie Gray and W.J. Holt, shouted for the Judge to call in Bill McCraw.

Anyone could see that Judge Moore was enjoying the uproar, although he banged his gavel and demanded order. When the courtroom settled down, he addressed Archie Gray, the First Assistant Attorney General.

"I am going to recess," he said, "and I want you to get Attorney General McCraw."

Archie Gray called the capitol, and the Attorney General arrived at the courthouse within fifteen minutes, entering through a back door. However, McCraw was a showman, and his entrance into the courtroom was not so quiet. He strutted down the aisle and through the gate to face the judge as if he were master of the situation. He started to speak, but Judge Moore cut him off.

"Mr. McCraw," he said sternly, "before you open you mouth, I want to warn you that you are in trouble."

McCraw's face fell; he dropped his swaggering manner.

"I am dissolving the receivership as of today," Judge Moore continued. "Do you want to hear testimony as to why you are in trouble?"

"No, your Honor," McCraw replied.

"Do you want to make a motion against dissolving the receivership?" the Judge asked. "If you do, we'll have to go into all the claims, which will bring up questions of malpractice, malfeasance, and barratry."

The Attorney General bowed his head and said, "No, your Honor. I'll follow the order of the Court."

The valid claims were proved and accepted in short order, and Judge Moore instructed the receiver to have a cashier's check ready by noon the following day for $28 million, Pacific Mutual's funds held in receivership in Texas.

The first battle had been won, but Pacific Mutual was still in receivership in 35 states. The next battle would be in Louisiana, which held about $16 million of Pacific Mutual funds.

We had sent insurance investigators into Louisiana well in advance, and they had put together all the information I needed before my arrival. In this case I was not dealing with an attorney general, but with Governor Dick Lesche and Lieutenant Governor Earl Long, who held complete control of the state government.

It was early evening when I met with the two men in the Governor's office in Baton Rouge. Governor Lesche was a reasonable man, but his Lieutenant Governor was less so. Earl Long was the brother of the great Huey Long, but there was little comparison between the two men.

I had laid out my case for the Governor and Lieutenant Governor. "I guess we don't have any choice but to dissolve the receivership and turn over the money," Lesche said.

"Nothing doing," Earl Long said angrily. "I'm not ready to give up so easily. Make them fight for that money."

"Whatever you want," I said with a shrug. "We can wash all the dirty linen in court."

That was my last word. The two men began to argue heatedly, and the argument quickly turned into a fist fight. Long had Lesche down on the floor and was kicking him with his cowboy boots. I intervened, separating them, and called for help. We had an ambulance take the Governor to the hospital.

The next morning Louisiana newspapers carried an announcement that Governor Lesche was in the hospital suffering from arthritis. The Pacific Mutual Receivership in Louisiana was settled without the case going to court.

The case in Minnesota was even easier, and that was because of Harold Stassen, Attorney General, one of the finest men I've ever met in political life. The only obstacle I faced there occurred before going to court and involved Pacific Mutual's general counsel for Minnesota, who was a son of a U.S. Supreme Court Justice. He, Butler, was an ethical lawyer, but unfortunately my reputation had preceded me to Minnesota. There had been considerable talk about the "rough stuff" I had engaged in during the court battle in Texas. Concerned that something similar might take place in his state, young Butler resigned as general counsel for Pacific Mutual.

Butler should not have been concerned. When we went into court, we managed to present only a small part of our case. Attorney General Stassen understood the situation immediately and stopped the proceedings. "Your Honor," he said, "the State of Minnesota will not be a party to any attempt to take money that belongs to policy holders. I suggest that the receivership be dissolved and all money be returned to Pacific Mutual."

The court agreed, and an order was issued to that effect.

As expected there was virtually no trouble in the other 33 states. Very quickly Pacific Mutual's money was returned, and Asa Call was given his opportunity to reorganize the company. One policy holder challenged the reorganization plan in the Superior Court in California and lost. He took the case on appeal to the California Supreme Court and then on to the U.S. Supreme Court, which gave its stamp of approval to the Pacific Mutual reorganization. Within a matter of 60 days the company was solvent, sound, and ready to do business again. When it was all over, I was given a good-sized bonus on top of the fee I had set.

Asa Call asked me then to take on another case, that of the old man who had embezzled the company's funds. I met with the former president of Pacific Mutual, but turned down the request, explaining it would represent a conflict of interest, since I had been attorney for the policy-holders. Of greater concern to me, however, was the old man's expressed hope that I would use my political connections to get him a presidential pardon. Although I had earned a reputation for using some rough tactics, I did not practice the kind of law he wanted.

Throughout my career—whether it has been business, law, or politics—a great many people have misunderstood my code of ethics; but that code has been quite clear in my own mind, which is the only place it's really important. Whatever the situation, whatever the issue, I've always been for the little guy. The ordinary citizen believes in honesty and fair play but he doesn't have much defense against those with power and money, especially when the rich and powerful play dirty. The powerful ones make the rules, but sometimes they are the first to break them, and the first to yell loudly when the little guy does. In defense of the little guy, I have occasionally found it necessary to meet dirty tactics in ways that don't always match the rules. The recording I used in the Pacific Mutual case may have been a form of blackmail, but it achieved justice for thousands of plain, hard-working policy holders who had put their savings into the insurance company.

I kept a good reputation with the little guys and with the honest judges, and that was where it mattered to me. In Longview, I also quickly gained a reputation for being a lawyer who never lost a case. This wasn't always because of skill or ability; sometimes I won cases from sheer luck. One case I recall involved a young man arrested for breaking and entering. He happened to be an identical twin. I put the twin on the witness stand, and the sheriff identified him as the prisoner. The judge threw the case out of court.

One day I was in a courtroom at the Longview courthouse, talking to another lawyer, when District Judge D.H. Meredith approached me. "You're always so cocky saying you've never had a client convicted," he said. "I'll bet you $1,000 you can't get the next man off."

I had no idea what the next case involved, but I agreed to take the defense and the bet. Judge Meredith liked to gamble on anything and everything, and he had plenty of money, so he could afford to lose the thousand without it impairing his professional judgment.

Being cocky, I said, "Okay, and I'll take the jury that's already in the box, without even reading the indictment." That jury had just found the last defendant guilty.

The case involved a man charged with possession of heroin. The evidence was a kitchen matchbox filled with white powder, which the prosecution claimed was heroin.

The first thing that struck me was that the defendant was not a wealthy man, and I knew enough about drugs to realize that a kitchen matchbox full of pure heroin would be worth a small fortune. I had no idea what was in that box, but I felt sure it could not be heroin. That meant that whoever had done the lab report on it could not have been very thorough. Luckily I knew about chemical testing because of my days at the Mellon labs.

The District Attorney put various witnesses on the stand, and I cross examined them routinely, looking for a clue as to what that matchbox contained. Then the defendant's father was put on the stand I saw the solution. The old many had a skin cancer on his nose, and I asked him what he used to treat it.

He told me, "Powdered alum."

I held my fire until the DA put the lab technician on the stand, a doctor from Dallas. He testified that the powder was positively heroin. I kept him on the stand for two hours, grilling him about first one test and then another, none of which he had used in his analysis. As the evening wore on, my questions were answered repeatedly by "I don't know." He was growing more embarrassed and flustered, and Judge Meredith was growing increasingly angry with the District Attorney for perpetrating such an "authority" on his court. The DA did not help matters by constantly jumping to his feet objecting to my questions.

It was getting near midnight when I finally decided enough was enough. I picked up the matchbox and dipped my finger into the powder. Then I extended my finger to the witness and asked him to taste it.

Reluctantly he did, and his face registered distaste.

"Now, doctor," I said, "will you tell me whether that is heroin or powdered alum."

"Powdered alum," he replied, crestfallen.

I turned to Judge Meredith and made a motion for an instructed verdict of not guilty, and he accepted the motion. My client was a free man, and I had won the bet with the Judge.

Interestingly, Judge Meredith was responsible for the first court case I ever lost, but we didn't have a bet going on that one. He came to my office one day. "I don't want to appoint you to this case, but I'd like to ask you to do some charity work," he told me. It was a boy from Gladewater who could not afford a lawyer. He was charged with shooting the manager of the Western Union office in Overton. Members of the boy's church claimed he was in church at the time.

I could tell from Judge Meredith's manner that he believed the boy innocent. I accepted the case.

The defendant's name was Carol Needles David, and he was obviously well-liked by all of the members of the Church of the Nazarene in Gladewater. I put ten of the church members on the stand, all of whom testified positively that David was in church the night of the shooting.

However, there was one lady who followed me around all the time begging me to let her testify. She struck me as the kind of witness who could be easily rattled or confused, and I preferred not to put her on the stand. Finally, she got the minister of the church to intercede for her, and he came to me to ask to let her testify. I believed I had the case won, so I agreed to put her on the stand.

She swore, as all the others had, that Carol Needles David was in church at the time of the shooting. However, on cross-examination, the District Attorney managed to elicit from her a piece of information that had not been divulged—the fact that the defendant had been going to Overton to see a doctor who was treating him for gonorrhea.

The District Attorney subpoenaed the elderly doctor and his appointment book. That record clearly showed that Carol Needles

David had been in Overton on the date in question and that he had left the doctor's office a short time before the shooting occurred.

After the case was over, Judge Meredith apologized to me, saying, "I could have sworn that boy was innocent."

The recounting of incidents in abbreviated form may seem as if my law practice involved one exciting case after another and that I was engaged in a constant crusade for justice. There is a considerable difference between the living and the telling. Every case was not as clearcut as those I've related. Many were more gray than black and white. It was necessary to take these cases to earn a living, but that did not satisfy a need to accomplish things of importance.

Having achieved my boyhood ambition to become a lawyer and "help people," it now seemed inadequate. It was true that every once in awhile a case would come my way where I felt I was needed, a case I could handle maybe a little bit better than some other lawyer. However, I saw another field in which I could better serve: the field of politics.

Part III
PARTY LINES

"PUT SADLER IN THE SADDLE"

The slogan for the 1938 campaign for Railroad Commissioner was "Put Sadler in the Saddle." (Above) A political cartoon, which appeared in Texas newspapers at the time. (Below) A campaign photograph.

13

Running for Railroad Commissioner

When I have been asked why or how I decided to go into politics, I have always told a story about sitting in a movie theater in Kilgore watching a Shirley Temple movie. My moment of decision came while watching *The Littlest Rebel.* That's not the whole story, because there were many other factors that led up to that moment. If that hadn't been the case, then that movie would have changed the lives of the thousands or millions of other people who saw it.

I had been aware of politics and government almost all my life. When in the oil business, I had been involved in politics to a limited extent, working to get candidates, whose views agreed with mine, elected. In working to knock out the NRA and in trying to get a fair hot-oil bill passed, I was involved with politics and government.

On one of my trips to California while working on the Pacific Mutual case, I had become involved slightly with that state's politics. At the time, California's politics were about as gray in color as Texas politics, and there was a power struggle going on. No matter who won that struggle, it appeared the big loser would be the voter. The man who seemed most likely to be the next governor was Neblett, the law partner of William Gibbs McAdoo, who was Woodrow Wilson's son-in-law. Neblett would ruin his own chances by getting involved in an extremely messy divorce before the election, but no one knew that when the group of businessmen asked me to go to see Leo Carillo to ask him to run for the office.

Carillo, a movie actor noted for his portrayal of the Cisco Kid's sidekick, Pancho, was also noted for honesty, integrity, and a genuine public spirit. The businessmen did not want to approach him themselves, feeling he might think they were trying to compromise him in some way, to buy his good name, or to curry favoritism. Being from out of state, I would represent an objective, disinterested voice.

I agreed and went to see Carillo at his home. I found him to be an immensely likeable man but also very familiar with California politics. However, he had no desire for political office. He told me, "Assuming I did run for governor and assuming I got elected and served two terms, then what would I do? I'd be an ex-governor and nothing."

His words impressed me, and I would think of them often in later years. But what I was most impressed with then was the great need for honesty in politics and government. I wondered what our government would be like if honest men like Carillo wanted to stay out of it.

Another factor in my decision involved a new court case in which I represented the owner of a Greek cafe in Houston. When I entered the scene, it was a civil case, involving an injuction against picketing cooks and waiters, but it became a criminal case before it was done. It was one of those gray cases, with no well-defined boundaries between right and wrong. I won the case for my client, and he gave a big party, but I was in no mood for celebrating. After it was over, I went home, went to bed, and tried to sleep, but I couldn't. I was troubled; I did not want any more cases like that one.

The last factor—and possibly the most important one—was a book I had recently read. It was the latest book by Walter Prescott Webb, entitled *Divided We Stand,* subtitled "The Crisis of a Frontierless Democracy." Today, most people are unfamiliar with it, but it still stands as possibly the best analysis ever made of the role of sectionalism in the United States. Webb traces the rise of Northern dominance over the South and West from the Civil War up to the 1930s. He compiled statistics and offered examples to show how the one section of the country controlled banks, insurance companies, and industries to drain the wealth and natural resources from the other two sections.

I don't think I had ever read a book that so excited me. Webb was voicing things I had sensed and felt when I was in the oil business but could not substantiate. As an independent oilman I had been constantly facing the problems of laws and government favoring the big oil companies, all of which were controlled in New York, New Jersey, or Pennsylvania. I read Webb's book many times.

Then, that 1937 summer Sunday afternoon, when I stopped in Kilgore, planning to kill some time, and chose to see *The Littlest Rebel,* with Shirley Temple playing the part of the tiny southern belle, I sat in the theater, my mind wandering, thinking about Texas as it must have been before the Civil War; about my great grandfather, W.T. Sadler, who had been in the war. I thought about the defeat my homestate was still suffering. I thought about the Texas Railroad Commission, and I knew that two of its three members were controlled by out-of-state oil companies. Wall Street wrote the orders for Ernest O. Thompson and C.V. Terrell. The people's only friend on the commission was Lon Smith, but he could do very little as a minority member.

That afternoon I decided to run for the Railroad Commission. If I were lucky enough to get elected, I could really do something for the people of Texas. I didn't know whether I could actually get elected or not, but just by making the effort I could get my message out before the people. During those lean years of the depression, oil was the lifeblood of Texas, and the wealth that belonged to the people of Texas was being stolen by the fat-cats of Wall Street.

At the outset I realized that I would not face the fat-cats directly. One of the ways they managed to maintain their control was to remain quietly and secretly in the background. They paid others to fight their battles for them. It wasn't difficult for them to get the most talented and best-educated men that Texas had to offer, especially during those years of the Great Depression. They held the honey jar, and they held it out for those who were ambitious to dip into it. Those who wanted money could be hired outright as public relations men or lobbyists. Those who wanted the sweet taste of political office could be bought off with large campaign contributions.

There was no word for those Texans who betrayed their fellow citizens by dipping into the honey jar, so I coined one. I called them the Honey-Money Boys. They were the ones I would be up against in running for political office. Later on, when asked to define "Honey-Money Boys," I replied, "They're the ones who sit under the Fritter Tree and drink out of the Honey Spring."

It was a difficult fight, possibly an impossible one. Money and power are an almost unbeatable combination. The people I could count on for help would have neither; all they would have would be their singular right to vote. They were the little guys, the plain people of Texas. Some call them the common people, but I—like most plain people—reject that term, because it carries a derogatory connotation.

When I left the Kilgore movie theater and walked down the streets, I decided to take an informal poll. I stopped one passerby and then another, introducing myself, informing each that I planned to run for Railroad Commissioner, and asking their opinions. I stopped about nineteen people in all, and their response was unanimous. They all thought I was crazy.

That convinced me to run. Their response had told me that the plain people knew what I would be up against, even if they could not offer examples or statistics as Walter Prescott Webb had done.

I went back to my office and talked to Fred Erisman about my plan, Even though he knew it might mean losing a law partner, he was all for it. He had been toying with the idea of running for political office himself, but had not reached the point of decision.

I had decided to try to unseat the strongest man on the Commission, the Chairman, C.V. Terrell. He had held political office for 54 years, on the Railroad Commission nearly fourteen of those years. For the kind of campaign I had planned, however, he was the right opponent. He was not a dishonest man, although the Railroad Commission under his leadership had come under the control of the oil monopoly. He was simply tired and old and ineffectual, running the commission on the buddy system, doing favors for favors. The real culprits were in the lower echelons, some of whom had been appointed by C.V. Terrell.

I did not want to challenge Lon Smith, for in my opinion he was the best of the three commissioners. Although he had been on the Commission almost as long as Terrell, his energy and his concern for fairness had not flagged. The third member was Ernest O. Thompson. I had less respect for him than for the other two men, and I felt that he could be swayed if I should be elected. Thompson was an opportunist, with no real convictions of this own at this point. The youngest member of the Commission, he followed the leadership of the other two.

Considering the kind of candidacy I planned, it was a foregone conclusion I would have to fund it on my own, with perhaps some help from family and close friends. If I started asking for campaign contributions, I could not be absolutely sure where the money came from, and I easily might fall into a political trap.

When I told my family about my intentions, a few of them thought I was crazy for wanting to run, but I had the support of all of them, right down to most distant cousins. Uncle W.T. Sadler, a doctor out in West Texas, had been a second father to me, and he supported me wholeheartedly; another uncle, H.F. Anthony, as well. But the one who would really bring in the votes was Cousin Harley Sadler, a highly successful tent showman. Cousin Harley was probably the most popular and most respected man in West Texas, and his shows pulled in big crowds wherever he went.

To handle my publicity, I called on my friend from my childhood days at Hickory Grove, Ernest "Bones" Jones. Ernest had, until recently, been the editor of the *Palestine Press,* which had been purchased by the *Palestine Herald,* to become the *Palestine Herald-Press.* While Ernest was looking for another job, I asked him to work with me on my campaign.

This would be my first time out as a political candidate, and since there was sure to be several candidates for the position, I knew that I would have to do and say extraordinary things to get attention. I persuaded the editor of the Longview paper, W.W. "Hick" Holcomb to serve as my campaign manager. He was a veteran of the Texas political wars, having worked on the campaigns of Governor Allred and Ross Sterling, among others. We agreed that I had to avoid being a one-issue candidate. I would need to make my speeches different for each major city if I intended to make headlines with them. I would need to speak to Texans in their own language, to show myself one of them, a plain man among plain people. I admit that this required an alteration in my habits. Since my financial success, I had grown accustomed to buying expensive Globe tailor-made suits. The plain man of the 1930s wore Curlee suits; at a price of $20 a suit, they were the cheapest available. I went out and bought myself a closet-full. It turned out to be a good investment. Many times during the campaign people would open up my suit-coat to look at the label.

It was my cousin, showman Harley Sadler, however, who came up with the biggest attention-getter of my campaign. He suggested that I organize a cowboy band to accompany me on the road. People who would not normally come to hear me speak would at least come to hear the band play. I found four musicians, named them the Sadler Stringsters, and they became so successful they got themselves a radio contract to continue when the campaign was over. The idea also prompted other politicians to organize bands of their own.

By the deadline for filing, a total of eight candidates had announced for the one position on the Railroad Commission. Besides Terrell, the opponents I had to face were: Will Martin, R.A. Stuart, John Wood, J.C. Christie, Gregory Hatcher, and Frank Morris. All of them had held high political office before. Terrell was, of course, the one to beat, but among the others John Wood was considered to have the best chance of winning. Two of the candidates—Hatcher and Martin—pulled out of the race in the early weeks to support Wood.

The attacks on me started even before the filing deadline had arrived. The first assistant District Attorney of Gregg County, running unopposed for District Attorney, took a few low, dirty shots at me. At first I didn't understand this; he had nothing to gain by attacking me. Then I realized that he had close ties to one of the large oil companies.

On the day of the filing deadline, I was complaining about this problem to Fred Erisman. "I would swear he's being paid by the oil company to make trouble for me," I said. "Otherwise he wouldn't be traveling around the state to make speeches against me."

We'll stop that," Fred said. "I'll go file for District Attorney against him. I'll make things so hot for him he won't have time to make speeches about you."

Fred's idea worked, and he ended up getting himself elected Gregg County District Attorney in the process.

The beginning of my own race was not as jubilant as I had intended it to be. On Texas Independence Day, March 2, 1938, my father, Claude Sadler, died. I had hoped that he would live through the campaign, might even possibly see me elected, but age would not allow it. After I was called to his bedside, he had little time left. He had lived long and knew what Texas politics was like. His last words to me were, "Be fair and square, and you'll never regret what you do." I told him I would always try to heed that advice.

I launched my statewide campaign in Dallas on April 4, with a speech broadcast over the Texas Quality Network, which included radio stations WFAA, WBAP, KPRC, and WOAI. The keynote speech of my campaign touched upon all the major issues I planned to use.

I hit hard at monopolistic trends in business. "Texans are engaged in a rolling game—rolling nickels, dimes, quarters, and dollars into the North where they are stored in the warehouses of those whose only thought is of luxury and dictatorship. The Railroad Commission is one of the few remaining bulwarks around which the independent can rally. The independent in the oil and gas business is one of the few survivors but his days are numbered unless he gets help."

If the voters would listen to my campaign slogan and "put Sadler in the Saddle," I promised I would provide that help. "I will ride the bronco of monopoly," I said. "I will boot him and spur him on the flanks and in the sides. I promise you that, if necessary, I will jerk the bridle off and hit him on the head. And I won't pull leather."

I pointed out that the controls exercised by the Railroad Commission affected far more than just the oil and gas business. By establishing freight rates, the commission's decisions could affect the price of cotton and farm produce. And I explained how royalties from oil affect such things as state school funds and the control of gas rates.

I brought up the war raging in Europe. I suggested that the decisions of the Railroad Commission could aid in preventing war, affecting the world far beyond the borders of Texas. "The gasoline that powers the motor that propels the bomber that kills the sleeping baby in its cradle comes, in many cases, from the sacred soil of Texas," I stated. "Modern wars, with all their attendant horrors, cannot be conducted without huge quantities of oil and the products of oil. The Railroad Commission of Texas regulates this industry in Texas, and Texas is the largest oil producing state in the largest oil producing nation in the world."

As I had hoped, I received a great deal of attention in the press, and I set people to talking about me, but most newspapers still ranked me eighth in a field of eight.

I didn't mind; that placement gave me a kind of advantage. Even when I was ranked sixth out of six, the other candidates spent more time attacking each other than they did speaking constructively to the public. I hit the campaign trail hard, speaking at no fewer than five towns a day, talking only about the issues and ignoring my opponents. Because of the Sadler Stringsters, I attracted big crowds, and always got a big play in the press. The people listened to me, and I kept my speeches short—about fifteen minutes, long enough to say what I had to say, yet not so long as to bore anybody. The plain people gave me their respect, and I began to believe I might also get their vote.

As we passed through the countryside, going from town to town, we had the loudspeaker going on the sound truck, playing music and announcing our appearances. Farmers plowing the fields unhitched their mules and followed us into town, ready for some free entertainment.

One of my early stops was in Weatherford, and we had a good crowd that afternoon, However, right next to where I was speaking, a farmer had parked a truck and trailer. In the trailer, there was a jack, a mule that's used for breeding purposes. Right in the middle of the speech, the jack started braying. That set everybody to laughing, and I was afraid nobody would be able to take me seriously after that. When the jack stopped, I said, "I didn't know any of my opponents would be here today." The people liked that, so I continued my speech until the jack begain braying again. I made another comment about my opponents, and waited for him to stop. I managed to get to the end of my speech despite the jack, and people applauded as if we were all good friends.

Before and after speeches, I would walk around a town and talk to people. I have mentioned that Franklin Roosevelt nicknamed me "Snuffy" because of the fact that I am a snuff-dipper. I had been dipping snuff for quite some time. In just about every town I ran into other snuff-dippers, and comparing notes on techniques turned out to be a good way to get a conversation going.

From the response I was getting at each stop, it didn't look as if I were the underdog in this race. I attracted even the attention of my opponents and candidates for the other state offices. One particular candidate was interested in my string band; W. Lee "Pappy" O'Daniel, a "flour salesman" running for governor, had a Ft. Worth radio show, on which he advertised his flour. He didn't have much of a platform for his race, except opposition to the "political machine" in Texas. When I was preparing to speak in Abilene, one of my campaign workers came up to me and told me Pappy O'Daniel had come to hear me. The Sadler Stringsters were playing and I waited in the background for them to finish.

"Is he out front?" I asked.

The worker shook his head. "No," he said, "he's sitting in the hotel next door. If you look up, you can see him in the window of his room."

A few days later, Pappy added a band of his own to his campaign appearances, and he did me one better by writing a song entitled "Beautiful Texas" for them to play. Very quickly the 1938 campaign was turning into one of the most colorful and most entertaining in Texas history.

Quickly, I moved up from last place in the race to fourth. As my chances rose, my opponents' attacks increased. Mostly they seemed concerned about my "youth and inexperience." I didn't really mind that. I considered those two qualities part of my qualifications. And their mentioning my name was that much more publicity. I chose not to reply to them by name, but referred to them as a group as "Ex Men"— three ex-senators, an ex-secretary to an ex-governor soon to be an ex-highway commissioner, and a soon-to-be ex-railroad commissioner. My audiences liked that.

As July 27—primary day—approached, I was still generally considered to be in fourth place, though one or two small newspapers were saying I had a good chance for second place. By far the majority considered Terrell a shoo-in for another term, but quite a few were predicting a run-off between Terrell and Wood.

When the votes were totalled, there was widespread astonishment that I came in a close second to Terrell, requiring a runoff. Runoffs were necessary for five other offices—Attorney General, Lieutenant Governor, Land Commissioner, Supreme Court Justice, and Associate Justice—but the race for Railroad Commission had caused the greatest surprise—and the greatest furor among the professional politicians and the big oil companies.

The primary runoff election was set for August 27. In the first exciting taste of success, I had no idea of the trouble that awaited me during the coming month.

14

Politics and Pugilism—A Fighting Chance

Political campaigning is one of the most strenuous activities a human being can engage in. After months of continual speaking, a candidate can begin to lose his voice. His hands become sore, swollen, and bruised from constant squeezes and handshakes. But the greatest fatigue is a mental one that comes from day after day of meeting thousands and thousands of people, with the necessity of remaining polite, attentive, and interested in the concerns of every one. Some campaigners lose weight, others gain. I was one of those who gained weight.

In a way, I thrived on the excitement of campaigning. I enjoyed the four months of constant traveling, the fervor of the crowds, but one of the things that helped me get through it all so well was the knowledge that, after July 27, whatever the outcome, I would be able to go home to my bed and rest for awhile.

I was delighted by my showing in the primary, and for the first time I truly believed I had a good chance of being elected. After one day's rest I was ready to hit the trail again. If I could pick up a good percentage of John Wood's voters, I knew I could win. I felt certain that Wood could be persuaded to support me in the runoff. He had waged a vicious campaign against Terrell, and it was inconceivable that he might now support the incumbent.

But the inconceivable occurred. All of the defeated candidates for Railroad Commissioner came out with one voice in support of C.V. Terrell. That struck me as suspicious, and my suspicion was confirmed when a witness came to me and told me a representative of a major oil company had invited all of the defeated candidates to Dallas to a room at the Adolphus Hotel and offered all a deal. That angered me, but I decided to say nothing about it.

The big oil companies had not taken me seriously during the first primary, so they had not gone all out to make trouble. This was the first indication they would fight me with all they had, and they had no intention of making it a clean fight.

In the four months of the first primary I had made two complete circuits of the state. For the runoff, I would have to make one swing through Texas in only one month.

I began my runoff campaign with a plea to Terrell to step down, claiming the voters had spoken, three-fourths of the votes polling for his opponents. Naturally he didn't respond; I hadn't expected him to. But I did begin to get hecklers in my crowds. I did my best to hold back and ignore them, but after the first couple of weeks the strain was getting to me, and I had a hard time controlling my temper.

In Denton, I finally lost it. While speaking, I recognized the heckler as a lobbyist for the Magnolia Petroleum Company (later Mobil), and the same man who had paid off other candidates to lend their support to Terrell. I would not give ground to the heckler, Bob Hoffman. However, I did stop speaking when another man—one who had not been involved in the heckling—stood up and asked politely, "Mr. Sadler, will you yield to a question?"

"What is your question, Brother?" I asked, not prepared for a trick.

"Why did all your opponents endorse Judge Terrell?" he asked.

Hoffman's heckling had made me so angry I blurted out the story. "Because Bob Hoffman paid them to do it," I said. "In case you don't know who he is, he's the man right over there who now gives me a hard time. He's a lobbyist for Magnolia Petroleum, and he was the college roommate of the General Counsel for Magnolia. Now, if you don't believe it, I have proof." I explained to the crowd there were two men that afternoon—McIver and Dotson—who were present at that meeting. They had worked for Judge Terrell at the Railroad Commission, and Hoffman offered them some of that money that day, but they wanted to have nothing to do with the payoff. "They're standing right over there, and if I'm wrong, I want them to say so right now."

The hushed crowd turned to look at the two men, who merely nodded to confirm the truth of what I said. I returned to my speech without further interruption. When I stepped down from the platform, Bob Edwards, the publisher of the *Denton Chronicle,* approached, a worried look on his face. "There's about to be some big trouble here," he said. "Hoffman's fighting mad. I think you ought to take the back way around the courthouse."

"No," I said, "my pa didn't raise me to be a coward. I'm going out to shake hands with the people the way I usually do."

I was in the middle of the crowd when I saw Bob Hoffman approaching, a look of uncontrollable rage on his face. When he drew near, he shouted at me. It would serve no purpose to list the foul names he aimed at me, but one was "son of a bitch," and another was "bastard." Now, I normally don't mind being called names as long as I'm the one being attacked. But I do take offense at terms that question the integrity of my mother.

"Mr. Hoffman," I said calmly, "you're a lot older than I am, and I've been taught to respect my elders. If you'll just apologize for what you said about my parentage, I'll forget about it."

Hoffman did not apologize; he raved on at me, not only repeating his earlier words but adding worse insults, then he lunged at me. I grabbed him by the lapels and shoved him aside.

Suddenly, from behind, I heard something that sounded as if an elephant had hit the wall. I turned and saw a couple of men scuffling and several tough looking men moved toward me, a murderous look in their eyes. One of them I recognized as an ex-Texas Ranger who had been kicked off the force for having killed another Ranger.

Deputy Sheriff Roy Moore slugged this man. It was the loudest lick I had ever heard delivered by a fist, and it knocked the ex-Ranger out. At that point fighting broke out all over the courthouse lawn. The Denton Police Chief came up to me. "I've had your car pulled up next to the curb," he said. "You start working your way down to it. We'll be with you and do our best to protect you. Just don't turn your back on these guys."

I was grateful that I had the police department and the sheriff and his men on my side, but I was touched to see the farmers and other townsmen from the crowd also coming to my aid. The courthouse lawn was a riot of brawling, fighting men.

As I edged my way toward my car, I noticed one young man, whom I recognized as Jim Gaddy Norris, the son of fundamentalist preacher J. Frank Norris, run across the lawn shouting. "You can't do this to Jerry! You can't do this!"

Suddenly a man clipped him, and he skidded backward and fell down. Young Norris scrambled to his feet, protesting, "I'm not in this! I'm not in this!"

As I drew near the car, Hoffman moved toward me again. This time he had a knife. A man pulled at his shirt, but Hoffman was determined.

The car door was open, and I reached in and took out my pistol. I pointed the pistol at him. "Mr. Hoffman, I suggest you calm down, and get your buddies to do the same."

Hoffman was beyond calming down, but the gun kept him at a distance until I got into the car. Just before we drove off, an old man, wearing patched overalls and a faded plaid shirt, ran up and tossed a silver dollar into the car. "This is all the money I have in the world, Mr. Sadler, but you take it and use it to fight these crooks," he shouted. I smiled and thanked him, then asked Bones Jones to take the man's name and address. Jones had been keeping a record of people who had gone out of their way to help us.

Our motorcade stopped in Gainesville to rest and prepare for another appearance. Only then, when I removed my Curlee suit jacket, did I discover that the back of it had been slashed from shoulder to shoulder. It looked like a razor cut, thin and smooth. It had not damaged my shirt underneath, so it was doubtful if it had been Hoffman. I had no idea who had done it or when, but it shook me up a bit.

I hoped that was as rough as the campaign would get. However, it got rougher.

In Waxahachie, when I finished my speech and was moving through the crowd, a hefty young man approached as if ready to shake my hand. Instead, he hauled off and hit me square in the middle of my forehead. He was a star football player for Trinity University who had been employed by John Wood for his campaign and, as it turned out, had been paid $100 to attack me. In the newspaper account that appeared afterward, he, Raymond Motley, claimed he had hit me after I had called him a "damn liar." Supposedly he had tried to explain Wood's reason for supporting Terrell. That was a face-saving move on his part; actually Motley followed us to the doctor's office, apologizing, saying that he had done the job because he needed money. Although I had a knot as big as a goose-egg right in the middle of my forehead, and it was very painful, I wasn't seriously injured.

We set out on the road again for our next appearance at Waco. Near the German community of West, Texas, we stopped at a public well to get a drink and refresh ourselves. The August day was extremely hot. (We didn't have air conditioned cars and buses in those days.) I pressed some of the cool well-water on my goose-egg and commented to Bones Jones, "If this kind of thing is going to keep up, I'm going to have to get myself a bodyguard."

To my great relief there was no brawl at Waco. The only thing that happened to upset me while I was there was getting the news that Pappy O'Daniel had announced his support for Terrell. Now, I must admit that I didn't have great admiration or respect for O'Daniel, but he had won election in a campaign directed at what he called the "common people," and he had voiced strong oppostion to the professional politicians. I had maintained some hope that he was somewhat sincere, that he wouldn't be such a blatant hypocrite. If he hadn't been willing to support me, he could simply have remained silent.

Most of all, what made me angry was the realization that he had sold out. I didn't have proof, but I could envision another of those hotel rooms and money changing hands.

Cousin Harley Sadler met me in Waco, looked at my injury, and insisted on taking me to see his friend, Dr. Siler, who treated my head and made me look less ridiculous.

I had another visitor while I was there, former Governor Pat Neff, at the time President of Baylor University. His visit was heartening. He offered me his support, expressed admiration for what I was trying to do, and asked me for a favor. Neff knew I didn't like to have anyone introduce me when I spoke, but he asked me to make an exception this one time. He requested I allow Judge Jake Tyrie to introduce me that evening.

I was reluctant to break my rule, even for Governor Neff, but he was very persuasive. Judge Tyrie was on the Court of Civil Appeals, one of the most respected men in the area. "He's an honest man, and the people know it," Neff said. He told me this was the biggest crowd in Waco since O'Daniel's appearance, and the Judge could help prevent trouble. "All you have to do is stay cool and not lose your temper," he added.

I accepted, and Judge Tyrie handled his introduction well. He talked about how I bore the scars of battle, fighting the minions of monopoly, and stated that the people of Waco were behind me and would see that there would be no similar trouble in their city. The crowd, nearly 50,000 people, gathered around the courthouse and enthusiastically applauded. Despite the pain in my head, I made one of the best speeches of my political life and received an overwhelming response from the people.

No one could judge the sort of vote I would actually be able to pull in the runoff, but there were signs that the tide was turning to me.

Newspapers and trade unions were beginning to announce in my favor. My opponents began to get desperate.

Right on the heels of O'Daniel's announcement for Terrell, Elliott Roosevelt paid a visit to Texas and announced his support for the candidate with "experience," implying that he was speaking for the President, though that was entirely untrue.

Then I received word that the opposition planned to issue a scandal-sheet on me, an illustrated broadside that would prove I was part-owner of a Longview bar, which served liquor by the drink. At that time in Texas history this was a sin that ranked alongside rape and murder, just about the lowest thing a man could do.

It was obvious that they had been searching every nook and cranny of my life trying to find something of a questionable nature. Unable to uncover a trace of scandal, they had located a slight connection with the Fountain Bar in Kilgore and had twisted it to make it appear that I was part-owner.

Earlier, when Stanley and I were in the oil business together, the town of Kilgore had no decent hotel. One had started construction with the excavation dug and steel girders placed, but work had halted when the entrepreneur went bankrupt. It stood unfinished for several years; then I joined with a group of Kilgore businessmen to finance its completion. I was involved in several facets of the hotel. I put in the pharmacy and owned it for several years. And I was indirectly involved in establishing the Fountain Restaurant, which had come to be called the Fountain Bar. The investors wanted to set up a restaurant next to the hotel ballroom, one that could be a gathering place for the town's leading citizens and reserved for private parties in the hotel. I agreed to loan the money needed to decorate the room and to help in designing it. R.D. "Fat" Adams would be owner, and he would repay my loan over a period of years.

The Fountain did not have a bar. It had nice booths, with leather-covered seats, mirrors in all sizes and colors, and a fountain in the center of the room, spouting water under a canopy of mirrors. At the time, liquor by the drink was illegal in Texas; it still is in many places. However, good friends of Fat Adams could get served whatever they wanted in the way of alcoholic beverages.

And I was still receiving payments on my loan.

This situation galled me. Everybody who knew me well—and this included everybody connected with the Fountain—knew that I was strongly opposed to drinking. Because of what liquor had done to my father, I was willing to support a Prohibition law. I very much wanted to obtain a copy of this scandal sheet before it was distributed. My informant told me that all the copies were sitting in a hotel room, waiting to be sent out all over the state, and that the person supervising the distribution was Myron Blalock.

Lem Frazee, on my campaign staff, was an excellent actor. He had black hair, was nice looking, and he could pretend to be anything—doctor, lawyer, professor—and carry it off with a straight face. We worked out a plan, and he went to Blalock's room at the Austin Hotel, pretending to be the pastor of a church in West Texas. He told Blalock he intended to preach a sermon attacking Jerry Sadler and asked for useful information for his attack. Frazee was convincing, and Blalock gave him one of the lithographed broadsides.

When I saw this scandal sheet, I was outraged. They had printed not only a picture of the bar with photos of me and Fat Adams, but had managed to secure cancelled checks from my bank as "proof" that I shared in the profits of the Fountain. These were the checks of payments from Adams on my loan to him. But the lie they printed was a credible one, much more credible to the public than would be the truth. If I attempted to defend myself, telling the truth, I could look like a fool.

I took the offensive at once.

I brought up the matter of the scandal sheet for the first time when I spoke at Huntsville, Texas. I held up the purloined copy and said, "This is what my opponents are coming out with in order to get rid of me. They are claiming that I run a saloon in Kilgore, and it's an outright lie. And the terrible thing about this is that it's not even Judge Terrell who is responsible. He's just too old and tired to care about what's being done in his name. The man responsible for this is sitting in the Governor's office right now, that professional politician Jimmy Allred and his henchman Myron Blalock. They don't want me in office because they know I can't be bought."

I pointed out that every sworn affidavit printed in their scandal sheet was a lie, bought and paid for. One affidavit was from a former Texas Ranger who was in their employ. Another was signed by a man who had been convicted of rape in Arkansas, and he had a vendetta against me because I had been attorney for his rape victim. Yet another from a Baptist preacher who had killed a Port Arthur man, and who owed his freedom to Allred and Blalock.

"One of these men is here today," I said. "I saw him just a moment ago standing right back there." And I pointed out the man, who identified himself by protesting angrily. Before he had a chance to defend himself, a man from the audience standing near him, hauled off and slugged him. The police broke up the fight, and I finished speaking.

I continued speaking against charges in the next few towns, and the response I received was favorable. To top everything else my opponents had been trying, the scandal sheet incident did nothing but create sympathy for me. In Madisonville, a man named Buddy Wakefield, who was the local campaign manager for O'Daniel, came to me in tears. "I want to ask you a favor," he said. "I persuaded a lot of people in this county to vote for Pappy O'Daniel." He said he regretted this and asked me to allow him to be on my platform and say so. "I'd like you to let me introduce you," he added.

I considered this a major political coup, and I agreed. Wakefield stood on top of my bus, weeping openly, and made a speech that had half the listeners in tears. He said that he had worked for O'Daniel because he wanted to get rid of the professional politicians, but now that he was elected, O'Daniel was the worst of the lot. It was too late to withdraw his vote for Pappy, he said, but it was not too late to vote for Jerry Sadler.

The Sadler bandwagon picked up momentum. The plain people all over the state were behind me. Then I began to pull some elected officials and civic leaders behind me. And quite a few of the small town newspapers came out with editorials supporting me. There were also political cartoons showing me busting the bronco of monopoly and helping to carry the coffin of professional politics.

From Madisonville, I went on to Corsicana and from there to Dallas. The state fair was still on, and I was scheduled to speak that night at Fair Park. When I got to the fairgrounds, Governor Allred was there waiting to speak to me. He was very upset. "I have not spoken out in opposition to your campaign," he said. "I want to know why you have brought my name into this fight."

"You may not have spoken out against me," I said. "But I have proof you are responsible for this scandal sheet, and I know why you've done it."

The Governor argued angrily. I knew he was simply testing me, trying to find out if I was bluffing.

"I regret having to do this to you," I said, "because you helped me out when I was beginning my career. But the truth has to be told. I know where and when you got together with O'Daniel and Jesse

McKee, and I know what was said in the meeting. I know that you want to keep Mr. Miller, your father-in-law, employed at the Railroad Commission, and I know that Jesse McKee reminded you that I had refused to go along with him back in 1935 when he wanted the Tyler Refining Company to give you a large campaign contribution."

Allred blanched. He knew that I knew the whole truth. "Look," he said, "I'm leaving office in January. I've had a good record as Governor, and President Roosevelt intends to appoint me to a federal judgeship. I don't want my name tarnished at this point. Won't you let up on me?"

"No," I said firmly. "I will let up on you the night before the election, and no sooner. I'm tired—and the people are tired—of politics in the state being run by secrets and lies. I'm going to keep on you and everybody else until the truth is out, the whole truth. On the last night of the campaign, I'm going to speak over the Texas Quality Network, and I'm going to tell all of it—the whole story of your involvement in this, with names and dates and places."

He knew there was nothing he could do about it. "I wish now I hadn't gotten involved in this," he said.

"You admit that you're guilty?" I asked.

"Yes," he nodded.

"Then I'll let up on you," I said. "I won't tell everything I know. I'll stop at what I've already said."

Allred gave me no more trouble, but the rest of the opposition forces did not stop. A few of those who were out to get me were about to become even more violent. Unable to silence me in any other way, they determined to kill me.

In the final week before the runoff election, I was in Brownsville, about to work my way up to Longview by the day of voting. I stayed at the El Jardene Hotel, and about two o'clock in the morning, someone knocked at my door. I got up and went to the door. It was the football coach of Texas A & I College at Kingsville, and he seemed highly agitated.

"Don't go to Kingsville tomorrow," he said. "Cancel your speech. They plan to kill you."

"How do you know?" I asked.

He said he had overheard a group of men plan an assassination. He explained the sheriff would be out of town, and the county commissioner had a bunch of Mexican workers from the King Ranch in on the plan with him. "When you finish your speech and walk out into the crowd, the commissioner will speak to you. Then the men will surround you, and one of them will kill you."

I thanked him for bringing me the information, but I told him I intended to go to Kingsville as planned, and I intended to leave there alive. I was not being particularly brave, but had made a decision finally to get myself some protection.

I got up early the next morning and went outside town to Duncan Wright's house. Dunc was the night Chief of Police in Brownsville, a former Texas Ranger, and he had worked on the Corpus Christi police force. He was a friend of Frank Hamer, and he carried a reputation of being one of the toughest of the Texas Rangers.

Even though it was early, it was already hot. Dunc sat in a chair in his front yard, quietly smoking a cigarette when I arrived. I walked up to him and—after we exchanged greetings—I told him: "It looks like I'm about to have a little trouble in Kingsville."

Dunc didn't ask what kind of trouble, and the cool expression on his face didn't alter. Without hesitating and without turning around to look at his house, he called out, "Mattie, pack my bag!" He knew his wife had listened from the front door.

He picked up his little satchel, got into the car with me, and we left Brownsville. We had one stop to make before we went to Kingsville, in the town of San Diego, Duvall County—"Parr Country." Of all the Texas political bosses, George Parr was the most notorious and the most ruthless.

Duncan Wright's brother-in-law had a drugstore right on the courthouse square, and we could use it to plug in the sound equipment. Dunc told me, "Don't be afraid to say anything you want to say. And don't spare George Parr. If there's any trouble, I'll take care of it."

With Dunc standing by, I felt safer than before, so I did throw in a few choice words directed at Parr. From my platform on top of the band bus, I could see through a courthouse window where Parr and a group of his men seemed to be counting poll tax receipts. I told the crowd, "George Parr would like to see you vote for my opponent, but he has no regard for you at all; he looks upon you as swine. Right now he's in the courthouse counting poll taxes so this time he'll know just how many voters are registered in this county."

Despite my bravery in speaking freely, there was no trouble in San Diego, Texas.

When we arrived in Kingsville, I went straight to the Sheriff's office,

Dunc accompanying me. As I had been warned, the Sheriff was out of town and not expected that day. There was a deputy who was not particularly friendly. I told him that I intended to speak on the courthouse square that afternoon and had heard there might be trouble, so I had brought some protection along. Dunc Wright didn't open his mouth the whole time, but the Deputy got the message.

We parked the bus alongside a long solid brick wall of a furniture store. The driver waited in my car behind the bus, ready for a quick getaway if it should be necessary.

I did not attract my usual big crowd. The warning had obviously been spread around the county for people to stay away. Except for the county commissioner and his cohorts, there were only a handful of spectators. While I spoke, the commissioner stood out front listening silently, with the other men—about twenty in all—lined up in a "V" formation around him. Duncan Wright stood quietly in the background, leaning against the brick wall of the furniture store, beneath the awning. All the time I was up on the platform his eyes never left the county commissioner.

I knew the man, and I was aware he had a grudge against me. He had once hired me to represent his son in a rape case. The father had wanted me to try to bribe the judge to get a verdict of innocent; I had advised the son to plead guilty and throw himself on the mercy of the court. The son was now serving time in prison.

The Deputy Sheriff was there, watching everything, but he represented an unknown factor to us. If trouble started, we had no inkling what he would do.

I concluded my speech without incident, which was something that had come to be unusual. After I was through, I climbed down from the platform and walked out to shake hands with the county commissioner.

As I approached him with my hand extended, he refused the handshake. "You son of a bitch, why didn't you tell the truth about yourself?" he said loudly.

I clenched my hand and pulled back, about to slug him. The Deputy reached for his gun. Suddenly Dunc Wright was behind me, grabbing my arm.

"Put up that gun!" Dunc commanded.

The Deputy did as he was told, saying, "I respect you, Captain."

Until he spoke, I did not know that Frank Hamer was there, that Dunc had called on his friend, the most celebrated of all the Texas

Rangers. "Get in your car, Jerry," he said, "and let's go. We'll be right behind you." He said to the county commissioner and his men, "We're going to leave town and leave Kleberg County. We'll stop on the other side of the county line. If any of you men want to shoot it out, you can follow and we'll do it there."

Dunc got into the car with me, and we raced off out of Kingsville as fast as my car could go, followed by the band bus and by Frank Hamer's car. We stopped just inside Nueces County, only a short distance outside Kingsville. The County Commissioner and his men gave chase, but they turned around before reaching us, deciding against a fight not heavily weighted in their favor.

In Corpus Christi, I had a hotel room reserved to clean up and change clothes. I had barely entered my room when there was a knock at the door. The Chief of Police wanted to talk to Duncan Wright. He told Dunc that he had been given reports of plans to break up my speech. He said that he intended to have no trouble in Corpus Christi. No matter which side they were on, anybody who tried to start a fight would be arrested immediately. "I don't want any shooting," he emphasized.

The police department was out in full force that night. And they had three Black Marias backed up alongside our vehicles, waiting for anybody who desired to disturb the peace. We had a good crowd, and there were a lot of hecklers catcalling during my speech, but no fights.

It was when I climbed down from my platform on top of the bus that a group of men suddenly tried to rush me. But the police were alert, and they moved in swiftly, grabbing men, literally lifting them up and throwing them into the paddy wagons. I was ushered into my car and driven off without further incident.

The next evening, I spoke in Houston, and faced another attempt to get me. It too passed without a serious confrontation. In Houston, I was to speak in Hermann Park, and the threat was greater there because it was not well lighted as were downtown areas. We parked the bus in an open area, but it was surrounded by trees, shrubs, and hedges, and the area beyond was in shadow.

I had worked out some hand signals to let my workers know where to look for trouble. They were interspersed in the crowd and so could not see too well, but I was up high, on the platform atop the bus, and I could see everyone and everything.

As I spoke that night I noticed a group of men on their hands and knees crawl along behind the hedge, working their way toward the bus. I signalled to my men, and they got to them and held them until police arrived to take them away.

The campaign was winding down to a close. My opponents had tried everything they could think of to get to me, but still had not managed to shut me up. However, they were not yet ready to give up, because a small group followed me from town to town. They still had a few ingenious tricks up their sleeves.

In Center, the next stop on the road after Houston, they tried another tactic. Only the day before, I had heard that Bob Hoffman had died. He was the lobbyist for Magnolia Petroleum, who had started the trouble in Denton at the beginning of the runoff campaign. He had walked through the front door of a Denton drugstore and had suddenly suffered a fatal heart attack.

After my speech at Center, a man named Leroy Garrison climbed up on my platform to make a short speech of his own. He claimed that I was wanted for murder in Denton, saying that Bob Hoffman had died of wounds I had inflicted in our fight. (In fact, I had done nothing more than shove Hoffman.)

Wardlow Lane, the Shelby County District Attorney, climbed onto the platform and Garrison left. Lane spoke in my defense. "If Sadler was wanted for murder in Denton County, I would have been notified. This man is clearly lying, attempting to smear Jerry Sadler."

Leroy Garrison moved back out into the crowd. An old man raised his walking stick and poked him in the stomach. "Now you get out of here and leave Sadler alone." The man was so old and feeble, Garrison did not respond to the badgering.

The climax of the election came at Carthage. It appeared everybody in Panola County had driven to town for my speech, as well as quite a few citizens from surrounding counties. There was such a crippling traffic jam in the small town of Carthage we had difficulty getting into the community. The courthouse square was packed, hardly a spare inch anywhere. It was a hot day and I was thirsty, so I worked my way with difficulty through the crowd to the drugstore to get a Coca-Cola. It too was filled with people. While I drank my Coke, I heard one farmer speak to another. "I reckon Sadler's gonna be fighting here tonight." "Yep," the other replied, "that's what I heerd."

I wasn't sure I liked the reputation I had acquired. I didn't mind being known as a fighter for the rights of the plain people, but I was beginning to fear that I was attracting attention for the fighting rather than for the principles I was fighting for. I decided to stay on an easy, even tone that night, still hitting hard at my opponents, but not straining too hard at the emotions of my audience. I knew that Leroy Garrison and his bunch had followed from Center, and they were still spoiling for a fight. As I spoke, I signaled to my workers and managed to keep each of Garrison's men covered so they would start no trouble.

Before I rose to speak in Carthage, we had discovered that Leroy Garrison and his men had parked their cars in the alley behind the courthouse. We worked out a plan in which my men would block off the two ends of the alley, preventing Garrison and his men from escaping, thereby providing an opportunity for a final showdown. I had noticed that Garrison had carried around a briefcase, when he followed us from town to town. I very much wanted to have a look at the contents. After my speech, I would pretend to leave town in my official, unmarked car, just outside the city limits. Then I would return.

By the time I returned, my men had the situation well under control. Garrison and his men were a little the worse for wear and in no condition to complain when we took them for a little ride in their own cars. On our way into Carthage that day we noted a stretch of road about halfway between Carthage and Tenneha had just been paved with concrete. In August there are very few things hotter than concrete in Texas, especially for bare feet. It stays hot far into the night. There's probably only one thing more unbearable for bare feet, and that is the grass burrs that flourish on the sandy shoulders of the road.

There we removed the shoes and socks from Garrison and his men, and we removed the rotors from all of their cars, taking them with us as "souvenirs."

The one other thing I took was Garrison's briefcase. In it, I found all the evidence my opponents had gathered against me—the cancelled checks from the Fountain Bar, photographs of the place, affidavits, and depositions.

They were a sad looking group as we drove off, leaving them alone in the dark. Later I heard that Garrison and his men managed to get back to Carthage about one in the morning, still barefoot, and they went to the Sheriff to file a complaint against me. He refused to accept the complaint, telling them he would give them 30 minutes to get out of Carthage and an hour to get out of Panola County.

Our campaign motorcade didn't stop until we got to the Sabine

River Bridge. I decided that would be a good place to get rid of our souvenirs. I kept the documents from the briefcase, considering them rightfully mine, but I did not wish the briefcase itself.

A young man on my campaign staff had wanted to make a speech ever since the start of the campaign. He was inexperienced and I had never given the okay. As we stood out on the bridge, above the flowing Sabine River, I told him, "You are finally going to get to make your speech. I want you to get up on the railing of this bridge and make a speech entitled 'Farewell to the Briefcase.'" I handed him the briefcase. "And when you get through, I want you to pitch the briefcase into the river."

He climbed up on the bridge's railing and made a brilliant, though somewhat humorous speech, and—to the accompaniment of applause from the entire staff—he tossed the briefcase out into the dark water below.

Two nights later I concluded my campaign in Dallas, with a speech broadcast over the Texas Quality Network, and beamed into most all of the other radio stations in the state. With that speech, I pulled out all the stops. In addition to the Sadler Stringsters, I had Floyd Tillman, Buck Creel, and Lew Childre on the program. The songs were the most heart-rending in the country and western repertoire—such as "If I Could Only Hear My Mother Pray Again" and "That Silver Haired Daddy of Mine."

When I spoke, I out-Pappied O'Daniel. I hit out at the Big Oil monopoly, at the Wall Street brokers and their pimps, and I lambasted the professional politicians of Texas who took their thirty pieces of silver and betrayed the plain people. I charged them with taking the food out of the mouths of old folks and children, suggesting that the reason Texas did not have an adequate pension and social services program was because its wealth was going into the pockets of men in the North. From my own experience as an independent oilman, I gave examples of the ways politicians were bought and sold, naming names and dates. I told about Jesse McKee and Jimmy Allred and Pappy O'Daniel. And I said that recent price cuts in East Texas crude oil were politically motivated. "Let us assume that it is," I added, "since Myron G. Blalock, one of Commissioner Terrell's ardent supporters is a principal owner and director of one of the companies which cut the price."

At that point, people in the audience cried out, "Pour it on 'em."

The broadcast seemed more like a country church meeting.

I pointed out that Terrell's recent years in office were a series of junkets—legislative junkets, hunting junkets, fishing junkets—noting that he had been away from his office a total of 192 working days in a single year.

I called on the people of Texas to join with me to work for change, asking the studio audience and the radio audience at home to join hands. It surprised me when they actually did as I asked. Later I learned that there were people who hadn't spoken to each other in years who joined hands that night. One story I heard was of former Speaker of the Texas House of Representatives Emmett Morse, who was out on the highway somewhere near Waco in a car driven by a police officer. The policeman told me that they were listening to my speech as they drove along. Emmett asked him to pull the car over to the side of the road and stop, explaining that he had to cry awhile.

I wound up my speech calling on patriotism. "The cry of the vanquished at San Jacinto was 'Me no Alamo! Me no Goliad!' When the returns are counted on Saturday, the cry heard in Texas will be 'Me no Dictator! Me no Allred.' "

When it was over, the applause was thunderous. I felt a little guilty about that, not because I had lied or said anything unfair, but because I had consciously manipulated the audience, using the same techniques of a fundamentalist preacher.

Even then I did not really believe I had a good chance of winning. I knew only that I had made a damn good race and that I had managed to get my message across.

When word came through about two o'clock Sunday morning that I had won the election, I was stunned.

Now I would have to make good on my promises.

15

Fighting Big Oil

The Fat-Cats and Honey-Money Boys of the big oil companies thought the end of the world was at hand. In the weeks that followed the primary runoff, newspaper headlines foretold instant disaster the day I would take office. Actually, I was not yet formally elected. I had merely won the Democratic Party nomination for the office, but in those days Texas was a one-party state, and nomination was tantamount to election.

There were demands for Governor Allred to call a special session of the legislature to nullify my election by appointing a special oil and gas commission. The Governor was the first person to call me to apologize for his actions during the campaign, and he said if he ever heard any of his aides saying anything against me, they would instantly lose their jobs.

To the press he announced that he would not call a special session of the legislature to create an oil and gas commission, stating, "The people elected a Railroad Commissioner. I do not see any occasion for a special session to create a new one."

Allred was the first of many people who had started off opposing me, then did an about face when they got to know me. The reason, of course, was that my reputation always preceded me, not only setting my opponents on guard, but also prejudicing some honorable men. Through the years I have been called many things, some of them true, some not—temperamental, obnoxious, demagogic, crude, belligerent, egotistical, and violent. I have no regrets about the things I've done to warrant those terms. What has been more important to me has been to be right and just and honest. When the truth is spoken quietly, it can't be heard. I managed to attract attention to the truth.

Immediately after the runoff, I went to Austin, telling the press I intended to create "some of the biggest headlines you ever saw." I was not yet in office; in fact, I would not even be officially elected until

November, but there was one issue that needed immediate attention.

Attorney General McCraw was engaged in a series of confiscation suits against East Texas oil companies. On the surface it appeared that his cases were just. He was doing his job according to the law, but he was attacking the tip of the iceberg while the law concealed the major part of the injustice.

With the help of the Railroad Commission, the major oil companies and some of the independent operators were still managing to get around the Connally Hot Oil Act and the state law that provided for the confiscation of all oil produced in excess of the proration allowances. The state was required to sell this confiscated oil at public auction, and the proceeds were to go to the school fund to improve public education. A state law had been passed to eliminate specific pits where excess oil had existed, but those pits were now appearing to be almost bottomless.

This oil was coming from several sources, all of them illegal. Some of it was coming from local wells, and some was being shipped in from other states as a way of getting around their own allowances. It cost the oil companies to do this, but in the long run they made money in the process, due to the Railroad Commission not putting the hot oil up for public auction. Once the Commission confiscated the oil, they would sell it back to the original owners for 27 cents a barrel. This then made it legal oil, and the companies could sell it for $1.35 a barrel.

Bill McCraw was playing right into their hands—wittingly or unwittingly.

When I arrived in Austin, I held a press conference and recommended that Attorney General McCraw appoint a special prosecutor to investigate hot oil. I offered my services and, as I had expected, my offer was refused. However, I met with Governor Allred and provided him with proof of what was happening. He acted immediately, calling a conference in his office. He invited Bill McCraw, T.J. Holbrook, chairman of the senate investigation committee, Senator Joe Hill, a member of that committee, District Attorney Edwin Moorhead, and me. After this conference, statements were issued avowing to change the hot oil situation.

I did create a few headlines on this and other important issues, but my opponents created just as many of their own, using scare tactics to try to undermine my influence. When the big oil companies had been unable to get Governor Allred to circumvent my election by pressing for an appointed oil and gas commission, they went to work on Pappy O'Daniel, the candidate for the Governor's office, persuading him to try to establish one in the Democratic Party platform, which would be adopted at the state convention in September.

To sway convention delegates to accomplish this, the oil companies managed to influence many Texas newspapers to conjecture about the sectional impact of my election, pitting West Texas, the Gulf Coast, and the Panhandle against East Texas. The basis for this conjecture was that, for the first time in many years, the East Texans on the Commission outnumbered the West Texans. Until my election, Lon Smith was a minority voice. Smith supported my campaign. Now, he and I represented a majority.

News headlines prophesied disaster for West Texas, predicting East Texas oilfields would be receiving preferential treatment. Lon Smith and I protested that no section of the state would be given advantage over any other, but seeds of fear were planted, and the sowing managed to take hold. There was no truth in the charges, but by giving no section an advantage over any other, West Texas and the Gulf Coast would lose the advantage they had possessed for years, while East Texas would be treated fairly for the first time.

However, neither my opponents nor most of the newspapers were concerned with fairness. Now, I don't mean to be too critical of the newspapers. I believe strongly in the freedom of the press, and I have a great respect for most newspeople, but they are human. Sometimes they can be duped; sometimes they don't look into a subject deeply enough before they write about it; and sometimes they deliberately tell only part of the truth so as to slant a story.

This was a perfect example of a slanted story. None of the facts were inaccurate, but the overall effect was misleading, because all of the facts were not included.

As a result, there was a strong chance that Pappy O'Daniel might get his oil and gas commission, at least on the party platform. If I did not want all of my efforts of campaigning to be a complete loss, I had to prepare to fight once more at the convention.

Only two of the candidates nominated in the Democratic primary were unsatisfactory to O'Daniel. I was one, of course, and the other was the nominee for Attorney General, Gerald Mann. Neither of us were delegates to the convention, so we had to find delegations who would appoint us as alternates even to get inside the front door of the convention hall in Beaumont. We certainly had no say on the platform committee unless we could find a way to force the issue.

Mann and I looked over lists of delegations from around the state and discovered that together we had quite a few friends and supporters among them. We also found that some delegations had vacancies to fill by appointment. We succeeded in arranging appointment as alternates for ourselves, and a few other friends and supporters were appointed as delegates.

I came up with an idea. Trying to think of friends who could be added to the Harris County delegation, I remembered one of my "mentors" when I was a bellboy at the Rice Hotel—Miss Gussie Windham. Miss Gussie was the manager of the Windham Hotel, which was actually not a hotel, but a brothel, and Miss Gussie its madame. Everybody in Houston knew about the Windham Hotel, but they pretended otherwise. Miss Gussie was something of a celebrity, if one calls someone who is publicly ignored a "celebrity."

When Miss Gussie was appointed to the Harris County delegation, I went shopping to buy her a special outfit to wear. I purchased a beautiful red dress for her—I mean, bright red. And I bought her a red hat, red stockings, red shoes, a red purse, and a red umbrella. When she dressed in this outfit, it was impossible not to notice her. She agreed to wear it to make her entrance at the Democratic Party convention.

Meanwhile, we went to work to get all of our supporting delegates to the convention. Many were plain people who couldn't afford to pay all their own expenses—transportation, hotel room, and meals. Some of our delegates were hauled to Beaumont on flatbed trucks, and some came on their own, although they had no place to stay. We rented the entire Crosby Hotel to provide rooms for those who had none. Some delegates had to double up, and since our group had the whole place to themselves a party atmosphere prevailed. Many—though not all—wandered the halls, drinking and having a good time. At one point, I walked down a hallway and discovered one delegate, a judge from Georgetown, so drunk he could barely stand up. For his sake, and for the reputation of our delegation, I decided I'd better put him to bed. I asked him where his room was. "Don't have one," he replied.

I approached a maid in the hallway and told her the man didn't have his key and needed to be let into his room. I picked out a likely looking door, and said it was his. The maid unlocked the door, and I took the judge in to the room and put him to bed. Unfortunately I had picked a room that belonged to a lady delegate. She saw no humor, when she returned to find a drunken man passed out on her bed.

That wasn't the only complaint, however. The next day, Carl Kennedy, the Beaumont Chief of Police came to me to say that it had been necessary to arrest a few delegates. He was willing to release them from jail to attend the convention if I would make sure they stopped prowling the halls of the hotel. I agreed, and all our delegates were present for the important day.

Everything was organized, with every delegate and alternate knowing his or her part in the plan. Some were to speak, others would organize and lead floor demonstrations. One delegate, posted at the convention hall entrance, would signal me when Miss Gussie arrived. I was to escort her to her seat myself.

Mrs. Oveta Culp Hobby, the parliamentarian of the convention, was at the microphone when I escorted Miss Gussie down the aisle. The expression on her face, when she recognized Miss Gussie, is indescribable. It was the only time I ever saw Mrs. Hobby, always the lady, lose her composure. I seated Miss Gussie in the very middle of the Harris County delegation; immediately other delegates began to leave. By convention rule, no one could stand in the aisles, and if they could not find seats with another delegation, they had to leave the hall.

She hadn't been seated long, with only a handful of our hand-picked delegates remaining near her in the Harris County seats, when a Fort Worth man, head of the Tarrant County delegation, came to me. "Jerry," he asked, "won't you please seat this lady someplace else?"

"Why should I?" I replied. "She had a poll tax. She's a voter. She's a Democrat, and she's a delegate to this convention. She has as much right to be here as anybody else."

A few moments later, I was informed that Mrs. Hobby wished to speak to me. I went to the podium. "Jerry," she said, her face ashen, "we'll do anything you want, if you'll just get that call-house madame out of the Harris County delegation."

"Will you let me write the party platform?" I asked. "And get Pappy O'Daniel to issue a statement welcoming me and Gerald Mann into the fold?"

"I can't promise that," she said. "That's up to Mr. O'Daniel. But I'll surely speak to him."

Oveta couldn't persuade Pappy, and Miss Gussie stayed to vote.

Texas politics is unpredictable, wild, and crazy, but what W. Lee

O'Daniel faced when he arose to address the convention was unprecedented, even in Texas. The party standard-bearer was booed off the floor. All over the hall delegates demonstrated so loudly against him that he could not make his address. Upset, he stalked off the podium, and left to Mrs. Hobby the restoration of order.

The boos and catcalls ceased; O'Daniel came again to speak; again, he met a raucous demonstration.

After a third attempt, he left the convention hall and returned to his hotel.

Mrs. Hobby and other leaders attempted to proceed with the convention agenda, but on signal, one delegation or another would interrupt their efforts. When the leaders realized they would be unable to conduct any business, they opened the floor to recognize anyone who wished to speak. One of our delegates, C.W. Kennedy, from Grapeland, addressed the convention. The theme of his speech was: "Any Son-of-a-Gun who Doesn't have a Poll Tax and Can't Vote Shouldn't be Allowed to Hold Elected Office." This subject referred specifically to Pappy O'Daniel, who couldn't even vote for himself.

After Kennedy had talked his subject to death and many delegates, growing bored, had left the hall, the leadership closed the meeting for the day. Unless something was done, the leaders realized they would face another day like the first. Our minority was so large, the sergeant-at-arms was unable to cope with us. The police could not be called in, partly because Chief Kennedy was our friend and partly because it would be poor public relations for the party regulars.

O'Daniel responded the way I hoped he would. That night, in my hotel room, I received a delegation from the future governor, headed by Frank Rollins of Ft. Worth and Sam Long of Dallas. They told me that O'Daniel wanted me to go to his hotel room.

"No," I told them, "I won't go to see O'Daniel, and I won't speak to him. I will give you a message to give to him: we will allow him to address the convention if he will allow us to name the committee who will write the platform and made sure there is to be no oil and gas commission included in it. Also, we want to issue a public statement that he is pleased with all of the candidates nominated by the voters."

The delegation indicated these were reasonable requests, and they felt sure that O'Daniel would agree.

As they were leaving, I cautioned them. "If anyone attempts to amend the platform from the floor to get the oil and gas commission onto it," I said, "the ruckus will start again. We'll take over the floor and stop the convention completely."

O'Daniel agreed to our demands, Jim Kilday of San Antonio was my man on the platform committee, but it was actually written by my campaign manager, Hick Holcomb. The oil and gas commission was effectively killed, at least for the next two years, and the party standard-bearer did make a public statement welcoming me and Gerald Mann onto the Democratic ticket and promising unity.

For the next two months, I was able to enjoy the kind of lighthearted and inoffensive activities that are part of our political system—attending county fairs, football games, barbecues, and rodeos. Controversy took a back seat to snuffdipping contests, posing on horseback for photographers, and crowning beauty contest winners. Yet I had to remain alert to my own ethics, being careful not to relax too much.

Several times I was offered large amounts of money to "cover" my campaign debt, often as much as twenty to thirty thousand dollars. Always I had to refuse, even when there appeared to be no strings attached. On one occasion I recall, when I was in Houston, Jack Dies offered me $20,000 in twenty-dollar bills for my campaign, with no witness present. In those days, candidates were not required to be precise in their campaign financial reports, and that kind of offer could be quite tempting. However, Jack Dies was the biggest of the Honey-Money Boys, completely owned by Humble. I turned it down. Of all the big oil companies, I certainly did not want to be indebted to the powerful Humble Oil and Refining Company.

Since the time when I announced my candidacy, I had not directly faced the Fat-Cats, the big boys in the oil industry—although I had a few run-ins with their Honey-Money Boys. They had tried to defeat me, to kill me, to circumvent me, and to bribe me, and all because of second-hand information brought to them by their underlings. I decided it was time to face the Fat-Cats, to let them know—straight from the horse's mouth—what to expect.

While in Houston, I went to see Mr. Harry Weiss, Chairman of the Board and President of the Humble Oil and Refining Company (which is now Exxon). I knew that the biggest fight I would have, once in office, would be with Humble.

"I know you have done your damnedest to keep me off the Railroad Commission," I told Mr. Weiss. "But I want you to know that is not going to make one bit of difference after I take office on January first. I am going to treat you as fairly as I do any other oil producer or refiner. If you are within the law, you don't have anything to worry about; if you're not, you're in just as much trouble as the biggest hot oil runner in East Texas. Nobody is going to get preferential treatment from me."

As a gentleman, Weiss accepted that. "I do have one demand to make, however," I continued. "If your money-totin' Honey-Money Boy, Jack Dies, ever comes to the Capitol after I'm in office, I'm going out and shut down every well that Humble has in the State of Texas, and I will reveal all I know about your company's activities."

Mr. Weiss thought for a moment. "Well," he said agreeably, "Jack is getting to be an old man, and his health isn't too good anymore." Weiss thought it was time for Dies to retire.

I waited until the week after the election in November to deal with the matter of the Banker's Tender Board. They were the group of the state's bankers appointed by the Railroad Commission to pass upon a company's application for permits to sell oil. Without a tender issued by this board, oil could not change hands; the Tender Board had engaged in numerous abuses of their power. As bankers, they were naturally inclined to favor the big oil companies, because ultimately, it meant more money for them.

This board was totally unnecessary, because it performed a function that should have remained in the hands of the Railroad Commissioners.

One member of the Banker's Tender Board considered to be honest and fair was Fred Florence, President of the Republic National Bank in Dallas. I asked him to arrange a meeting for me with the most important bankers involved—Nathan Adams, President of First National Bank of Dallas, and Bob Thornton, President of the Mercantile National Bank.

These three men did not constitute the entire Tender Board, but formed the committee who appointed numerous other members in cities around the state. Many of the bankers who sat on the board were also owners of oil producing or oil refining companies. These banking leaders also hired lawyers, who constituted the Petroleum Council, to give them legal advice. It was a large network of power—appointed power, not elected.

When I arrived in Florence's office that November evening, I shook hands with the three men, thanking them for meeting on such short notice. "Now that the votes are counted," I said, "and I am officially elected to the Railroad Commission, I have something to say, and I wanted to say it in person, so there's no misunderstanding. You have almost two months to get the Banker's Tender Board in order. After midnight of Janaury 31, 1938, you will no longer have any say in who can or cannot do business in oil in the State of Texas."

Florence sat quietly listening, but the other two began to protest angrily. "He means what he's saying," Florence interjected calmly. "And I think we'd better hear him out."

"If you want a fight," I continued, "I'm willing to give you one, but I don't think you gentlemen will want to air your dirty linen in public. What I suggest is that you notify Ernest O. Thompson of your intention to dissolve the Banker's Committee voluntarily, turning all responsibilities back to the Railroad Commission."

Clearly, Adams and Thornton were not inclined to follow my advice, but Florence was calm and persuasive. "I think we ought to do as he suggests," he told his associates. He told them they had the reputation of their banks to consider, as well as their own reputations. He pointed to a number of abuses by the other members of the board. "I haven't been as guilty as others have been, but I, and my bank, would suffer with the rest if there were to be a public scandal."

Eventually Florence persuaded the other two men to dissolve the board voluntarily. I had one parting comment for one of the men, Nathan Adams. He had written a letter to all Texas bankers, warning them that my election would destroy the state's economy. "If Jerry Sadler is elected to the Railroad Commission," he said, "grass will grow in the streets of your town."

"Mr. Adams, I have a great respect for you," I said. "However, you might prove to be wrong about one thing. After I am sworn into office, I don't think grass will grow in the streets of every city and town in Texas. We might just have more progress than we've ever had."

I'm sure that Mr. Adams and others considered this action a spiteful one. I held many accusations of being spiteful after my election. I guess simple justice does look a little like spite to those who suddenly have to take a little of what they're used to dishing out. Others who are more radical might think I let the bankers off too easily, but I gave a lot of thought to the way I would handle this situation. The banks these men represented held a lot of money that belonged to the plain people of Texas. It had taken quite awhile to restore people's confidence in banks. If I had forced the issue publicly, the state's economy might have suffered just as Adams had predicted.

I admit to one spiteful action during this time—and I admit to enjoying it wholeheartedly. It took place one day when I was visiting Corpus Christi. I was talking to two of the town's leading citizens, one of whom was a lawyer. We discussed the politics there. "There's one thing that happened in Corpus Christi during my campaign that I don't understand," I said. "There was a radio show, and most all the lawyers in town went on the show to speak out against me. Why did they do that?"

The lawyer, not among the radio speakers that evening, explained: "It was set up by one of the oil companies here. Every one of those men were hired to do it. The scripts were written for them." He said the lawyers read their scripts and collected their fees.

That made me angry, not that these lawyers opposed me, but that they were willing to sell their good names. I had always considered the legal profession as sacred, almost holy. Shysters and ambulance chasers always made me angrier than anything or anyone else ever could.

The more I thought about how they had sold their ethical profession, the angrier I became. That evening, sitting in my hotel room, I collected a list of those lawyers who had participated in the radio program, and I found their home phone numbers in the telephone book.

One by one, I called them, telling each the same story. I gave a fictitious name, identifying myself as a cattleman. I said I desperately needed a local lawyer because a truckload of my registered cattle had been hit and overturned by a switch engine in the Corpus Christi railroad yards. I didn't know how many of my valuable animals had been killed, but it looked like at least thirty. I said I was from out of town and I didn't know any lawyers there. "A witness to the accident recommended I call you," I told each lawyer.

Almost every attorney reached by telephone was interested in the case, saying they would go immediately to the scene of the accident. I had selected an open area of the railroad yards for my mythical accident, and I gave each man precise directions.

I finished my telephoning and went to the railroad yards to observe the excitement. There were men in cars all over the yard, looking for the accident. It was such mass confusion that—before it was over—the police were called to clear traffic.

I hoped the Lord would forgive me, but it had been a long time since I had had a good laugh. And it made me feel good.

16

The Railroad Commisson—Big Changes

The last meeting of the Terrell Commission took place in December of 1938, just prior to my installation in office. I chose not to attend the meeting, even though they were to consider two important matters that would affect the first months of my tenure—proration allowances for January through March, and enforced shutdown of oil wells for four additional days each month. I felt I had hurt Terrell enough by defeating him in the election, without making his last days in office miserable.

Despite appearances, I have a soft heart. I honestly liked and sympathized with the old man. After I was in office, a strong bond of affection developed between us. He stayed on in Austin and would wander up to the Railroad Commission offices most every day, lonely and looking for someone to talk to, something to do. Once he was out of office with no power, the people he once called friends had no time for him. When I could find a spare moment, I invited him into my office—once his office—and we would talk. Before he died, he told me, "Out of all of them, you're the only real friend I had."

My first months with the Railroad Commission were hectic ones. I had promised voters I would initiate changes, and together, Lon Smith and I lived up to those promises. Decisions and actions that might have seemed to require weeks or months of deliberation were packed into single days. And in most of those early days we were besieged by literally thousands of people seeking appointive offices.

One thing I had sworn, however, was to cut the number of Railroad Commission employees, especially people collecting state paychecks but performing little useful work. Before it was over with, I believe I eliminated about 69 unnecessary jobs, keeping the firings from being a political issue. Although I did remove some of the abusers from their power positions, I tried to keep those who were honest, capable, and interested in working, even if it meant moving them to different services. I did bring in my own secretary, but I found another job within the department for Terrell's secretary.

Some newspapers accused me of spite in the job cutbacks, but the legislature voted to commend me for the economies, and then went on to make cutbacks in other departments of the government.

One of the most important appointments I made was to hire Stanley Bean for the Kilgore office of the Commission. When I got down to serious work, I anticipated some big trouble in the East Texas fields, and I felt I could trust Bean to handle it. He had been a Kilgore policeman and a Longview deputy sheriff, and he had a good reputation for being a tough lawman. In East Texas, I had observed his actions against some really bad criminals.

Conservation was the major problem facing the Railroad Commission when I assumed office; and it was not just a local problem. There was too much oil on the world market, far more than the demand. This glut was a threat to the oil industry as a whole, a national—and to a certain extent an international—problem. A portion of this problem stemmed from greedy oil producers within Texas, but they represented only a part. Lon Smith and I had plans to take care of the hot-oil runners in East Texas and the excessive prorations in West Texas and the Gulf Coast. A major crisis came from the other oil-producing states, particularly Louisiana, Illinois, and California, where there were no effective controls on oil production.

President Roosevelt was extremely upset about overproduction of oil. The federal government had the Connally Hot Oil Act, intended to control the flow of oil, but there was no federal authority to enforce it. Enforcement (reduction) was left to the states. However, in some cases, those responsible for the excesses were state officials. Roosevelt and Secretary of the Interior Harold Ickes made plans for a federal authority such as the Texas Railroad Commission, to take over the regulation of the oil industry. As Congress assembled that January, 1938, much of the discussion concerned passage of such law.

I understood the problem, but I wished to avoid federal control at all costs. I was acquainted with FDR, having met with him on several occasions, but we were not as yet on friendly terms. We had, I believe, a mutual respect for one another. In principle, we generally agreed. On specific issues, we were often in opposition. We each considered ourselves Jeffersonian-Jacksonian Democrats, but our thinking was as different as our backgrounds. He has always been painted as the

Liberal's Liberal, but he was far more conservative than people believed. He had been reared in a world of wealth and privilege; as much as he might have tried to understand the problems of the little guy, he understood them only from a businessman's point of view. His solution to almost any problem was to set up a centralized agency to deal with it, thereby removing the power one further step from the people.

If FDR managed to get his federal agency to regulate oil, the man who would have the power would be Secretary of the Interior Harold L. Ickes. I did not trust him—or any appointed official—to handle matters of such importance fairly. He would be an oil czar, with few effective checks on his authority.

After my election, Roosevelt had called me to offer his congratulations and to express the need for us to work together. On the matter of federal control of oil, I asked him to give me a chance to try to bring the other states in line before pressing Congress to enact legislation.

He told me that Congress would appoint a committee to study the matter, and I would have about six months, at the most.

During my first week in office, I arranged a meeting with Governor Lesche of Louisiana. Lesche promised to call together the oilmen and government officials involved in that state's illegal oil activities at an informal meeting at his hunting lodge. Lon Smith and I arrived in Louisiana to learn the other men had been "unable to make it." Although Dick Lesche was the Governor and presumably the most powerful man in the State of Louisiana, he could make no promises to curtail his illegal activities without the approval of his two "partners"— Lieutenant Governor Earl Long and LSU president Monroe Smith.

Lon Smith and I attempted to reason with Lesche, explaining that his personal greed was threatening the entire oil business and the national economy. But he seemed not to care.

We left the hunting lodge and issued a statement to the press, expressing regrets that the government officials did not see fit to meet with us. We threatened an oil war with Louisiana if that state did not make an effort to halt the flow of hot oil into Texas.

Lesche retaliated, issuing a statement that he welcomed a war with Texas and declared that he would join with Oklahoma and New Mexico to pursue a policy of encirclement to drive us, Texas, to economic ruin.

To Roosevelt I appeared to have failed in my mission, but I was not through with Lesche. Moral persuasion was only the first step. The law was my next course of action, and I quietly began to collect evidence to be used in the courts.

Meanwhile, there were plenty of problems to be taken care of in Texas. Of immediate concern were abuses in the West Texas oilfields. As a result of the prorations set there by the last meeting of the Terrell Commission, two oil companies—Texhoma and Cities Service—had filed suit against the Railroad Commission.

Lon Smith and I traveled to Amarillo to investigate the situation in West Texas and to hold hearings on the abuses there. We found the big oil companies were exceeding their allowances and covering up by taking less oil from the small independent companies than the amounts set by the Commission. We filed charges against fourteen companies— among them Phillips Petroleum, Shamrock Oil & Gas Company, Skelly, Shell, Magnolia, Continental, and Mid-States, some of the biggest companies in the business.

I had taken office January 1; Pappy O'Daniel was sworn in as Governor of Texas, January 17. One of his campaign pledges had been a pension of $30 a month for all people over age 65, promising that he would approve no sales tax to achieve that. He now proposed something quite different: that the legislature pass a guaranteed income of $30 a month for those over age 65, and acceptance of his presentation of a plan for a "transaction tax" to accomplish it.

I immediately attacked the plan. "The transaction tax is a sales tax plus, a glorified sales action tax," I stated publicly. "A 1.6 percent tax looks like about an 8 percent tax for the consumer. And I didn't have to figure that out by lantern light." (This was a reference to a small furor I created when I complained that the electric lights in my office were not on long enough to suit me. I worked from early morning through late evening; it became necessary for me to bring a kerosene lantern to my office.)

I was not the only one to cry "foul" at Pappy O'Daniel. The legislature set a record of 163 days debating his proposals before finally turning them down.

In February and March I turned my attention toward the hot oil situation in the East Texas fields. Here, I decided, neither gentle persuasion nor lawsuits would be effective. The only way to tackle the problem would be by swift and sudden action—moving in on companies while they were in the midst of their illegal acts.

Soon after taking office as Railroad Commissioner, Jerry Sadler complained because the lights at the Capitol were not turned on by 5:00 A.M., when he started work. Supporters sent kerosene lanterns and lamps for him to read by. (The framed photo in the background is of Cousin Harley Sadler.)

Pausing in a busy schedule as Railroad Commissioner for a favorite pasttime—barbecuing.

A political cartoon, which appeared in the Austin Statesman *in 1941.*

Sadler "in the saddle," during the Railroad Commission years, with hunting dogs.

I knew the East Texas field like the back of my hand. I knew which wells were dry and which were producing, as well as how much they were capable of pumping. I knew where the pipelines ran and the extent of their capacities. I knew who was doing what illegally, and when. But knowing wasn't proving!

With the Bankers' Tender Board no longer in operation, I insisted that all reports from the oil producers be mailed directly to the Railroad Commission. I went over every report carefully, checking each well against its allowable. I found 27 dead wells listed on the reports, wells I knew were incapable of producing oil. That meant that the oil reported as coming from those wells was coming—illegally—from someplace else, more likely from wells that were exceeding their allocations.

I went to Kilgore to see Stanley Bean. Without any publicity, we went out into the fields to scout around, inspecting pipelines, storage tanks, and refineries, when owners and managers weren't around, pinpointing each infraction. Some of the owners guilty of illegal activities were very prominent. They included the director of the State Prison System, the director of a Dallas bank, the president of the Cotton Bowl, and a man I had known all my life. It included one group of men I had warned before taking office to clean up their business because I intended to crack down. At that time they had replied, "Oh, we're as clean as a hound's tooth."

One of our sudden, nighttime raids revealed a very unusual setup. It was near the town of New London, in Rusk County. There, a well was listed on property where no well seemed to exist. We found one well nearby, however, that was pumping 24 hours a day, far more hours than it should have been for the amount of oil the records showed it was producing. We went into Henderson and obtained a warrant from the district judge to search the house of the supposed owner of the non-existent well.

That house was locked behind a chain-link fence that was electrified and had barbed wire running around the top. A very elaborate setup to protect the run-down little house on the one-acre of land. With several other officials from the Kilgore office of the Commission, Stanley and I went to the house equipped with wire-cutters, flashlights, and a sledgehammer, its handle wrapped in soft rubber.

We smashed our way through the chain-link fence and entered the house. Inside, the only person seemed to be an old lady, sitting placidly in her rocking chair.

"Granny," I spoke politely. "We're gong to have to ask you to get up and move out of the way, so we can have a look under your rug."

"I ain't movin'," she said. "And you can't make me."

"Then we'll have to move you, chair and all," I said.

Two of our men lifted her chair—overriding protests—and moved it (and her) to the edge of the room. We pulled back the rug and, as I suspected, found a trap door.

Under the house a small cellar had been dug, and installed there an illegal switching device, a valve that allowed oil to be diverted from the constantly pumping nearby oil well. In the cellar was the switcher, the man who operated the device and who owned the house. I was certain he had not devised the scheme. Eight-thousand barrels of oil a day came from his activity, but he would not be living so modestly if he had been getting the full profit from this.

We arrested him, hoping he would give us the names of the men he worked for, but he wouldn't talk then. Only after he was convicted and sent to prison—without his bosses coming forward to help him—did he finally name the names of those we suspected were behind the operation. However, by that time, the men had grown scared and had shut down their refinery.

That spring we managed to clean up the East Texas oilfields. It became the only oil-producing area in the United States operating in strict adherence to the Connally Hot Oil Act and other federal regulations. In the process of cleanup, we uncovered plenty of evidence against the Governor of Louisiana.

Next we attempted to bring the rest of Texas into line, and then moved on the matter of equitable allocations in order that the East Texas region would not suffer for obeying the law.

With the three months of proration set by the Terrell Commission coming to a close, the Commission meeting of late March, 1939, was the first in which I would have some influence in allocations. With that meeting we returned to monthly proration hearings, a situation I preferred for a number of reasons. Monthly allowances seemed more equitable for the smaller companies, and made it possible for the Commission to observe any suspicious activities of the larger companies. They also helped us keep oil prices stable; if we observed too much oil on the market in one month, we could cut production the next.

There was a lot of activity going on in the capitol at Austin at the time. The legislature considered a bill that would allow the Railroad Commission to regulate refineries in the same way we regulated oil producers. The Interstate Compact Commission, the federal regulatory board set up by the Connally Hot Oil Act, met in Austin to discuss problems of regulating in the states of Illinois, Louisiana, and California, whose producers still glutted the market. The practices forced Texas producers to cut back in order to keep the price of oil stable.

The excess supply of Texas oil was somewhat reduced since the extended shutdown, but it had not been as effective as it could have been. The big refiners—such as Humble, Phillips, and Magnolia—had been importing the excess oil produced by non-complying states. They, and big oil producers along the Gulf Coast and West Texas, demanded that the Railroad Commission extend the enforced two-day a week shutdown of Texas oil producers. What had been an eight-day a month shutdown of wells would, in April 1938, be ten days because that month had five weekends.

Ernest O. Thompson agreed with the big oil companies, but Lon Smith and I had been working on a plan that would resolve all of the problems within the state. It would make the proration allocation for East Texas more equitable with the rest of the state; it would maintain the flow of oil at its present rate, keeping the price stable, even with the flow of imported oil from other states; and it would allow wells to return to pumping six days a week. (The big producers had managed to get waivers from the commission before Terrell left, so that all but the East Texas field had been pumping a full seven-day week.)

In that March meeting of the Commission, Lon Smith and I voted to lift the Saturday curb on Texas oil production. At the same time we voted to cut the total state output of oil by 302,000 barrels a day, increasing the quota in the East Texas field by 78,000 barrels a day. The cuts came primarily from the Gulf Coast fields and West Texas fields. The ones to suffer the most were the Old Ocean field and the Yates field, located in the Gulf Coast Region. It seemed only fair; the producers had been shamelessly pampered for years. Their allowables under the Terrell Commission had each been approximately twenty times that of the entire East Texas region.

We also announced that there would be no private commission hearings with individual companies to adjust their allocations upward as there had been in the past. The allocations would stand as announced.

All hell broke loose the next day. While receiving numerous letters and telegrams of praise, not just from East Texas and North Texas, but from the whole nation, we were beset by crowds of angry oilmen from the other regions, storming the hallway outside our offices, protesting our decision.

Admittedly, it was the most radical change in the proration allowances made by the Commission since its beginnings, and we had expected resistance. In fact, we had planned for it by cutting the allocations far more than was finally accepted when the furor calmed. However, we did not expect the loud ruckus to last an entire month before it was settled.

The Abercrombie Oil Company and the Harrison Oil Company, which together operated the Old Ocean field and a large number of the others that had been cut, acted immediately by having their lawyers file an injunction in a Houston court to prevent our enforcing the cuts. Meanwhile a group of state legislators from the offended areas got together to write a bill that would extablish a natural resources commission to circumvent the Railroad Commission. Nothing came of that bill, but for the next month, the court action occupied a great deal of our time.

Federal Judge T.M. Kennerly of Houston issued the ten-day injunction, and a three-judge federal court was selected to hear the case. Two days later, Lon Smith and I attempted to avoid the court case by issuing revised orders, adjusting the allocations upward somewhat, but the oil companies were unwilling to compromise. Because of the hue and cry from all over the state, they thought they had us on the run. From my first appearance in Judge Kennerly's court, acompanied by two lawyers from the Attorney General's office, I was ready to fight. The case presented by Fouts, Ammerman, and Moore, attorneys for Abercrombie and Harrison, attempted to destroy the Railroad Commission itself, by questioning its legality.

We set hearings for the May proration allocations early in April, giving the oil producers a month to air their grievances about the stringent April allocations. When we issued our orders for May, the allocation figures were set approximately at the amounts Lon Smith and I had been aiming for all along. They were accepted without protest. We were willing to adjust April allocations to conform, but had to await the court hearing.

The three-judge panel, which met in Houston at the end of April, consisted of Judge Kennerly, Judge Foster, of Yazoo City, Mississippi, and Judge Macmillan, of San Antonio. It lasted for several days, and they called upon a great many people to testify before calling me. Five lawyers represented the oil companies, but Joe Moore, of Fouts, Ammerman, and Moore, did most of the questioning. Joe Moore can be easily described as a *mean* lawyer. He didn't question witnesses; he raked them over the coals.

Commissioner Ernest O. Thompson was questioned, and he stated he had not participated in the writing of the proration orders, and that he refused to sign them when they were presented to him. He considered the April orders to be unfair and disastrous for the Texas oil industry. He prophesied that—if they were allowed to stand—there would be numerous bankruptcies.

He read from a prepared report. "If we tried to restrict the flow on eight wells in the Old Ocean Field, due to the high gas pressure, it would blow up all that part of the country," he stated.

This had long been part of the propaganda issued by Abercrombie and Harrison in order to obtain waivers and exceptions to Railroad Commission rules, and it was patently untrue. As I would later prove.

The judges called C.M. Langford, Jr., an engineer with the Commission, and a buddy of Thompson's, who testified that he had warned us of dangers in cutting the allocations for the Old Ocean Field. He claimed that we had already set the figures before holding the hearing.

Joe Moore's interrogation of Lon Smith was disgraceful. He treated the Chairman of the Railroad Commission as if he were a convicted criminal, but Smith maintained his dignity by answering the questions simply, honestly, and politely, a strong contrast to Moore.

In the end, Moore got what he deserved from one of the judges. At his summation, his law books piled high on the table, he started off speaking in his dictatorial manner, instructing the court what they could do and could not do.

Judge Foster interrupted him. "Counsel, you should read the law."

Moore replied, "Your Honor, I have read the law, and I have the law here."

"Counsel, you should learn to interpret the law," Judge Foster said.

In the end, the case was dismissed, since we had already issued new orders adjusting the allocation upward, and those adjustments had been accepted by the oil producers. Meanwhile in the state legislature there was a lot of talk about the impeachment of Jerry Sadler. House and Senate members from the offended oil producing regions, unable to get anywhere with their natural resources commission bill, made personal privilege speeches from the floor, trying to get sufficient strength to try me for malfeasance. That, too, came to naught.

One other lawsuit that was filed against the Railroad Commission's new allocation procedures would have far reaching effects. This was the Rowan and Nichols Case.

At first the petition filed by Rowan and Nichols Oil Company of Ft. Worth in Austin's Federal Court of Judge R.J. MacMillan seemed routine, less important than the Harrison and Abercrombie Case. However, it went beyond the question of the company's allocations to challenge the legality of the formula we had used in figuring the prorations. We had determined our allocations on a well by well basis, allowing each to produce daily 2.32 percent of its hourly capability with a minimum of twenty barrels per day per well. There was a degree of inequity in this, particularly in the East Texas fields, where numerous exceptions had been granted over the years to Commission Rule 37, which required wells to be distantly spaced.

The East Texas region was settled earlier than the rest of the state; it was more densely populated. A landowner might have a plot of a quarter-acre or less and have a well on it by getting an exception to Rule 37, while another landowner with hundreds of acres would be forced to space his wells at the required distances.

There were other issues involved in the Rowan and Nichols case, such as the density of the sand, the depth of wells, and the size and pressure of the oil pools, but the spacing issue was the major one.

Judge MacMillan decided in favor of Rowan and Nichols, and his decision voided our proration orders, forcing us to formulate a new basis for our allocations, taking into consideration the spacing of wells. With effort, Lon Smith and I managed to adjust our formula, maintaining the overall regional allowables while making the individual well allocations in East Texas more equitable.

All these major changes took place in the first six months of my tenure in office. The partnership with Lon Smith worked well; we had accomplished much in a short span of time, leaving Ernest O. Thompson on the sidelines doing little more than interjecting objections to our actions.

However there was one flaw in my plan, one factor that I had not taken into account, and it now began to surface. Lon Smith was an old man, and the strain began to take its toll on him. As proration hearings for June, 1938, approached, he wanted to slow down. I was adamant about maintaining our schedule of setting allocations on a month by month basis, in order to closely monitor activity.

For the first time, he sided with Ernest O. Thompson to overrule me, and the June hearings set the allocations for a three month period, and restored Saturday shut-downs.

This provided the Commission a kind of summer vacation. The offices wouldn't be closed, but activity would slow, and Smith would be able to get some rest. As it turned out, it wasn't so bad; it gave me the oportunity to direct my attention to matters I had neglected. There were two matters of major importance—the threat to the Texas oil industry from states not adhering to federal guidelines and the proposed legislation to set federal control over the oil industry.

To face these two matters, I took a trip east to Washington to visit the President.

17
Snuff-Dippers, FDR, and Icky

On the way to Washington, I had a vacation—of sorts. I stopped off at Grenada, Mississippi, for the Snuff-Dipper's Convention.

Several weeks earlier, I had received a letter from a rural mail carrier telling me that the people of this small town in Mississippi planned the first national convention for snuff-dippers. I was asked to be their principal speaker. I accepted. I asked if the town had an airport, explaining I would be flying in my private plane. They reported they had a landing strip, but no airport. So I decided to fly into Memphis and drive down to Grenada with a group who planned to party the night before the start of the convention.

On July 1, I arrived in Grenada and learned that the planners had managed to persuade American Snuff Company to underwrite the expense of broadcasting the event nationwide. A half-hour broadcast was arranged, and my speech would take up a major portion of time—nineteen minutes. Other events were a snuff-spitting contest between an attractive young lady and me, narrated by a sports announcer; the naming of Prettiest Dipper, Ugliest Dipper, and Oldest Dipper; and spoken testimonials from some notable dippers. I began my speech by referring to great snuff-dippers among our forefathers—Thomas Jefferson, George Washington, and Benjamin Franklin. "If, in this modern age, we need anything more than anything else, it is the simple, God-fearing faith of our fathers, mothers, and grandmothers and grandfathers—all of whom were snuff-dippers," I said. "My granddad and yours didn't expect the government to keep him in idleness and supply him with a radio to enjoy his comfort.

"My grandmother and yours didn't have all the complexes and psychoses that modern women have. She just took a dip of snuff and went on about her business of raising her family and having her children. These modern women with one baby could learn a lot from these pioneer women who laid the foundation for this nation."

I told them that "cigarettes are the ghost of tobacco, chewing tobacco is the body, and snuff is the soul of nicotine." I said the reason so many snuff-dippers were such brilliant men was because "with their mouths half full of snuff all the time, they couldn't talk, and so they had to think."

As I talked, a messenger from the Western Union office, which was situated a couple of doors away from the platform, began to bring me telegrams from the radio audience, most of whom were snuff-dippers. By the time I had finished, those telegrams were really rolling in by the handfuls. A lot of them referred to my comments about "one-babied cigarette smoking mothers." One from a woman in Houston, the sister of Mrs. Dan Moody, asked, "Jerry, how are the twins?"

When the time arrived for testimonials, a well-dressed man arose. "I'm the president of the First National Bank in Jackson," he said. "When I left this morning to drive here, my wife and children were upset with me. They wanted to know why I was coming down here to be with all these hicks. Well, after hearing this young man from Texas, I have to make a confession. For forty years I've had snuff hidden in the drawer of my desk at the bank, and I've used it when people weren't around. I've kept it a big secret, but now I don't care who knows."

Photographers were present from *Time* and *Life* magazines. They took many pictures, and there were articles in both magazines about me. A few weeks later, when I returned to Texas and went to visit my mother, she met me at her door with copies of the magazines, which my sister had sent her. She was upset. "Here you have inferred that your daddy and I were snuff-dippers. That's a lie, and you know it. Neither of us ever used snuff in our lives." That was the angriest I had ever seen my mother.

Some time later, I ran into Senator Bilbo and learned that he had been their first choice for speaker at the convention, but he had turned them down. "I have to hand it to you," he said. "I thought I had tried everything there was to get publicity, but you beat me to hell and gone."

When I arrived in Washington, I learned that the radio show had also reached the White House. I walked into Roosevelt's office and he greeted me, smiling. "Hello, Snuffy."

I had arrived prepared to do battle with the President, expecting resistance from him. He had initiated the legislation to create a special federal authority to regulate the oil industry, the legislation that had reached as far as a special committee—the Cole committee—which was then traveling around the country holding hearings on oil industry practices. I saw that legislation as potentially disastrous for Texas, and I was prepared to challenge its legality.

I reminded him that such a law might prove unconstitutional as it applied to my home state, Texas. We had entered the union on a basis considerably different from all the other states. We were an independent nation and had accepted annexation with the provision that we would keep our public lands in return for paying off our own national debt.

"Our oil is a part of our land," I told him. "We lived up to our part of the bargain, and the federal government can't renege on that agreement just because oil was later discovered and we've profited from it. If the Cole bill is passed, we will be prepared to fight its constitutionality in the courts."

To my surprise, Roosevelt did not argue with me. He seemed not to care about the Cole bill at all, claiming that it was a baby of Secretary of the Interior Ickes. "My only concern is," he said, "that the oil business be kept in control. If the states can take care of it, that's fine. If not, we have to find some way of doing it on a national level."

He told me that he had no doubt Texas could keep its own house clean, but he was concerned about the situation in Louisiana, Illinois, and California. I told him that the federal government already had the needed power with the Connally Hot Oil Act to take care of that problem. "All you have to do," I said, "is set up Federal Tender Boards in Baton Rouge, New Orleans, and Houston. We have only one such board now, the one in Kilgore, Texas, and it's doing its job well."

I said I had lived up to the promise I made to him in our phone conversation six months earlier, and I presented him with the evidence he needed to convict Governor Lesche and the other offenders in Louisiana.

I think the President was surprised that I had managed to do what I had promised. I do know he was pleased with the information I gave him. With a delightful laugh, he said, "We'll send that lying son-of-a-bitch to the penitentiary, before he knows what happened to him."

With his laughter, his friendly manner, and even his vulgarity, Roosevelt charmed me completely that day, turning our relationship from one of polite opposition to one of deepening friendship and mutual conspiracy. I learned most about that man that day, and I liked what I learned. Roosevelt enjoyed intrigue as much as I did. He was an extremely witty man and probably the most foul-mouthed man I've ever met in politics. His favorite term was "son-of-a bitch," and he came up with more adjectives to put with it than I thought existed. I liked some of them so much I began to use them myself.

Gradually, in a deceptively casual manner, he turned our conversation around to the real reason for inviting me to the White House.

He talked about Texas politics, and proved he knew the state's peculiarities very well. That didn't surprise me a great deal, because he was surrounded by Texans in Washington; what did surprise me was that his view of those Texans coincided with mine. He intensely disliked his Vice-President, "Cactus Jack" Garner. He didn't trust that "flourselling son-of-a-bitch," Governor O'Daniel. Former Governor Allred had been the mainstay of Roosevelt's New Deal program in Texas, but as a federal district judge he was now out of politics. Maury Maverick, the mayor of San Antonio, had stepped into Allred's place in the New Deal, but Maverick had gotten himself into hot water over the issue of freedom of speech for Communists. In Congress, Roosevelt depended on Senator Tom Connally as an ally and on Congressman Sam Rayburn, although in a pinch, he wasn't sure how loyal Rayburn would be.

In all the talk about Texas politics, Roosevelt worked the conversation around to the subject of the 1940 presidential election. "I've got to start thnking about who will succeed me in this office," he said. "Vice President Garner is the most logical choice, and he wants the job. What kind of president do you think he would make?"

"If you want my honest answer," I said, "I think he'd be the worst choice you could make. He's less than honest, and he's drunk more often than he's sober."

There was a twinkle in his eyes. "The country is going to need a sober mind in this office in the next few years," he said. "As much as I dislike the idea of war, there's a strong chance we may have to get into the difficult situation in Europe." He said the choices of politicians we had to lead us into war weren't the kind he'd like to have. In the Democratic Party, he pointed out, we had only Garner, Jim Farley, and Cordell Hull.

"Why not Franklin Roosevelt?" I asked.

"A third term?" His eyes twinkled again. "No president has ever done it."

"There's nothing but tradition to keep you from it," I said.

"But tradition is very strong," he said. "No, I don't think the people would stand for it. I don't think I could get elected again."

Despite his words, he seemed to like the idea of a third term. I had the impression it would take only a little persuasion to get him to run again for office.

He continued to talk about the prospects of war in Europe, saying he had reason to believe that the major European powers would be fighting each other before the year was out. He was concerned about the part the U.S. oil industry would play in the war, and his concerns were large that some of the major oil companies' leaders had strong German sympathies. This was the urgency that prompted him to push for federal regulation.

A few days later, to my surprise, my visit with Roosevelt was the subject of Boake Carter's column in the New York *Daily Mirror*. I had revealed nothing to anyone about my conversation with the president.

> Into Washington a few days ago blew a chunky, rawboned Irishman with a jaw that might have been hewn from El Capitan and a drawl that made you think instinctively of wide open spaces.
>
> The Big Boss summoned him. The Texas Irishman hopped aboard his own plane and flew to Washington. Unobservedly the two men met.
>
> The chunky Texas Irishman who faced the Big Boss wanted to know who was destined to be "It" for the Democrats in 1940, before saying "Yes" or "No."
>
> The other man sought to discover whether this Texas politician who preferred to be a king-maker rather than a king could be utilized as a successful spearhead to undermine Mr. Garner. Both men knew that Texas is due to play a critical role in 1940.
>
> The Garner-for-President boom is not meeting with overwhelming success in Mr. Garner's own home state, but it is rolling like a prairie fire in other Southern and Southwestern States.
>
> The gentleman from Hyde Park desired the gentleman from Longview to put his weight and his millions in a drive to take the "oom" out of the Garner boom.
>
> But the gentleman from Longview wanted

> from the gentleman from Hyde Park an itemi-
> zation of what lay upon the cards for 1940; who
> was to be the standard bearer and what were the
> policies to be before saying "Yes."
>
> The gentleman from Hyde Park laughed and
> fenced. The gentleman from Longview was non-
> committal. The result? The proceedings were
> adjourned temporarily.

In the column, Carter conjectured that the real subject of the meeting might have been that Roosevelt intended to run for a third term, and had been seeking support. Since no one else was present at our meeting, I had to assume the President planted the story himself as a way of testing the public's response to a third term.

Roosevelt acted immediately on the information I had given him about the Louisiana situation. He sent an attorney to Louisiana to handle the matters. Governor Lesche was soon indicted and convicted. I had not been able to obtain necessary evidence against Earl Long, so no case was possible against him. Long became Governor after the resignation of Lesche. A Greek oilman involved with Lesche managed to escape the country. Dr. Monroe Smith, president of LSU, also planned to leave the country, but at the last minute changed his mind and stayed to face the music. He, too, was convicted.

I recall later seeing a photograph of Lesche and Smith on a prison farm, cutting sugar cane.

Soon after, Roosevelt telephoned me and asked me to go to Illinois to see if I could help to resolve the problem there. As far as I knew, the situation in Illinois was totally unlike that in Louisiana. As oil states go, Illinois was new to the business, and the state government had simply not passed legislation to conserve their resources. With their newfound wealth, Illinois was going wild on production, with no consideraton for what they were doing to the overall oil market, or for their own future.

Although Illinois Governor Henry Horner had made a few rash statements to the press opposing proration for his state "until it catches up with the rest of the oil producing states," he was not unsympathetic to the problem. He also had considerable respect for Roosevelt, and he had been informed I was coming at the request of the President. He invited me to be his guest at the governor's mansion.

Together we wrote the legislation, and he arranged to have it submitted to the Illinois House of Representatives. It passed the House without difficulty, and we expected it to pass the Senate as well.

However, one night, the Lieutenant Governor came to the governor's mansion and announced to us, "I've changed my mind about this bill. I'm not going to let it pass the Senate."

Governor Horner asked why.

The Lieutenant Governor replied that he owned some oil royalty, and he would stand to lose if the bill passed.

Governor Horner spoke angrily. "You didn't own that royalty when we started trying to get this legislation through."

"Well, I own it now," he replied, "and it's profitable royalty."

The oil companies won that round, but the state of Illinois lost. Without conservation measures, in a few years their fields were quickly drained by excessive pumping and waste. I refused the next Presidential request—that I travel to California to work on establishing proration there. Trouble had erupted in Texas, with lawsuits, oil prices dropping, and a pending major investigation against Humble Oil. Above all else, I had to think of my responsibilities to the people who had elected me.

I continued to see the President regularly, traveling to Washington approximately once a month, usually for only a day or two, if the only reason was to go to the White House. When I had to testify before the Cole Committee, or to see Secretary of the Interior Harold Ickes, I stayed longer.

Early in September, I began denouncing the sale of crude oil to the Nazis, pointing out that Germany was getting 25,000 barrels of Texas oil a day from three South Texas fields. The oil was shipped out of Port Arthur, and although I did not name the producers involved, I knew their sympathies lay with the Nazis rather than with the Allies. I released a statement to the press, suggesting that we should drop neutrality and sell oil to the Allies, who defended Europe's freedom and democracy. Naturally, I was severely criticized for such warlike statements.

On September 18, Lon Smith and I flew to Washington to appear before the Cole Committee and protest their plan for federal oil control. On that flight the weather was terrible; halfway between Columbus and Pittsburgh, we hit the damnedest storm I'd ever flown in. I'm a pilot myself, and normally I'm not scared, but that time I was. We had to get down below the clouds, and there was barely enough room above the treetops for the airplane.

I looked at Lon Smith. He was whistling, as if enjoying it all. "Aren't you scared?" I asked.

"No," he replied calmly. "Not with my Baptist religion."

We were forced to stay overnight in Pittsburgh. Once settled into our hotel, all Lon could think of was dominoes; at any opportunity, he pulled out his ivory dominoes and tried to get a game going.

The following day we took a plane into Washington. As soon as we registered at our hotel, I had to leave to testify at the committee hearing. Lon told me, "I'm going over to see Senator Bankhead of Alabama. I hear there's a Baptist Convention in town."

When I returned to our hotel suite after testifying, I found more Baptist women than I'd ever seen in my life. Contrary to my impression of Baptists, they were all imbibing heavily.

On that visit, I had several meetings with Secretary Ickes, prompted by Roosevelt. He wanted us to patch up the many differences we had been airing in the press. The month of August had been difficult for the Railroad Commission. With lawsuits, the Humble Investigation under-way, a sudden drop in oil prices, and a fifteen-day shutdown of the oil business in six states, I had experienced great pressures. This condition was aggravated by the fact that somebody had put a "tail" on me. I was followed everywhere I went. At first I thought it might be private detectives hired by the oil companies, but these men looked too professional. I finally determined that they had to be federal agents, and there could have been only one man responsible for that—Secretary of the Interior, Harold L. Ickes.

Then, when it finally appeared everything in Texas was beginning to be resolved, Ickes issued a statement in the press, saying that he intended to suspend the Conally Hot Oil Act and permit uncontrolled production, unless oil-producing states brought themselves into line.

I hit back with a telegram, which I also shared with the press:

> I have read with a great deal of amazement your statement as quoted by the News Wire Services to the effect that you stand ready to "suspend the Connally Hot Oil Act" in the event of an emergency. In view of the fact that the regulatory bodies of five states have successfully met the attack of the Standard Oil Company and its affiliates in their vicious attempt to rule or ruin the industry it strikes me that your statement is poorly timed and uncalled for. I must warn you Mr. Secretary that your desire for federal control, which has long been your objective does not

conform to the ideas of the people of the oil producing states nor to the rest of the nation. I fear that your lust for power in this connection is coloring your viewpoint and is in no way whatever in accord with the views of our illustrious President. While you have the authority to suspend the Connally Act you of course realize that to do so would encourage promote and stimulate violation of state laws in all the affected states. I must also call your attention to the fact that Texas has been the only state in which you have even shown any interest in placing into effect the provisions of the Hot Oil Act. In other words your administration of that ban to date certainly does not justify placing the whole industry into your hands. Quite the reverse is true. The oil situation is well in hand Mr. Secretary. Although I am not familiar with your many and complex duties I nevertheless feel that they are sufficient to occupy your full time and attention. Your interest in the welfare of the consumer is commendable. But your domination or interference in the present situation is completely wholly and entirely uncalled for.

Needless to say, I did not think highly of Mr. Ickes, and he certainly did not like me.

The day after testifying before the Cole Committee, I had an appointment at the White House. I told the President that I was tired of finding somebody following me every time I turned around. "I can't even go courting," I told him, "without having a damned federal agent or two tagging along. Yesterday I was crossing a street in Dallas and I met one coming toward me. As soon as he recognized me he turned around and followed."

"Are you sure they're federal agents?" the President asked in amazement.

When I assured him that they were, he called the Attorney General and asked him to come to his office. Then he called Ickes and asked him to come over. In a matter of minutes, Attorney General Frank Murphy and Secretary Ickes were in the oval office. Roosevelt asked them, "Have there been FBI agents following Jerry Sadler?"

"Yes, sir," the Attorney General replied.

The President turned to the Secretary of the Interior. "Did you request those agents, Icky?"

Ickes replied yes.

"What was your reason?" Roosevelt asked.

Ickes explained. It seemed every day his office received letters, telegrams, and phone calls of complaint about Jerry Sadler. Some were signed by oilmen, some were anonymous, but he felt he had to check on the accusations.

"How many agents have you had assigned to him?" the President asked.

Ickes said twenty-six agents were the most at one time.

"Did Mr. Hoover approve this investigation?" Roosevelt asked the Attorney General.

"No, sir," Murphy replied.

"With so many agents on the job," the President said, "you must have been able to do a thorough investigation. What were you able to find out?"

"One of our agents from the Federal Tender Board says that he has come close to catching Sadler taking bribes on several occasions. If he had been there about two hours earlier, he would have caught Sadler in Sweetwater." Ickes reported the agent came close to getting what he needed in Corpus Christi, and again in Wichita Falls.

Roosevelt's eyes twinkled. "An investigator who almost obtains evidence isn't much different from the girl who is almost a virgin. I think perhaps you ought to get rid of him. If you ignore this man's reports, what can you conclude from your investigation?"

Ickes was slightly embarrassed. "I would have to say that Sadler is either the smartest crook in the world or the most honest man that ever held office in the United States. We can't find a penny anywhere that he has obtained illegally. When he has traveled, he has even paid his expenses out of his own pocket."

"Then I thnk you can stop wasting the taxpayer's money on him," the President told the Secretary. "Icky, you and Sadler have been at each other's throats long enough. I want you to kiss and make up. We're all working on the same team, and we can't have this kind of fighting. Now that Maury Maverick has gotten himself into hot water,

Sadler is going to be my man in Texas. Maverick is here in Washington right now, and I want you all to get together and talk over the problems we have in Texas. And I want you to come up with some solutions."

Ickes and I didn't exactly kiss and make up. There was no way we could become close friends. We declared a truce and developed some direct lines of communication to discuss our differences calmly.

At this time there were some subtle changes taking place in Roosevelt's administration. Just as he had predicted, full scale war had broken out in Europe. The United States was still bound by the Neutrality Act, and the Allies suffered from this far more than the Axis powers. In the face of the isolationist views of the majority of people, with some strong Nazi sympathies in powerful places, Roosevelt had Senator Tom Connally push through Congress a new Neutrality Act that permitted sale of critical war supplies to belligerent nations on a "cash and carry" basis. The object was to aid the Allies without appearing to do so.

One of my responsibilities was to try to see that Britian and France had the oil they needed; a job easier said than done.

I believe Roosevelt had accepted the fact he was the only man who could lead our country into war, but he continued to pretend that he would not run for election to a third term. He had already endured charges from some quarters that he was "power mad" and "dictatorial." He realized it would have been foolhardy to openly seek the Democratic nomination again. It would have to appear that his nomination was a draft. He maintained this attitude even with his closest advisors and associates.

Publicly, his main objective seemed to be to prevent his Vice President from being nominated, and I was the man he had picked to lead the "Stop Garner" movement. *Time* magazine revealed this on October 23:

> The word in Texas last week was that President Roosevelt has picked a baby-kissin', sniff-dippin', vote-gettin' man to replace Mayor Maury Maverick of San Antonio as front man for the New Deal forces working against John Nance Garner on his home base. This snuff-dippin', vote-gettin' man: Railroad Commissioner Gerald Anthony Sadler.

This was the first public indication that Roosevelt opposed Garner's aspirations. I learned later from the President the effect it had on the Vice President. "There is a photograph that was taken of Garner with ink and blood on his cheek," Roosevelt told me. "There are only a few people who know what happened. General Watson knows, and one of my secret service men knows. I think you are entitled to know as well, since you are involved to a certain extent."

After reading the *Time* magazine article, Garner stormed into the oval office. He demanded to know why Roosevelt opposed him so strongly.

The President said something to the effect that Garner's behavior at that moment was a good example of his reason. He pointed out that the country could not afford to have a heavy drinker in the White House.

Garner shot back, "That's no worse than having a goddamned cripple for president!"

That he was confined to a wheelchair was one thing Roosevelt was sensitive about. Paralyzed from the waist down, he had compensated with added strength in his arms. Angrily, the President grasped the heavy inkstand on his desk and hurled it at the Vice President, hitting Garner on the cheek.

The next day, John Nance Garner left Washington, returning to Uvalde, Texas, and would not return to the Capitol until his term of office was over.

I learned of this event when I visited with the President on the first of November; the meeting that was, I think, my most memorable one with him. It was a meeting instigated by my new "friend," Ickes. He had called me to say that something had happened to change the President's attitude. "He's saying he absolutely will not run for a third term, even if he is drafted. He's adamant about it, and he gets angry if anybody brings up the subject." Ickes said I might be the only one who could get away with talking about it, but we could not let FDR think that was the reason for the meeting. "I'll arrange the appointment and tell him it's to discuss the matter of supplying oil for the Allies," Ickes said.

On October 31, Lon Smith and I flew to Washington, giving that purported reason to the press.

While I went to the White House, Lon Smith played a domino game with some friends. There were three of us in the meeting with the President—Secretary Ickes, General Edwin Watson, and me. We discussed problems of supplying oil for the Allies, weighing the risk of shipping on U.S. tankers against the small quantities they could obtain, being limited to their own tankers by the "cash and carry" policy. And we discussed the need for a refinery regulatory act to keep oil supplies at a stable level.

When we were through and made motions to leave, I asked the President if he had given much thought to my suggestion he run for a third term. There was a change in his manner, almost as if a cloud had drifted over his face.

"I've decided that's out of the question," he said. "I think William O. Douglas would be the best candidate."

"That stuffed shirt!" I exclaimed. "Even he admits that's what he is. He could never get elected. If you try to push him off on the party, Garner will get the nomination for sure."

It was then that he told me about the confrontation with Garner, adding that he thought that the Vice President could be persuaded to stay in Uvalde and retire from public office. As Roosevelt told the story, I sensed that I understood the reason for his change of mind. Garner's remark about his handicap had struck far deeper than the President wanted to admit. As a peacetime President, he managed to do his job regardless of that handicap. A wartime president might need an able body as well as an able mind, and Garner had made him wonder if he shouldn't step aside for a more physically able candidate.

I could not argue with Roosevelt on that point without making matters worse. The only way I felt I could convince him to change his mind again was to give him evidence that the people wanted him and that the men he most respected were convinced he was the only choice.

"Garner is already lining up his delegates all over the country," I said. "I've talked to a number of men, and they agree that—if you don't run—Garner has it sewed up. I was just talking to Felix Frankfurter yesterday, and he is convinced of it. And Jesse Jones agrees as well. He's been a lifelong friend of Garner's, but he believes it would be a great tragedy for this country if Garner becomes president. Come January, you're going to see how the people feel about it. I'm scheduled to speak at a Jackson Day dinner in Houston, and it's going to be radio broadcast. The subject of my speech will be a third term for Roosevelt, and I am going to tear into Garner with everything I've got. Now, I won't call him an alcoholic, but I will say that we need a sober, sane head to guide us through the troublesome days ahead. All you have to do is tune in your radio, and you'll hear how the people feel about you, the plain people, because this isn't going to be one of those hundred-dollar-a-plate dinners. It's going to be the two-dollar plain people's dinner."

When I left the White House, there were a few reporters outside. They recognized me, probably because of the recent *Time* article and photograph, and they wanted to know about my meeting with the President. I told them "problems with the oil business." Then they asked about Garner. I told them I considered Garner to be the "first American casualty of the war," and I said that I would support Garner for a third term as vice president, but not for president.

Then one of them asked if I had tried to convince the President to run for a third term. "No," I replied, "I tried to convert him to snuff-dipping."

"What was the result?" one asked.

"I failed," I replied. "The President said he never dipped snuff so soon before lunch."

In the middle of December, the Cole Committee hearings went to New Orleans, and Ernest Thompson and I went to testify, still fighting against a federal oil bureau, but pressing for Federal Tender Boards in Louisiana. The committee for those hearings consisted of the Chairman, William P. Cole, of Maryland; Carl E. Mapes, of Michigan; Edward A. Kelly, of Illinois; and Charles A. Wolverton, of New Jersey. (The most energetic questioner on the committee was Congressman Mapes. When after a long and hard day questioning Thompson, Mapes returned to his hotel room and suffered a heart attack. He died early the next morning after a second attack. The committee recessed and Mapes' body was returned to Michigan for the funeral.)

A few days after that Congressman Cole asked me to Washington to meet with him. I planned a full week there, so I would have a chance to talk to the President, and then return home to Texas for Christmas. I arrived on Friday, had a long meeting with Cole, and finally began to convince him that a Federal Oil Commission would be a mistake. He invited me to his home in Maryland for the weekend—a beautiful colonial estate with nicely tended grounds—and continued our talks in these pleasant, relaxed surroundings.

On Monday we returned to Washington and went to the White House together to see Roosevelt. "It is the unanimous recommendation of the Committee," Cole told the President, "that we should not have federal control of the oil businesss. We find that it can—and should—be left to the individual states. Would you like us to provide you with an official report of our findings?"

"No," President Roosevelt replied, "That's not necessary. But I would like you to stay while I get Icky over here."

He called the Secretary of the Interior, and within a few minutes he was in the oval office. The President greeted him jovially. "Well, Icky, it looks like Jerry has won, and you're not going to get to be Czar of the Oil Industry."

Ickes accepted the announcement with good humor. "I figured some time ago that's the way it would be," he said. "Jerry traveled all over the country, appearing at every committee meeting, and he always seemed to have one more card up his sleeve."

Thursday, that week, I returned to Roosevelt to discuss plans for an Oil for Britain Day, one day in which every oil well in Texas would donate its production to England. I knew the idea would face resistance from most of the major producers, so our strategy had to be planned carefully.

Most of the government employees had already left for Christmas, and Roosevelt himself was getting ready to leave for his estate at Hyde Park, New York. When I arrived, two men were in the oval ofice with the President; Missy LeHand, FDR's secretary, told me to wait in General Edwin Watson's office, since he had departed on vacation. The door between the two offices was open, and I could not help but hear the conversation going on, because the three men were shouting at each other. The two men opposing the President were Henry Ford and Joseph Kennedy.

The subject under discussion was the manufacture of airplane motors for England. At the point I came in to overhear the discussion, Henry Ford was speaking. "I will manufacture all the airplane motors the United States can use, if and when they are needed, but I will not manufacture even one for England." It surprised me to hear Ford so adamant on the subject, but what was more surprising was to hear Joseph Kennedy siding with Ford against the President.

Roosevelt tried to reason with them, explaining that ultimately any airplane engine built for England would benefit the United States, telling them that—if England and France couldn't hold back Hitler— we would eventually have to go to war with Germany. Both men refused to accept that, insisting that Germany had no designs against the United States.

The President called Ford and Kennedy—individually and collectively—stupid sons-of-bitches, and then threw in a few other choice expletives as his anger rose.

All three men knew, I heard and saw what was going on, so I decided I might as well join them. Roosevelt was so angry, I was afraid he might pick up the inkwell again and do injury to one or both men. My presence did help to quiet the President, and he finally told Henry Ford and Joseph Kennedy to "get the hell out."

That night, on the train home to Texas, Ralph Budd, president of the B. & O. Railroad, came up to me and told me that Mr. Jesse Jones was in his private car at the rear of the train. Jones wanted to know if I would care to join him.

Jesse Jones was a good friend of the President, and while we talked I told him what had taken place in Roosevelt's office that day. At first he was bewildered, then surprised, and then angry. "I can't imagine Henry Ford and Joseph Kennedy taking that kind of stand," he spouted. "They know we are going to be in this war before it's over with."

On January 6, 1940, I addressed the "Old Hickory Dinner" of the Andrew Jackson Democrats at the Lamar Hotel in Houston. My speech was broadcast, and President Roosevelt listened to it on his radio. As I promised, I hit hard on the subject of a third term for Roosevelt, praising the President's record and stating again and again that he was the best man to lead us in troubled times. As I had hoped, the audience response to my call was tremendous, with long thundrous applause and loud cheers breaking out.

As soon as I finished speaking, a message was brought to me that the President was on the telephone wanting to speak to me. "Well, Jerry, you've convinced me," came Roosevelt's familiar voice. "I'll run for a third term."

18

The Railroad Commission—The Fight Gets Rougher

The decision of the court in the Rowan and Nichols case set off a chain of lawsuits that resulted in the biggest crisis the oil industry and the Railroad Commission had ever had to face. For over a year, oil regulation was virtually ruled by injunction, as the major oil companies attempted to destroy the power of the Railroad Commission and to drive the independent producers and refiners out of business.

The formula we arranged for allocations, as a compromise in the Rowan and Nichols case, was the most equitable the Railroad Commission had ever used. However, there were a few flaws, and major companies picked up on these to challenge the legality of state regulation itself. The battle against our authority was led by Humble Oil and Refining Company, and it centered around Rule 37, the famous well-spacing regulation.

In resolving the Rowan and Nichols case, we revised Rule 37 to permit the drilling of more oil wells by large leaseholders to compensate them for greater withdrawals on adjacent small leases that were more heavily drilled. Humble, the largest of the lease-holders in East Texas fields, refused to accept this as an equitable solution.

On July 27, 1939, Humble Oil obtained a temporary order from Federal District Judge Duval West of San Antonio, awarding them an East Texas allowable increase of about 50 percent of their quota; a three-judge federal court would be set up to hear their case. Nine other companies followed their lead and went to court to file suit against the Commission. The effect of these injunctions was to permit the big companies virtually wide-open production. Within a matter of weeks the market was glutted with oil.

On August 11, the Humble injunction was made permanent by the three-judge panel. On August 12, Standard Oil Company of New Jersey, which owned Humble, cut the price of crude oil by 32 cents a barrel. Shell Oil Company followed suit, dropping its price on Texas crude by 40 cents a barrel, and Sinclair dropped its price 20 cents a barrel. Suddenly, the nation's oil industry balanced precariously on the brink of disaster. It was a situation that the major oil companies could survive, while independents would be forced into bankruptcy. Major companies, all owned or controlled by the North and East, tried to squeeze out independents, particularly those in Texas, which had 40 percent of the world's known oil reserves. In effect, the Wall Street boys, the Fat-Cats, declared war on the State of Texas.

From the moment I began my campaign for office, charging Wall Street with domination of the Texas oil business, I felt at some point I would have to face them. Now they had acted, and I knew the Railroad Commission had to meet their threat swiftly and decisively.

On August 14, we issued an order to shut down all Texas oil wells for a period of fifteen days; with the possibility the shutdown would be extended if the problem of surplus oil was not quickly resolved. The order was effective at 7:00 the following morning. Oklahoma and New Mexico were the first to follow our lead, shutting down all their wells the next day. Then Kansas did the same, followed by Louisiana and Illinois. Within 48 hours, 70 percent of the nation's wells ceased to produce oil.

At the time we issued this shutdown order, I wired W.S. Farish, president of Standard Oil, requesting that he slash the retail price of gasoline by five cents a gallon or restore the crude oil price to it original, stable position.

> Unless one of these two courses is pursued, Standard Oil would stand convicted of serious charges now being made in Texas to the effect that the Standard Oil Company, through its subsidiary, the Humble Company, has determined to (1) rule or ruin the oil industry, (2) to run every independent out of business, (3) to deprive the state of money to take care of its aged, blind, and dependent, (4) deplete the state's vast oil reserves to the benefit of the money barons of Wall Street, (5) turn control of the oil business over to the federal government.

Farish replied that Standard Oil had no control over its subsidiary, Humble, thereby choosing to ignore the charges. Perhaps he thought the shutdown was all I had planned and felt confident his company had large reserves to weather the storm.

However, I had other cards up my sleeve. On August 15, I officially requested that Texas Attorney General Gerald Mann institute an investigation into the relationship between Standard Oil and Humble, charging them with violation of state anti-trust laws. Former Governor Ross Sterling had built Humble Oil as a Texas company. Standard Oil could not obtain a permit to do business in Texas. When Standard offered to purchase all of the stock in Humble, Sterling managed to achieve a special bill passed by the state legislature, allowing Humble to continue its business so long as it was a separate entity from Standard. I obtained a photostatic copy of the contract between Standard and Humble, which proved it was in fact a fully controlled subsidiary.

My request to Attorney General Mann stated:

> I must respectfully request your investigation of the contract to determine if the anti-trust laws of this state have been violated or if the Standard is seeking to operate in this state by subterfuge.
>
> In either case I implore your early action in the matter to the end that the laws of this state shall be respected and that officially we shall not . . . ignore rank violations.
>
> It is of course an open secret that the Humble is a subsidiary of the Standard Oil Company of New Jersey, and it occurs to me that the enclosed document is proof of that fact.

Mann acted immediately, and sent eight assistants to Houston to talk to Humble officials and obtain the company's files. At the same time, the Railroad Commission sent its workers to the oilfields, pipelines, and refineries to do a bit of investigating to find precisely how much oil was on hand, its location and its source. In addition to making sure that the oil wells were indeed shut down, this gave us the opportunity to learn if the crude cut was made because Texas was overproducing.

I had another recourse, but I did not have a great deal of faith that it would do any good. I called upon Governor O'Daniel to persuade him to call a special session of the legislature to levy a tax on crude oil. While I had welcomed the chance to fight the big oil companies, I was concerned about the cost that was being inflicted on the state and its people. The cut in the price of crude oil represented a loss of about $100,000,000 to the people of Texas; the state alone expected to lose about $400,000 in oil production taxes. I pressed O'Daniel to try for a tax of five cents a barrel on crude oil, which would allow the state to meet its social security obligations, something it was not yet able to do because of his determination to have a transaction tax.

O'Daniel declined my request, as I had expected.

Meanwhile the court battle with Humble continued, becoming bogged down in technical details, such as determining the thickness of oil in the load-bearing sand. Humble's attorney Rex Baker, presented a plan they considered equitable, a plan so complex it was impossible to prove its fairness, or even if an individual producer's allocation was accurate. I doubted the sincerity of Humble in proposing it in the first place, suspecting it was merely a delaying tactic.

As the case continued, however, Humble's deeper motives became increasingly clear to the general public. Articles appeared in the newspapers interpreting the case as an attempt by Humble to freeze out the independents. If we did not have the courts on our side, we did have the people.

The month of August drew to a close, and the time approached for the Railroad Commission to choose extending the shutdown or returning to production. It was evident many independent refineries were hurting because of lack of oil. However, Humble had done nothing about raising its crude rates to normal. At the last hour, we announced an extension of the shutdown for an additional two days. Almost immediately, Humble restored its prices, and we responded by allowing the wells to begin pumping.

A national crisis was over. At this point, Interior Secretary Ickes came into the act, announcing ludicrously that—if the states could not handle oil matters—he would step in and take charge.

The major oil companies had welcomed federal control, because it would have favored them over the independents. I don't say that all of the trouble they caused, in 1939 and 1940, was aimed at bringing about this change, but they were aware that the trouble was making it increasingly likely that the Cole Committee would propose legislation that would make the Railroad Commission unnecessary.

In September, we worked out a new proration order for East Texas, granting Humble Oil a considerable increase (allocating nearly the total number of barrels they requested); but Humble refused to accept it, because we had not altered our formula to that which they had requested. Their lawyers went before the three-judge federal court to request an injunction to prevent us from enforcing our proration order. The court refused, stating: "Under the law of Texas, the holder of an oil lease is the owner of the oil in place under the lease and is entitled to produce his fair share of oil drawn from the common reservoir. The Railroad Commission has authority to prorate the amount each well shall be allowed to produce, but its orders must be reasonable and fair."

The court considered we were reasonable and fair with Humble in this case. Refusing to grant the injunction, the Railroad Commission had won a first-round victory.

However, the original case continued, and in February of 1940, the three-judge panel decided in Humble's favor, but giving us thirty day's stay to prepare an appeal to the Supreme Court.

Combined with the Rowan and Nichols decision, this was a serious blow to the functioning of the Railroad Commission. We had already planned an appeal of that case to the Supreme Court; now we would join that appeal with the Humble. Despite lower court decisions, I felt we had a strong case. However, I did not feel we should rely totally on the "nine old men" Roosevelt had been quarreling with. As a safeguard, I went to Governor O'Daniel and asked him to call a special session of the legislature to pass new and stronger laws on oil regulation. O'Daniel refused.

Angrily, I issued a statement to the press, charging that the major oil firms were "running the governor's office," and announcing that I would go to Houston to meet their officials to try to work out some operational plan acceptable to them as well as to the Railroad Commission.

I arranged a meeting with Harry Weiss, president of Humble, at a Houston hotel. I tried to persuade him to allow a minimum of ten barrels a day per well, the least I felt could be produced safely and economically. (Originally, I wanted a minimum of twenty barrels a day per well. Under the federal court order, the independents on a ten-acre tract of land would be allowed only 2/10 of a barrel a day, an amount that would bankrupt them.)

"Nothing doing," Harry Weiss told me. He had the law on his side.

When I got downstairs in the hotel, the press awaited me. They asked for a statement. "I'm going back to Austin," I told them, "to get me some clean drawers. Then I'm going to Washington."

The afternoon before I left for Washington, I received an unexpected visitor, Jim Abercrombie, of the Abercrombie Oil Company, one of the owners of the Old Ocean Field (and one of the men who had previously given me much trouble). He arrived at my office in the late afternoon, and he did not depart until late that night. He spent six hours trying to persuade me not to appeal the Humble and the Rowan and Nichols cases. Abercrombie was smart enough not to offer me a bribe, but he used every argument he could, including repeating over and over that Commissioner Thompson wasn't in favor of appealing. He could not know I considered that one of the best reasons for being in favor of it.

When those cases were decided in our favor by the U.S. Supreme Court, Ernest O. Thompson took the spotlight, issuing the first statement that the court's decision was "a great victory for the people."

As it turned out, Humble's greatest mistake was in suing the individual commissioners along with the Railroad Commission itself. That permitted me to file as *amicus curae,* and I was permitted to present to the court the fact that all of the exceptions to Rule 37, concerning the spacing of oil wells, had been granted by my predecessors on the Railroad Commission. This opened up for the court's consideration the overall function of the Commission, rather than allowing Humble to concentrate only on the amount of oil pumped from wells of varying depth and pressure and spacing.

Justice Felix Frankfurter wrote the opinions in both cases, stating that the question was one of an economic nature, where no court should substitute their judgment for the wisdom of a body of experts. He suggested that it would create economic chaos if the decisions of the lower courts were permitted to stand.

After leaving the Supreme Court, I stopped by the Capitol to see Senator Tom Connally. He was in his office with several other Senators. I was truly happy about the court decision, and I wanted to celebrate, so I invited all of them to be my guests for dinner that evening at the Russian Troika, then an excellent Washington restaurant. Connally and two other senators accepted. With Ted Read, who had accompanied me to Washington, we made a party of five.

The restaurant and kitchen were in the basement of an old house. They served Russian food and had a fortune teller and an accordion player, and that night there was a particularly festive atmosphere. There were several tables of Texans present, all merry and getting merrier. Senator Connally was having a grand time, lifting a few and talking of the joys of the single man. (Connally was at the time a widower.)

I was interested in all the Russian dishes, and so I wandered off to the kitchen to ask some questions. Talking with the kitchen staff awhile, I gave a $20 tip and returned to the table. A short time later, the accordion player stopped by our table, and I requested he play "The Eyes of Texas."

He knew the song, and began to play it. Immediately a big, beefy Texan at another table leaped to his feet, proclaiming, "Everybody stand up when they play 'The Eyes of Texas.'" He didn't receive much response, so when the accordionist finished, the Texan gave him a five dollar bill, asking him to play it again.

"This time," he announced to the entire restaurant, "all of you damnyankees better stand up."

Most of the customers still didn't feel like standing, so the man (from Sugarland, Texas), decided he would force them. There began one of the biggest fights I'd ever seen. Chairs were thrown, tables overturned, and fists flew, just like in the western movies. Connally and the other senators departed as soon as the trouble began; Ted Read tried to get me to leave, but I was enjoying the show.

With a fight, however, you just can't stand and watch. It was Texans vs. Yankees, and I moved in on the Texan side. When the kitchen crew came into it, they joined my side. The cook must have had a long standing grudge against the fortune teller, because he really seemed to enjoy joining us.

Finally, Ted Read managed to whisk me from the place, and we returned to the Mayflower Hotel. The next morning the Mayflower's manager called my room to say the lady manager from the Troika was downstairs and wanted to charge onto my hotel bill the damage to her restaurant. The Mayflower's manager wished to know if this was all right.

"No, it's not," I said. "I didn't cause the trouble in her place, and she ought to have insurance to cover things like this." I considered telling her to send her bill to Senator Connally, but thought better of it.

In any event, the Supreme Court decision was a victory for the Railroad Commission, but it did not put an end to many challenges from the major oil companies. There were legal suits from Mobil, Gulf, and Conoco. Standard Oil even got into the act again through Sinclair.

In July of 1940, Sinclair Oil posted a price of a flat 75 cents a barrel for crude oil, representing an incredible drop, on top of an already very low price. We did not want to shut down the entire East Texas field again, so we tried another course. We cut Sinclair's crude allowable in the East Texas field to 2,240 barrels a day. Naturally, Harry Sinclair, Chairman of the Board of Consolidated Oil Company, owner of Sinclair, was not happy with that action. He announced he would prefer federal control of oil to the present methods of the Texas Railroad Commission, saying that he would take the matter to court if necessary.

We set the Railroad Commission statewide oil hearings for August 1, and requested the heads of all major oil companies to be present. At that hearing, we placed two witness chairs, one at each end of the bench.

I suggested Harry Sinclair take the chair at one end, and Humble's Harry Weiss take the chair at the other end. Then I asked Sinclair if we didn't have kinfolks in the two chairs.

Patrick J. Hurley, Sinclair's attorney, jumped up and asked me to clarify that statement.

I told him to sit down a moment and he'd have full clarification. I asked Sinclair, "Does Standard Oil Company of New Jersey own a percentage of Sinclair Oil Company?"

Harry Sinclair hesitated, obviously avoiding answering.

"I'll refresh your memory a bit," I said. I pulled out a copy of a secret operating contract between Sinclair and Standard. When I began to read off the document, lawyers for both companies hit the floor, protesting that I was not supposed to have that contract, that it was confidential.

I read aloud part of the contract, then entered the full contract as part of the hearing's record. The part I read made reference to 25 percent of Sinclair's stock.

"Now, you can both answer this question, at the same time or separately," I said. "Doesn't this make you kinfolks?"

Weiss admitted that this did bring them closer together, but Sinclair gave in completely. "Yes, they own 25 percent of the stock in my company," he said. "I decided at one time it would help to have a Rockefeller on my board."

"At that point, you kinfolks ceased to be kissin' cousins," I said.

At the conclusion of this meeting, Harry Sinclair announced that he was restoring the price of Sinclair's crude oil back to its normal amount, retroactive to the day of the cut.

There were numerous other fights waged in those first few years on the Commission. In March of 1940, we caught one of the Commission's deputy oil supervisors taking a $5,000 bribe from the Shasta Oil Company. The oil company cooperated in our investigation, and eventually we were able to uncover evidence that hundreds of thousands of barrels of excess oil had been cleared through the Commission's Midland office during the three years before I took office.

And in 1941, the requirement to have oil producers file their reports with the Commission by way of registered mail finally paid off. We had managed to collect a large number of false reports from around the state—primarily from the Panhandle fields and the East Texas fields. For years the oil producers had been able to get away with reporting falsely, because there was no serious penalty, only a fine. However, by using the U.S. mail to send their false reports, they were guilty of mail fraud, which carried a prison sentence. I called in the chief postal inspector, and the federal courts took over.

Slowly but surely, the Railroad Commission began to clean up Texas oil business. I was proud that my election had been largely responsible for the changes.

Perhaps too proud.

19

Politics 1940—Too Much of a Good Thing

Admittedly I've made a few mistakes. One of the biggest was my decision to run for Governor in 1940. From my first moments as Railroad Commissioner, the press talked about me as the next governor, and speculation about whether I would run increased for twoyears. It wasn't entirely that this talk went to my head. There were good reasons, as I saw it, for me to run for Governor.

O'Daniel was one of the worst governors in Texas history. As the state's chief executive, he tried very little, and accomplished even less. As an elected railroad commissioner, I had accomplished most of my promises to the voters. I was praised and damned, but I had never been idle—a strong contrast to Pappy O'Daniel. In addition, I had been handpicked by President Roosevelt to be his "man" in Texas.

There's also the fact I had nothing to lose. While the Texas governor is elected every two years, the railroad commissioners are elected for six year terms (with a commissioner up for reelection every two years). I had four years to go on my term; Lon Smith's term was up in 1940. If I was not elected governor, I still had my place on the Commission.

I had less respect for O'Daniel in 1940 than I had for Terrell in 1938. I thought by now the public saw through the Light Crust flour salesman, knowing him as nothing more than a radio personality with a smooth voice and some big businessmen behind him. Anyone who ever met him face to face had to realize it! He was the kind who would never look at you when you talked to him; his eyes circled about, never looking straight into another person's eyes.

During his first campaign, Governor O'Daniel offered the voters only one real pledge—to provide the elderly of Texas with a $30 pension, without a sales tax. He failed to provide the pension, and in his attempt to get a $30 monthly "guarantee" for the elderly, he had proposed a sales tax in the form of a "transaction" tax. The legislature had met for the longest session on record without arriving at a bill. I had great faith in the voters of Texas, and I believed they would see the truth about the man and not reelect him.

O'Daniel and I were never on friendly terms, but I began attacking him in earnest early in 1940. I mentioned that if some qualified person did not announce against him, I would run for office myself. One of my attacks backfired, causing some embarrassment; though now that I look back on it, the situation was funny. It was announced in newspapers that General Foods offered Pappy $75,000 to write verses for their advertising after he retired from office.

"I think that's a bit high for his talents," I said to the press. "The poet laureate of Texas is already making $12,000 a year," I quipped. "And that's twice as much as the poet laureate of England makes."

I didn't know that Texas actually had an official poet laureate, until a lady, Lexie Dean Robertson, stepped forward, protesting that her title was an honorary one and that she received no income from public funds.

At least my gaffe acquainted the people of Texas with a little-known fact. I recovered from my embarrassment with a public charge that the governor's office was run by the big oil companies, pointing out that the day O'Daniel had refused my request for a special session of the legislature to strengthen Texas' proration laws in the face of the Humble decision, he had met privately with the head of major oil companies.

By the time the political race got under way, there were a total of six candidates who had filed for Governor—Governor W. Lee O'Daniel, Railroad Commissioner Ernest O. Thompson, Highway Commissioner Harry Hines, Former Governor Ma Ferguson, a man named "Cyclone" Davis, and me.

It was a one-issue campaign, concentrating on the question of a suitable tax program to finance social security. The five challengers attacked O'Daniel, each proposing some form of taxation that differed from his transaction tax.

I led the way, announcing my program early in March, well before the other candidates had filed for the office. Mine was a program of natural resources taxes that would raise $23,000,000 in annual revenue for payment of pensions, care for crippled children, blind, dependent mothers, and teachers' retirement. It would include a 2¼ percent gross receipts tax on oil, which under normal producing conditions would raise $13,000,000 a year, plus a one-cent per thousand cubic feet tax on natural gas, which under producing conditions at the time would raise

$10,000,000. I believed teacher retirement could be funded by changes in the franchise tax and increase in the sulphur tax, and a pipeline tax.

It was my contention that Texas' natural resources belonged to the people, and that those who took them from the state—often far too cheaply—should be required to take care of the people's social programs. A sales tax, or a transaction tax, would place the burden on those least able to pay. I still believe it was the fairest of all the programs presented in that election.

A month later O'Daniel announced his program. He still favored the one percent transaction tax, but he stated that he would "support any plan that produces fifty million annually for financing social security, old age pensions, aid to the blind, aid to dependent children, and teacher retirement." He issued a plea to the voters to reelect him and to elect legislators who would pass a tax bill. He had little more to say about government programs; he spent most of his time talking of the Ten Commandments and the Golden Rule.

His hillbilly band grew disgusted with him and four of its members came over to the Sadler camp. Leon Huff, the lead signer, and Kermit Whalen, the guitarist, known as "Horace the Lovebird," were the first. Soon they were followed by Buck Creel and Cliff Bruner. With Lew Childre, they made up the "Cowboy Stringsters."

I no longer had the bus from the 1938 campaign, with its platform on top. Instead, I picked up a truck and trailer from a junkyard and managed to rig up a platform on its back. Ted Read resigned as a Railroad Inspector with the Commission to work on the campaign. I pulled together a staff, insisting that those working for me could not be holding government jobs. The campaign was set up much like my 1938 campaign. We circled the state, traveling from town to town, hitting five or six a day. I would speak, and then while the band played, I moved out to meet the people.

Every week I had a poll taken to show voters' opinions and to gauge the effectiveness of my campaign. In the early weeks, I was far ahead with a majority. O'Daniel hardly campaigned at all. He issued occasional statements to the press, and spoke on the radio a few times, but he announced that he would appear publicly for only one speech— in Waco on July 2.

With less than two weeks to go before primary day, he changed his tactics.

I got wind of it the night I appeared in Gilmer. While the sound system was being set up, I walked around the town and talked to people. A hotel owner told me that O'Daniel's treasurer and number one campaign advisor, Jesse McKee, had registered in the hotel for the night. McKee was very concerned about the hotel's telephone facilities, telling the owner that he had to make a very important phone call that night after my speech.

I knew immediately that McKee had come to observe public reaction to my campaign, and that his phone call would be a report to O'Daniel. I was staying the night in the hotel. So I went downstairs and became acquainted with the man who operated the switchboard. I arranged with him to notify me when the call went through to McKee and to connect the line to my room so I could listen in on the conversation.

That night the rally was the biggest so far on the tour, and the audience response was phenomenal. When I went into the crowd, people grasped my hands, crying and blessing me. Some slapped me heartily on my back, others grabbed at my neck and patted my head. I wore a ring on my left hand, and so many people grabbed my hand tightly that the ring cut my finger. Both hands were sore and swollen and my back was bruised from the slaps of encouragement.

McKee stayed on the edge of the crowd watching, but my men observed him; they were instructed to inform me when he left.

Soon I received the message. I apologized to people near me, telling them I had a telephone call waiting. I overheard Jesse McKee tell O'Daniel he had to get out and make speeches or he'd lose the election. "You have no idea of the response Sadler's getting. He practically had them down on their knees praying. They're for him," he said.

O'Daniel protested, "Oh no, they're not. You're just exaggerating. He knows the people are behind Pappy."

"If you keep hiding in the governor's mansion," McKee said, "they're going to forget all about you." McKee revealed that he had a $15,000 truck set up for O'Daniel and told him to get out there and give the people a better show than Sadler's. "It's the only way you can be reelected."

I was curious about the $15,000 truck McKee mentioned. I was to find out soon enough, for O'Daniel did get out to campaign. That truck alone drew crowds. Not only did it have an elaborately designed platform and sound system, but it also had a capitol dome, which hydraulically lifted high atop the truck, lit by floodlights, so that

O'Daniel could be seen speaking beneath it. A very impressive sight to the country folk.

He got himself a new band and wrote new songs, throwing in some church hymns to give his rallies the feel of religious revivals. In speeches he skirted around political issues, preaching the keeping of the Ten Commandments and practicing the Golden Rule, giving people the impression he was God's chosen candidate.

I hit hard, charging that "O'Daniel appears to be trying to save the rich man's money and the poor man's soul," trying to get people to listen to the issues. "The question I want O'Daniel to answer," I said, "is why with 91 house members and 21 senators, the largest working majority in the legislature of any governor, he failed to pay the old age pensions?" And I attacked his expensive $15,000 truck, a gift from a Ft. Worth oilman.

It seemed to do little good. I dropped in the polls, and O'Daniel began to rise. Other candidates seemed unaffected by his entrance into the campaign. O'Daniel was taking his increased votes from me, and I was not gaining any votes from the other candidates. Pappy was outdoing me at my own game. I had felt justified in giving people entertainment, because I was also getting them to listen to the issues of the campaign. Pappy just gave them the entertainment, and his show was bigger and more expensive than mine.

In the early weeks of the primary race, there was no serious trouble at my rallies as in the 1938 election campaign. With O'Daniel's active entry, the heckling started, and with each town it seemed to grow worse. To handle trouble, I had Stanley Bean on the trail with me, and I also had the Kimbrough boys, John and Jack. The Kimbroughs were the most celebrated college football players of that time—both played for Texas A & M, and John was an All-American. They were handsome and personable men, and they spoke at many of my rallies. They also made excellent bodyguards.

One incident took place at Brownwood. There was a guy at the back of the crowd, standing beside a car, heckling me. John Kimbrough was tall, I could always see him in the crowd. While I spoke, I watched him work his way back to the heckler. John walked up to the guy, propped his foot on the car bumper and talked to him. The conversation didn't look threatening, but very soon the heckling stopped.

Later, leaving Brownwood, I asked John what he had said to the heckler.

"I asked him whether he liked Jerry Sadler or not," John told me. "He said he didn't, and I said yes you do. Then he said 'I guess I do,' and that was all there was to it."

Trouble always seemed to be hotter when I hit Corpus Christi. There, on July 23, we had a big rally in Artesian Park. The boos and heckling were the worst I had experienced in this campaign. Again, the Kimbrough boys took care of the problem.

A man had been following us from town to town, organizing the heckling. He had several helpers in Corpus Christi, and they started in as soon as I began speaking. It was so loud and disruptive, I was barely heard over the noise. John and Jack knew they couldn't handle so many people alone, so they went for the police.

At one point in my speech, I pointed out the main troublemaker to the crowd. "This man has been following me around and setting up these demonstrations."

I stepped down from the platform; the man came toward me with a knife. Instantly, John Kimbrough was behind the guy and had him around the neck. John's hands were large, only one being used to reach all around the neck; and as soon as he squeezed, he told the man to drop the knife. The man obeyed, and the police moved in and took him away.

The biggest disturbance of that campaign took place at Longview, two days before the primary. Two brothers—one, an out-of-work barber from Louisiana—had been hired to kill me. They had followed me for some time, fortifying their courage with alcohol. This time Stanley Bean saved my life.

He and Gene Milner, my bus driver, and the Kimbrough boys had kept their eyes on the two men and also had alerted the police. Physical threats always seemed to occur when I left the platform, while the band played for the crowds. My men were all around the brothers when one of them pulled his gun. Swiftly Stanley Bean knocked the gun from the would-be assassin's hand. When it hit the pavement, however, the gun discharged, and two policemen were injured.

On primary election day, I knew I had lost, but I had no idea how sorely I was defeated until the returns came in. I placed a humiliating fifth out of six candidates, beating only "Cyclone" Davis. O'Daniel was so far in front of second-place Ernest O. Thompson, there was no need for a runoff.

My deepest regret was not the losing; I was able to take defeat in stride and joke about it. I regretted I had chosen to run in the first place.

Part of a crowd gathered for a Sadler rally during the unsuccessful 1940 gubernatorial campaign.

With Hick Holcomb in 1940, planning strategy for the gubernatorial campaign.

With the Kimbrough brothers—John and Jack, football stars at Texas A&M—and Lewis Dickson of Houston, during the 1940 campaign.

It was a mistake, which voters had been able to see, although I had not. They had elected me to a six-year term as railroad commissioner. I had done a good job and lived up to my pledges, but I had served only a year and a half of that term. It was my first elected office, and voters sensed I was pushing myself too far too fast.

Moreover, it was evident to them that the Railroad Commission was barely functioning during the campaign. Crucial issues confronting the oil industry were left hanging unresolved while Commissioner Thompson and I fought each other for another job. Only Lon Smith stayed in his office minding business, and he was a lame duck commissioner, havng announced he would not seek reelection.

It was my fault that Smith did not run again. With all we had gone through together, I had observed him rapidly growing more feeble. I know he would have preferred to die "with his boots on." He had every intention of running again, but I felt he might have a few more years if he slowed down.

He and I were returning from Brenham, where we had spoken to the Chamber of Commerce. We stopped on the road somewhere near Bastrop to take a leak. I knew Smith intended to announce his candidacy the next day. "You're not going to make that announcement tomorrow," I said, as we stood in the dark, relieving ourselves. "You're going to announce your retirement. You've had enough of this fight, and you need to spend a little time with your wife and family."

At first he was angry at me, but in time he understood and was actually glad that he had retired in the bloom of success.

This paved the way for the election of Olin Culberson. Though Culberson and I usually agreed on issues, I did not have great respect for him as a man, at least at that time. This is one thing that most people have never understood about me. I don't care if a man disagrees with me politically, as long as he is personally good, honest, and ethical. I have never believed that the end justifies the means.

Culberson had been an employee of the Railroad Commission, appointed to the Public Utilities Commission by Lon Smith. He had done a good job, but his manner created a great deal of disruption. From my view, he was self-centered, egotistical, and dictatorial; but, as far as I was concerned, that was still no reason to fire him. What upset me the most was that he was constantly criticizing Lon Smith, the man who had hired him, and he did not keep his criticisms within the confines of the Commission offices.

I knew Olin's motives. He was paving the way to run against Smith in the 1940 election. He had no idea Smith would not run for reelection. I had warned Olin several times to stop his criticism. Finally, I felt the only choice I had was to fire him. And I did, giving him 45 minutes to clean out his desk and leave his office.

That was the only disagreement he and I had; although I did not support him in his campaign for the Commission, after the election we worked together closely. On issues, our thinking was always in agreement, and we had an arrangement when one was absent from the office and an order had to be signed, his secretary could sign on the instruction of the other.

His egotism did bother me, but I reached a point I could laugh about it. When he took office, he did not have a simple swearing-in ceremony as was customary for railroad commissioners, but ordered a full-scale inauguration, with invitations, programmes, and a gala celebration, more elaborate than the Governor's. And when I took him to Washington to meet the President for the first time, he strutted about Roosevelt's office pompously instructing the third-termer on just how he ought to run the country.

Eventually Olin became my best friend ever. I teased him unmercifully about his egotism, and he took it in good humor, even laughing at himself. For years afterward, up until he died, Olin told people, "When Jerry tells you something, you can depend on it; and when he tells you to do something 'or else,' you'd better do it. I can vouch for it, because he once fired me for not listening to him."

In this most political of all my political years, I also had the responsibility of leading the "Stop Garner" movement in Texas. In the middle of my campaign for governor, the Texas Democratic Convention took place at Waco, on May 28. Roosevelt's chances for a third term were heavily dependent on the outcome of that convention. Garner had considerable support from other states, but in order to get the nomination, he had to be able to control his own state's delegation to the National Convention.

Many of the state's strongest "New Dealers" were caught in the rift between Roosevelt and Garner, and most had decided their loyalty to the Vice President was greater than their loyalty to the President. On his side, Garner had Sam Rayburn, the most powerful man in the House of Representatives and soon to become Speaker. Also, Senator Tom Connally, and young up-and-coming Congressman Lyndon

Johnson. The important Texans remaining on Roosevelt's side were Jesse Jones of Houston, Undersecretary of the Interior Alvin Wirtz, and me.

Unfortunately I had to be in Washington at the time of the Waco convention because of the appeal of the Humble case to the Supreme Court. In a conference with the President, it was decided that Alvin Wirtz should handle things at the Waco convention. When the time came to apply pressure to Garner, we would—if we had to—call on Jesse Jones.

The only time I ever worked to get convention delegates was before that 1940 Waco convention. I managed to get a good number committed to Roosevelt, but victory was not certain. From the time the convention began, I kept in touch with what was happening through Hick Holcomb, who would call me to give reports. I was at the Raleigh Hotel in Washington, but as the critical time approached I went to the White House, leaving Roosevelt's unlisted White House number with the hotel switchboard. I did not, however, give the location; I merely stated that I could be reached at it, in the event important calls needed forwarding.

Shortly after the Waco convention was called to order, Emmett Wilborn, a "good old boy" from Shelby County, was given the floor. He was an elected district attorney and something of a comic. He did not come straight to the point; few, if any, of Garner's people knew the reason he had taken the floor. Wilborn talked about how far he had come from the time he had been a country boy studying law by correspondence. He told of the day he had gone down to his mailbox, with the birds singing and the sun shining, to pick up his law diploma. Now he was honored to be elected District Attorney of Shelby County. Not only that but chosen a delegate to the state convention, and even more, chairman of his senatorial district. But what he was most honored to do was to put before this convention a motion to nominate Franklin Delano Roosevelt for President for a third term.

Immediately the big demonstration started, with delegates marching up and down the aisles waving banners and placards. At that moment the Garner candidacy was doomed. Myron Blalock, Garner's state campaign manager and long one of my enemies, struggled and manipulated and negotiated all day, with little success.

At about four o'clock that afternoon, a call came through to me at the White House—from Myron Blalock. With Roosevelt listening on an extension, Blalock conceded defeat but he pleaded for a "favorite son" designation for Garner in order to save face. I said I would agree to allowing Garner the honorary title of Chairman of the Texas delegation with a favorite son vote on the first ballot. However, I insisted Garner had to sign a statement withdrawing from the race as anything more than a favorite son, and the entire Texas delegation had to sign a pledge not to stop a third-term draft for Franklin D. Roosevelt. Hick Holcomb would write Garner's withdrawal and release it to the press with a photograph of Garner. Blalock agreed. The papers were drawn and signed, and Holcomb released the press statement with a photo I had selected—a picture of Garner in a tuxedo—which he hated. "It looks like a mule in buggy harness," Garner said.

With little opposition now, the way was paved for Roosevelt's third-term nomination in July at the Chicago Democratic Party convention. I had lost my own campaign that summer, but I was pleased I had succeeded for Roosevelt.

There was one other thing that happened that summer that pleased me even more. One really wonderful thing came from my gubernatorial campaign. On a very hot July day, while I was speaking in Cleburne, a beautiful young lady got up to wipe the sweat from my brow. Her name was Laura Jones, and her kind act started a romance that would last the rest of my life. A little more than two years later, Laura became Mrs. Jerry Sadler.

20

Oil, Britain, and a Fire in the English Channel

Despite the strong isolationist feeling in the United States, people did talk about the possibility that we might again be drawn into a European war. The German blitzkrieg and sudden surprise attacks caused people to speculate on how to defend their homes and families if German armies swept up from Mexico or down from Canada.

One spring evening of 1940, after Hitler's assault on France had begun, I was sitting in the Stephen F. Austin Hotel, talking with Byron Utecht, a veteran reporter for the *Fort Worth Star-Telegram*. We got to the subject of why the French didn't seem able to stop Hitler's tanks. "I can understand the problem with stopping an air assault," he said. But he thought there ought to be some way to stop the ground forces.

"There is," I said. "If the United States was attacked from Mexico, I'd pour oil on the Rio Grande River and set it afire. With enough oil, we'd keep the fire burning for years."

"Could that really be done?" Utecht asked, growing excited.

"Sure," I said. "They could do it in France, too."

"Do you know anybody in the French government?" he asked. "Someone we could send a cablegram to?"

"Well," I said, "I've met the mayor of Le Havre. He was over here recently to talk about buying oil. Since we're neutral, I couldn't do much for him. I guess I could send him a cablegram."

We put together a carefully worded cable, explaining the idea, and sent it to the mayor of Le Havre that night. The next day I got an answer from him, saying, "Good idea, but no oil."

I told Byron, and he was disappointed. He had liked the idea of doing a story about a Texan saving France. He asked if he could write the story of the idea as I had originally presented it—a way of defending Texas against an invasion across the Rio Grande.

I agreed, and Byron's article appeared in his newspaper. It set off a tempest all over the country. There were many articles and editorials in newspapers and magazines, criticizing the idea. It was termed insane, ridiculous, impractical, dangerous, and foolish. In Harlingen, Texas, the editorial accused me of trying to destroy their citrus crops. Another newspaper questioned: "What if the Rio Grande should be dry?" Even *Liberty* and *Colliers'* magazines got into the act, ridiculing the concept.

Meanwhile, France fell to the Germans.

Not long after the French fell, a man came to my office in the Capitol building, introduced himself, and asked to talk to me. He was British Consul in Houston.

"You are the only real friend my country has in Texas," he said. He appreciated the efforts I'd made to move oil supplies to England. He knew what I'd been up against. "The oilmen are not our friends; they want to produce their oil for Germany and Italy," he said. We don't want to place you in a difficult position, but Lord Halifax, the Ambassador to the United States, wishes to meet you."

The letter he handed me was sealed with wax and stamped. He said it would be appreciated if I would present this letter at the British Embassy in Washington. (That kind of thing will impress anyone, even Texans.)

It was all very mysterious, and I was intrigued by it. So I agreed. When I arrived in Washington, I did not go directly to the British Embassy; instead I called the White House and asked General Watson, appointments secretary, to arrange a meeting with the President.

Watson suggested six o'clock that evening.

"No," I said. "It must be earlier and in his office. I'm not here to drop by for his Old Fashioneds." (At the end of a day, Roosevelt would throw down three or four good stiff drinks before he would start social conversation, and visitors had to do the same.)

General Watson made an office appointment for that afternoon. I showed FDR the sealed letter and explained how it came into my hands and what I had been asked to do.

"I don't want to see that," FDR quickly said. "I don't want to know anything about it; you know I have to remain neutral. I've also told you before, I'm like the yell leader at the Army Navy football game when the officials want the crowd to be quiet. While I'm waving for silence with one hand, I've got the other behind my back encouraging the crowd to keep yelling." He looked at me a moment. "I know nothing about your communication, but at the same time I'm telling you to get your ass over to the British Embassy."

So I moved my ass to the Embassy. It was getting late now. I was met at the entrance by security men, who asked what I was doing there at that time of day. I showed them the envelope. "I have a letter for Halifax," I said.

Almost immediately, the Ambassador himself came out to greet me. He took me to a secluded, private room in the Embassy.

Polite amenities were exchanged, then Lord Halifax got to the point. He spread before him newspaper articles reporting about and commenting on my idea of setting fire to the Rio Grande. He said their intelligence sources indicated Germany planned an invasion of England. "It is likely to be soon, within the next three or four months," he said. England was not ready for an invasion, and Hitler knew it.

He pointed to the clippings on the table. "Now this is the only idea I've heard that could save us, if it's really possible."

"It's possible," I said, "despite all the people who think I'm crazy."

"Could you show us how to do it?" Lord Halifax asked.

"Sure," I said.

"How soon could you go to England?" he asked.

"Under normal circumstances," I said, "I could go tonight. But under our Neutrality Act, I can't go at all. If I showed up in England tomorrow, I would be in deep trouble. I'll give you all the advice and help I can, but it has to be here in Washington."

Lord Halifax understood. He asked me to tell him everything I needed, and we would set to work immediately.

"The main thing we need is a draftsman," I told him. "I will need to know everything about the English Channel—tides, water temperature, seasonal changes, and so on."

He arranged for the draftsman and the necessary information. Discussing the concept, Lord Halifax wondered if it might work just as well to pour oil along the English coast and on the Cliffs of Dover and set that afire. "It wouldn't be as effective," I said. "With what I've got in mind, you'll have the advantage of surprise. The English Channel is a lot bigger than the Rio Grande. You can't just pour oil and set it afire. You'd eventually run out of oil, and the Germans would just wait until you did. If your intelligence operation can learn when the Germans plan their attack my plan will be more effective."

When the draftsman arrived, we set to work. I explained we would design aluminum tanks, or canisters, that would hold the oil, but look like buoys when taken out into the channel and set into place. They'd have to be weighted or anchored in order to stay precisely in the same location.

I had difficulty describing the tank's shape, so Lord Halifax got some bars of soap from the Embassy lavatories, and I carved them up with my pocket knife. As I hashed out the problems with the draftsman, I also used brown wrapping paper, folding it into workable shapes. The shape of the aluminum tanks had to be roughly oval, and weighted with lead at the bottom to keep them beneath the surface of the water.

Lord Halifax arranged for food and coffee, and we worked far into the night, until the draftsman completed the blueprints. Then I turned my attention to the mixture of the fuel that would be needed to create the best fire on water. Here, I had to be careful about the water temperature in the English Channel. With what was available to the English, with their limited supplies, the best mixture seemed to be 80 percent Grade C fuel (which is what railroad locomotives use), combined with 15 percent gasoline and 5 percent propane. I worried about the propane. If the Channel's water got too warm, the tanks might blow up spontaneously. We checked varying temperatures, and they never seemed to get really hot.

The final part of the plan involved the Royal Air Force. When the tanks were set into place in the Channel, there would need to be an airplane pilot assigned to each one. When word would come the German invasion force was crossing the Channel, the British air force had to fire-bomb all the oil tanks with perfect accuracy.

The plan was top secret, and it has been kept secret to this day. There was great concern that it might be a breach of the rules of war. Hitler might retaliate with nerve gas, and England might be condemned by non-belligerent nations. The tanks were constructed, filled with oil, and on a moonlit but foggy night taken out into the Channel and anchored in place.

The plan worked: it probably is one of the best kept secrets of World War II. German invasion forces were repelled twice in 1940 from the English coast, once in August and once in September. There was a leak to the press in this country—in December of 1940—but it was quickly covered up.

Early one morning in December, I stood outside the front entrance of the Baker Hotel in Dallas, with a newpaper reporter. As we talked a newspaper delivery truck came by and tossed off a bundle of *The*

Dallas Morning News. I pulled a copy out of the bundle and left my money on top. I looked at the headlines: GERMANS FRY IN OIL AS BRITISH FRUSTRATE 2 INVASION ATTEMPTS.

Datelined Washington, December 14, the article was written by Boris Nikolayevsky, identified as a distinguished Russian publicist and historian who lived in France for many years before his arrival in New York a few days earlier. He had close contacts with French political circles and was a friend of former Premier Leon Blum.

The article stated in part:

> There have been at least two attempts by the Germans to invade England from the French coast and in both instances the Nazis were literally consumed by fire.
>
> This is the story told in France by workers from the occupied area along the channel coast and confirmed by nurses who worked in hospitals attending German soldiers who escaped the British flames.
>
> The first invasion attempt was made in August, the second early in September. Both failed as a result of the application by the British of Drake's method in destroying the Spanish armada, except that it was done not through the use of ships but of tanks of oil and gasoline set on fire by incendiary bombs from airplanes.
>
> As disclosed by Frenchmen in a position to know, the British sowed the channel with oil tanks anchored sufficiently beneath the surface to be hidden from view. Parallel with these the British anchored thousands of gasoline tanks. Then they waited for the Germans.
>
> On the first occasion the Germans advanced in 1,200 specially constructed aluminum barges, each bearing about fifty soldiers and equipment. They struck the oil and gasoline line about midway between the French and British coasts. At the same time British planes in the skies began raining indendiary bombs. In a few minutes the channel was a mass of fire enveloping the Nazi barges.

"We were caught like fish in a frying pan," was the way a German soldier who escaped from the debacle told a French nurse. Only a few thousand Germans succeeded in reaching the French coast. The rest perished in the sea or were burned to death.

The Germans tried again in September, via another route, and suffered a similar fate. People in the occupied French ports estimate as many as 80,000 German troops perished in the two attempts.

The fact is that hospitals in occupied France are filled with Nazi soldiers, all of them suffering from severe burns. Thousands of German bodies have been washed ashore.

According to reports brought back by persons who succeeded in making their way to the unoccupied zone, there was a wave of mutinies in the German army in September, many of the troops declaring they would not face again the burning sea, when they learned that a third attempt at invasion of England was being planned.

There are few German troops in the occupied French ports now, most of them having been moved inland. The population of the northern coastal area has been driven into the interior. The British appear to be well informed about German military movements in France, for no sooner is a division staff or any important military unit transferred from one place to another than it is bombarded by British planes.

I barely had time to finish reading the article before the delivery truck came speeding back and came to a screeching halt in front of the hotel. I quickly folded up my copy and hid it under my overcoat. A deliveryman jumped from the truck, grabbed the bundle of papers, tossed it back into the truck, and sped away. They did not bother to pick up the dime I had set on top of the bundle, but allowed it to fall onto the sidewalk.

The newspaperman wondered at the odd behavior, and did some

checking to learn the reason for it. He got no information from the *Dallas Morning News;* they denied any such incident had taken place.

When the early edition of the paper again hit the streets about an hour later, the article was no longer included in the makeup. As far as I know, I managed to get the only copy to survive.

Naturally I was permitted no further contact with British lesders so long as the United States remained neutral, and I could not discuss the matter with Roosevelt at this time, although we met numerous times on other matters. When we finally joined the fighting, I did visit England, and I met with many of their most important officials in government. I was kissed on the cheek by King George VI, and I was hugged by Winston Churchill. I was a guest of both Field Marshall Montgomery and Lord Louis Mountbatten. No reference was ever made to the burning of the English Channel. I was referred to as a "great friend of the British people" and remarks were made about my "great services" to them.

As a token of friendship, Mr. Churchill gave me a Meerschaum pipe, telling me that if I needed any help from the British, anything of any sort, all I had to do was to show them the pipe and they would respond. In return, I gave him a box of El Trellis cigars, which were made in San Antonio, and at the time cost about 50 cents each. He took out one of the cigars immediately and smelled it.

"Oh it is so sweet I could eat it," he said. "I could eat it." The United States was well into World War II before Roosevelt finally broke down and talked about what had happened, and then he did it when no one else was present. He said he knew I understood why it had to be a secret and why it had to remain a secret. Even the members of the White House staff and the U.S. military leaders could not be permitted to know about it. It was not just the question of U.S. neutrality, though that played a part in the secrecy. There was also an ethical or moral question involved. The massive loss of life and the pain in which the German soldiers must have died could be considered to go beyond normal rules of war. It could be argued that extreme situations might warrant extreme measures, but Roosevelt wasn't sure it could be argued convincingly.

It was then that the President shared with me a part of another important secret of the war. He gave me no specific information, but I was able to look back on the conversation later and know that he was referring to the atomic bomb. He was drinking Old Fashioneds that night, and was in a mellow, almost melancholy mood. He said something like, "Snuffy, can you visualize something so powerful that it is capable of burning a hole in a six-inch steel wall from a mile away? We are working on something right now that may have the ability to do that. It is not completed; it's still only theoretical, but we are very close to a breakthrough." He said this weapon will be the most destructive power on earth, and we will have it. He wondered aloud, though, if he had the moral and ethical right to use it.

It is a question that has been argued since atomic capability has been publicly known. It is a question that applies not just to nuclear weapons, but other modern weapons as well. In recent years it has applied to victims of Agent Orange, some of whom I have represented in lawsuits, victims who were soldiers of the nation who came in contact with the chemical. It is a question I can not attempt to answer.

However, looking back on the burning of the English Channel, I feel the British were justified in using that extreme method at the time. With Russia and the United States not yet in the war, they stood alone in the world against the wave of tyranny. Without this extreme measure, they would have been overrun just as had the rest of Europe.

Without England and North Africa as launching bases for a European invasion, the United States might have been forced to fight a war on its own shores without allies.

Today, few people remember the attitudes in the United States during 1940 and 1941, before the devastating attack on Pearl Harbor brought the American people to their senses, forcing them to look at the terrible happenings in the world. A handful of men in the government were aware of the truth and wanted to act, but they were hampered because the vast majority of the voters preferred to hide their heads in the sand. There were some American citizens who were concerned about the fact that democracy was rapidly disappearing from the face of the earth, but there were just as many—if not more—who expressed great sympathy for the cause of Hitler and Mussolini, and quite a few of them were in positions of leadership or power.

From my position on the Railroad Commission, I observed an alarming number of Nazi sympathizers, most of them in the oil business.

President Roosevelt was extremely concerned about this, because oil was crucial to the war. We discussed the problem numerous times and tried to arrive at ways of turning Texans' sympathies away from

Germany and Italy and toward Britain and France. I issued press releases and spoke out as often as possible about the need for supplying the Allies with oil, but it did little more than plant thoughts in the minds of the public. I started speaking out immediately after my first meeting with the President in the summer of 1939.

After the fall of France in 1940, we decided that something more than talk was needed. So we conceived the idea of an "Oil for Britain" day, one day in which all of the Texas oil companies would be asked to donate all of their production to England. Public sympathy for the Allied cause had increased, and we hoped that even Nazi sympathizers would feel compelled to respond in order to avoid public criticism.

However, we misjudged the depth and extent of the Nazi sympathy among oil companies, even after the United States was gearing up to join the Allied cause. We also faced the problem of the Neutrality Act. That law did not prevent oil companies from giving supplies to belligerent nations, only from selling it, and transporting it on U.S. vessels. For some time, we skirted this problem on a technicality. We had sold oil to Britain, but it was oil produced in Venezuela and refined in Texas. Texas oil producers had received very little of this market, and I feared some otherwise sympathetic oilmen might resist for this reason.

I suggested to the President that some alteration in this procedure should be made before the Oil for Britain day was announced.

In June of 1941, Roosevelt had Secretary Ickes announce that American producers would get a share of the British export trade. He urged that the Gulf region be allowed to ship some of its reserves in international trade, and stated that oil for export was not subject to restrictions of proration.

Finally, it was decided that I should not be the person to announce Oil for Britain day. Considering the way the major oil companies felt toward me, we had a better chance of compliance if their friend, Senator Pappy O'Daniel, made the official designation and issued the plea. I would do the organizational work, along with the other Railroad Commissioners.

O'Daniel made the announcement at the end of July, setting aside August 10 as the day for producing the oil. However, it had to be postponed to August 17; the invited public officials—President Roosevelt, Secretary of the Navy Frank Knox, Secretary Ickes, and British Ambassador, Lord Halifax—were to arrive in Austin the following day for presentation ceremonies.

Almost as soon as Oil for Britain Day was announced, the furor started. Although I had worked out the details to accomplish the event, major oil companies protested that it wasn't possible, crying that the amount of oil could not be properly calculated; that it could not be separated in the pipeline from other oil; and that individual shares could become confused. All that was for the benefit of their public image, to keep them from looking bad when they did not comply. The whole procedure was very simple. England would not be shipped the actual oil produced on that day, but would receive warrants for free oil for the amount donated.

A great many of the independent oil companies complied willingly. None of the majors complied, and most of them—including Humble, Standard, the Texas Company, Shell, and Rowan and Nichols—fought actively against it.

As a result, only 11,332 barrels of oil were produced for the British war effort, barely enough to cover the bottom of a tanker.

Oil for Britain Day was a fiasco. It had been sabotaged by the major oil companies, and they had managed to do so without damaging their public image.

Part IV
SUPPLY LINES

With Laura Jones Sadler in New Orleans, the day after the military wedding.

The Meerschaum pipe, a gift from Winston Churchill.

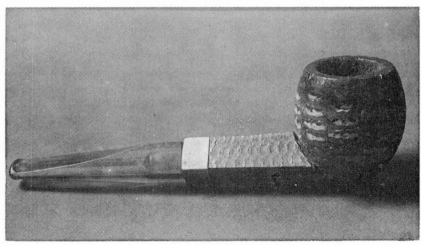

21

Preparing for War

In January, 1941, the Railroad Commission went through two changes. Olin Culberson replaced Lon Smith, and Ernest O. Thompson became chairman of the Commission. The alignment on most issues, however, remained two to one. Olin and I held the deciding vote against Thompson. Culberson had not been the choice of the big oil companies in the campaign, but neither had he been my choice. For a time they had hoped he might be brought—or bought—over to their side, but his integrity quickly became clear to them.

Since they couldn't buy themselves a Railroad Commission, they decided to try to buy themselves a legislature.

As soon as the state legislature convened in 1941, the big oil companies revived the idea of an oil and gas commission. They hired Clint Small, Sr., a lawyer from Amarillo and a former state senator, to get the bill introduced and passed. They also hired two men, one a former member of the legislature and the other an ex-convict, to handle payoffs to the legislators. The big oil companies had contributed over a million dollars for payoffs.

This time they meant business, and it was clear they had a winning chance. We decided that the Railroad Commission would need to hire some lobbyists. As principal lobbyist, we engaged Bob Calvert, later to become chief of the Texas Supreme Court. However, our lobbyists could use only their power of persuasion in rounding up votes against the oil and gas commission bill. They could not—and would not—offer bribes.

Naturally the big oil companies had the advantage. Money has a way of talking louder than words. We had Dorsey Hardeman, a representative from San Angelo, and Lester Boone, of Ft. Worth, as our floor leaders in the legislature, and they did their damnedest to get the votes we needed, but we, and out lobbyists, were restricted to the gallery and to the halls outside. They were able to get one of their men, the former congressman, onto the House floor. The only advantage we had was that our man, Bob Calvert, had formerly been the Speaker of the House. He knew which men were honorable. He also knew the political tricks to use to get a bill through or to get it blocked.

During the debate on the bill, we watched as their man on the floor went around talking to each legislator, offering "back campaign expenses." If the legislator was interested, their lobbyist would point up at the gallery, and their bag-man would hold up his bag of money. If the legislator was interested, their floor man would come up to the gallery, get the needed amount from the bag, and return to the floor.

Before too long it appeared we would be outvoted. They were clearly making enough pay-offs to get a majority vote in favor of the bill.

Good luck arrived in unexpected form. Clint Small's son was a student at the University of Texas; he had some trouble and had been arrested. When the trial came up, the father took a day off from his lobbying to go to court to help his son. It was our good fortune he took a number of his friendly legislators with him to serve as character witnesses.

We moved swiftly. Our floor leaders, Hardeman and Boone, brought up the oil and gas commission bill out of order. In the absence of the leading legislators who favored the bill, they moved to strike out the enacting clause of the legislation. Their motion passed, and the bill was effectively killed.

The big oil companies were desperate. They had tried every legal means (and quite a few illegal ones) to get rid of an unsympathetic Railroad Commission. In 1941, they revived the idea of trying to impeach me. They had no basis for an impeachment, so they groped about to manufacture one and pay for evidence against me.

I had no warning of what was happening until Augustine Salaya, a member of the legislature from Brownsville, came to my office. He told the receptionist he had to talk to me immediately; it was an emergency.

I went to the reception room. Salaya told me, "There's a group of legislators ready to file impeachment charges against you." He named the legislators. "I don't know what the evidence is, but it was given to them by a lobbyist for the Magnolia Petroleum Company."

I knew the lobbyist, and I didn't like what I knew. However, there was one lobbyist, recently hired by Magnolia, who was honest and respectable. "Is Hugh Steward involved in this at all?" I asked Salaya.

"Hugh is embarrassed about the situation," he replied. "He's been trying to shut the other lobbyist up, but he says he's taking orders direct from above."

That man was general counsel for Magnolia (and he had been a college roommate of Bob Hoffman, who started the Denton trouble during my 1938 campaign and had died shortly afterward).

One man I knew pulled considerable weight in the Magnolia organization—former Governor Dan Moody. I knew a few things that Moody would prefer not to have revealed, so I carried considerable weight with him. His office was near mine. I called Moody and asked him to come to my office. I also called Hugh Steward.

I asked Hugh to tell Moody everything. Hugh revealed the fact that the affidavits Kennedy had obtained from supposed "witnesses" were outright lies, bought and paid for. He also told him that the other lobbyist was taking his orders directly from Magnolia's General Counsel. "I've tried to get this thing stopped," Steward said finally. "I don't have any authority. Orders come from the attorney, but I don't want to have anything to do with this."

"I want you to talk to the Board of Directors of Magnolia," I told Moody. "I want you to tell them that I'm giving them until midnight tonight to get rid of both those men. If they don't, I am going to go out and shut down and padlock every Magnolia well in the state of Texas by noon tomorrow. And I'll tell the public why I did it."

Dan Moody hated to fly, but he chartered an airplane and flew to Dallas.

I gave him my unlisted home phone number and told him to call me as soon as he had a decision. His call came through late that night.

He told me, with a note of relief in his voice, "The General Counsel has resigned. He will announce his retirement."

"There's a difference between resigning and retiring. Which is it?" I asked.

Moody said he was resigning.

"What about the lobbyist?" I asked.

"There's a complication there," Moody said. "The Board of Directors is still here. They're willing to fire him, but they want me to ask if you'll allow them to give him a farm-out in Louisiana. They're in a difficult spot with him. If they fire him without giving him some kind of compensation, he might be inclined to shoot off his mouth."

A farm-out is a lease where there is a guaranteed production of oil.

"No farm-out," I said. "If they give him anything, I'll padlock the wells. You can tell your board that it's up to them to brush the buffalo chips off their shoulders and wipe their fannies."

I held the phone while Moody went back to the Board of Directors. In a short time, he came back to tell me, "It's settled. The lobbyist gets nothing. He's fired."

That was as much as I could expect from the Board of Magnolia. Two other men were involved in this, but they were not official employees of Magnolia. They were in the government, so I had to take care of them myself. One was a judge in Longview, the other a Texas Ranger known as "Lone Wolf," who had an undeserved reputation as a gunman. (He had gained his reputation by killing a man "in self-defense." Somehow it was never revealed that the man he had killed had been a paralytic in a wheelchair. No longer able to pull the wool over the eyes of Texans, he went to Hollywood where he obtained work as an advisor for a television series.)

At the time, the three individual members of the Public Safety Commission had the power to send Texas Rangers out on assignment, without majority approval. On the judge's order, Lone Wolf had been sent to collect the affidavits against me, offering $50 to anyone in Gregg County who would sign that they had witnessed wrongdoing.

I arranged for a full meeting of the Public Safety Commission, telling the other two members what had happened. In that meeting, the Safety Commission passed an order that no single member of their board could issue orders to Texas Rangers. And then they went into an investigation of the Ranger's activities. It was the beginning of the end for Lone Wolf, at least in Texas.

By the middle of 1941, the big oil companies began to realize they could not circumvent the law and get special privileges in the State of Texas, at least not as long as Olin Culberson and I were on the Railroad Commission. There were a few other businessmen, however, who had not learned that lesson. The Railroad Commission in Texas regulates more than just the oil business. It sets freight rates, regulating both railroad and trucking lines, and approves utility rates.

From the time I joined the Railroad Commission, I was involved in many landmark decisions on these matters, but most were not as spectacular as the ones involving the oil business, and the fights and battles that resulted from them weren't as far-reaching. There was one disgruntled trucker who was upset at a decision on freight rates who one day burst into my office with a gun. He threatened to kill me, but there were so many attempts on my life they got boring after awhile.

In 1941, however, there was one important battle involving public utilities. The Railroad Commission had received numerous complaints against the Lone Star Gas Company for excessive rates. A number of cities, led by Dallas, asked for an investigation. Lone Star was getting a gas gate-rate of 40 cents per thousand cubic feet. Dallas felt a rate of 19 cents per thousand cubic feet was sufficient.

The question of fair gas utility rates had been a major issue of Olin Culberson's campaign. That had been his specialty, and he had considerable experience with the utility companies and knew they were overcharging the customers. He felt a rate of 34 cents per thousand cubic feet would be fair.

Before we could get into our investigation, the Lone Star Gas Company went to court, seeking an injunction to prevent us from having access to their records and account books. Roy Coffee, the attorney for Lone Star, made the mistake of stopping by my office on his way to deliver the opinion he had written for the Texas Supreme Court to issue on granting the injunction.

Coffee was rather proud of the fact that the Chief Justice of the Texas Supreme Court had asked him to write the opinion, and he was eager to let us know that we would not be permitted within 100 feet of Lone Star's offices, books, or records. He left a copy in the Railroad Commission office, and then proceeded to go upstairs to give the original to the Chief Justice. Apparently Coffee was not aware that most government offices stamped any document with the date and time received.

Olin and I made a few choice comments about the Chief Justice to other officials in the Capitol building. The next day, the Chief Justice came down to see me saying angrily he'd heard that Olin and I had spread lies about him and the way he did his job. "If you don't stop, you're going to be in trouble," he said.

"Now Judge," I said pleasantly. "I'll tell you exactly! I've said that I saw your opinion before you did, and it's the truth. Roy Coffee brought a copy by my office on his way to you. If you'll compare the stamp on mine with the stamp on yours, you'll see a difference of about twenty minutes. If you don't want it said that an opinion of yours is written by a Lone Star lawyer, then don't have a Lone Star lawyer write it."

I took him in to Olin Culberson. "Judge, I'll tell you what I said

about you, and it's the truth. I said you're a damned political whore,"
Olin said.

The Chief Justice turned purple, spluttered a moment, then stalked
out of the office.

A day later I studied a map of gas lines and happened to notice that
Lone Star Gas had a seventeen-mile loop into Oklahoma. That meant
that the Federal Power Commission could be brought into the matter. I
told Olin about it. "Let's go to Washington."

The Federal Power Commission agreed to join us in an investigation. The Texas court injunction did not prevent the federals from
access to Lone Star's records. When the audit of the company was
complete and we began the hearings in Washington, Deck Hulsey,
president of Lone Star, called me into the hall.

He said we could call off the hearings. "We've decided we'll take a
rate of 32 cents."

"Deck," I said, "we were willing to compromise on 34 cents, but you
took us to court and fought us and got it overturned."

He said they had decided they could make money at 32 cents.

"One of the auditors knows the reason," he said. "I think you know
the reason, too."

"Have you cleared this rate with your holding company in
Pittsburg?"

He assured me that he had, so I went back into the hearing and
announced that the Lone Star Gas Company had decided to take a 32
cent rate.

There were also some important changes in freight hauling rates in
1941. For fifty years, Texas had had both intrastate and interstate rate
differentials that had made shipping within, from, and to the state
much more expensive than it was in the East and North. The freight
rates were somewhat lower even in the states surrounding Texas. Texas
had been very generous to the railroads, giving them 30 million acres of
state land to help them establish rail routes, yet they were overcharging
Texas shippers about $17 million a year.

We had investigated this and worked on a new set of rates from the
time I had first taken office. In 1941, the Interstate Commerce
Commission began its own inquiry into freight differentials throughout
the United States, and we joined with them in adjusting the rates for
Texas, making them more equitable.

Many of the matters we had to consider in 1941 involved mobilizing the nation for war. Special freight rates had to be established for war supplies and war priority items. Oil production had to be set for military production and home use. Plans had to be drawn for possible rationing of critical supplies. And perhaps most important, we planned for interstate pipelines in case of war, since tankers had to move in international waters between the East Coast and the Gulf of Mexico.

This problem would be the most troublesome, not because pipelines were difficult to build, but because of the involvement of Harold Ickes.

I had fought the Cole Committee for months to keep them from passing legislation giving Ickes control of the oil business in the United States, and I had succeeded. Now, because of war preparations, it appeared all of my effort had been for nothing. In early June of 1941, the President called me to Washington to meet with him to discuss several matters, none of them particularly pleasant to me.

The most important matter was the need for federal control of oil during wartime, and Roosevelt wanted to appoint Harold Ickes as Federal Oil Coordinator. We discussed the subject at considerable length. I could see the need for federal coordination of natural resources in a time of crisis, but I was concerned about the possibility that it might be maintained when the crisis passed. And I was very much opposed to placing the power in the hands of Ickes, our agreement to be "good friends" notwithstanding. But Roosevelt had a good memory, and he was able to point out all of the failures of the states to control the flow of oil on their own.

I pointed out that invariably Ickes favored the major companies in all his proposals and actions. And the President pointed out that, "Icky will admit when he's wrong. He respects you and listens to you."

Finally I gave in and agreed that I would support the appointment publicly. On June 11, in Washington, I issued the following statement to the press, after denying Ickes would be an "Oil Czar":

> Texas, California, and Illinois must get their houses in order if they expect to avoid federal control of the oil business. Naturally, Texas should lead the way since it is the most vitally affected state when it comes to oil regulation. I believe authorities here in Washington had rather see states get their own business straight than be forced to take over.

Interest which Texas oilmen once manifested in trying to keep federal control out has sadly waned. These men, whose industry affects over 1,000,000 Texans have gone to sleep at the wheel, and it is now high time they get ready to cooperate or the state will have the most stringent form of federal regulation. These statements are not threats. They are not imaginative. They constitute firsthand information and are true facts.

Now pending in the Senate are House bills 942 and 199, the latter making oil proration permanent. It is imperative that both of these bills receive approval or we will have Washington regulating and controlling our oil business. This fact cannot be too strongly emphasized. After talking to Administration leaders and conferring with Coordinator Ickes it is my sincere and honest opinion that House bills 942 and 199 are compulsory in preventing unwanted federal regulation.

I had hoped that my statements, added to the Ickes appointment, might scare the oilmen into cleaning up their act. Some responded positively, but most continued to "sleep at the wheel." On the other hand, Ickes listened and took my advice on many matters, at least in the beginning. And he graciously shared the credit for the fifty percent sharing plan when it was announced, granting domestic oil producers part of the European war market. However, less than a year later, we were at each other's throats over the proposed interstate pipeline. He wanted the line from the Texas Panhandle to Chicago, which would increase oil production in the Panhandle and cut out the little guys. I insisted on the construction of a pipeline from East Texas to Salem, Illinois. I also believed that we needed a pipeline from Texas to the East Coast, to avoid excessive shipments through the Great Lakes.

Another unpleasant matter Roosevelt wanted to discuss with me that day was his desire to have Congressman Lyndon Johnson elected to the U.S. Senate. Senator Morris Sheppard had died in April, and a special election had been called in Texas to fill his office. Several candidates had already filed, including Governor O'Daniel and Congressman Lyndon Johnson.

I could understand why the President would not want O'Daniel elected, but I was not particularly keen on Johnson.

"Why would you want Johnson elected?" I asked. "He's a son-of-a-bitch."

"Yes," Roosevelt replied. "But I don't mind if a man's a son-of-a-bitch, as long as he's my son-of-a-bitch."

I reminded him that only a year ago, Johnson had been Garner's son-of-a-bitch, but that didn't seem to matter to the President. "We've got to have two good loyal senators from Texas. Johnson's got to be elected, and you've got to see to it that he is. Do whatever you have to do, but get him that Senate seat."

Reluctantly, I did what the President asked. I returned to Texas and organized all of my loyal supporters to work for Johnson's election. With some of those who knew me very well, such as Owen Kilday of San Antonio, I had to be honest. I had to tell them that the order had come from the President, and I quoted his words to me.

Of course Roosevelt did everything he could to help. Undersecretary of the Interior Alvin Wirtz, who had done much at the "Stop-Garner" Waco convention, resigned his job in Washington to serve as Lyndon's campaign manager. As election day drew near, the candidate was getting good responses wherever he appeared. It was going to be a tight race, but Johnson had a good chance of winning.

I went down to Houston for Johnson's last campaign speech. He threw his arms around me. "Every place I've gone to speak, I've had ten to twenty people come to me and say they were there because of Jerry Sadler," he said. "I want you to know I appreciate what you've done."

On election day I went to San Antonio, and I spent the day and evening at our campaign office there. We had a direct line to the Election Bureau in Dallas, and we could keep up with the votes as they were counted.

At one point, one of our workers came in and asked how far behind Johnson was. I didn't think anything about it; workers were always asking. I told him, "about 10,000 votes."

I went home to Austin that night, and Johnson seemed to be ahead, but it was still close. The next day, Lyndon seemed to be sufficiently ahead for the Election Bureau to declare him the winner, although there were a few counties still unreported. I soon found out why Johnson was so far ahead. There were about 11,000 more votes in the boxes at San Antonio than there were registered voters. It was too late to do anything about it; all I could do was hope O'Daniel's men didn't notice the discrepancy.

I was sitting with Alvin Wirtz at my house in Austin, when Lyndon came by to thank me. He was really excited about the outcome of the election. He was so eager to be Senator, he already had his bags packed and was ready to fly to Washington that day. He was effusive in his gratitude to me, saying he knew how much I had done. He assured me he would never forget it. He hugged me, shook my hand, and put his long arm around my shoulder. Nobody could gush like Lyndon Johnson if he thought you were kissing his ass. He certainly gushed that day.

When he had finished, I got my secretary, Ted Read, to drive Johnson to the airport to take a plane to Dallas, where he'd transfer to another plane for Washington.

After Lyndon left, I looked at Alvin, and he had a funny little smirk on his face. Alvin Wirtz was a man who didn't talk much.

"It looks like Lyndon might bubble over completely before he makes it to Dallas," I said.

Lyndon couldn't have been more than halfway to Dallas before my phone rang. It was Roosevelt. He said one of his men keeping tabs on the election told him, "They've brought in Jasper County, and it's thrown Johnson behind."

"That's impossible," I said. "They don't have that many votes in Jasper County. What's the count?"

He told me, and I exclaimed, "That's five times the number of poll taxes in the county. But that's not too unusual in Jasper County; the chairman down there is one of Jim Ferguson's men." (Ferguson was managing O'Daniel's campaign.)

"Can you come to Washington tomorrow?" he asked.

"Yes," I replied, trying to figure out how to tell him about the votes in San Antonio.

"Come to my office as soon as you get to town," he told me.

By the time I arrived in Washington, all of the election returns had come in, and it had been announced officially that Pappy O'Daniel had been elected Senator instead of Lyndon Johnson. In a way I was relieved. The matter of the extra votes in San Antonio might never come up.

As soon as I arrived at the White House, General Watson pushed me into the President's office.

"Well, Snuffy," the President said, "we're going to impeach O'Daniel, and then we're going to send that impeached son-of-a-bitch to the penitentiary."

"Before you do anything," I said, "I think you ought to know that there were 11,000 unregistered votes cast in San Antonio, and they were cast for Lyndon Johnson."

Roosevelt was startled for a moment, but then he grinned. "Well, Snuffy," he said, "I guess we're not going to impeach the son-of-a-bitch after all."

22

Joining the Army

The biggest dispute Roosevelt and I ever had was over my decision to resign from the Railroad Commission to join the army. It continued for over a year, and it was the one subject on which we were unable to compromise. He was adamant that I remain on the Commission; and I was just as adamant that this was a free country and even the President could not keep me from serving it as I saw fit. The country needed fighter pilots for the Air Corps, and I was a trained pilot, which made me one step ahead in the game.

I talked to General Henry H. "Hap" Arnold about it, and he was interested. Because of my previous military record, I could go in as a captain. General Arnold had already begun to process the necessary papers when the President got into the act.

The showdown started because of Ernest O. Thompson, who had returned to uniform, reporting for service in Louisiana. He had not resigned his position on the Railroad Commission to do so. (By law, elected officials did not need to resign for military service.) One day Thompson called the Commission office from his military base. He wanted me to set up a press conference for him. There were always reporters around the Capitol building, and with three phones in the Commission office, the reporters could gather around them to listen to what Thompson had to say.

Thompson was masterful at manufacturing publicity. He told the reporters there had been a mock battle involving the troops in Louisiana (a "battle" between the North and the South). He—Thompson—had commanded the troops from the South, and they had whipped the hell out of the North.

The story appeared in the newspapers the next morning, and within a matter of hours General Kreuger, who commanded the troops stationed in Louisiana, appeared in my office. He brought with him a Sergeant, a trained court reporter. General Kreuger was a very angry man.

"The Sergeant will take down everything you say," the General told me. "And I'm going to ask you to sign the statement."

I told him I would be glad to make a statement.

"Did he ask you to call in the press and put them on the telephones?" he asked.

"Yes, sir, he did," I replied. "But before I answer any more questions, would you tell me why you're asking them?"

"Yes," General Kreuger said. "Colonel Thompson didn't know what the hell he was talking about. He wasn't even in the battle. He was drunk in a honky-tonk at the time. The army cannot tolerate this kind of irresponsible behavior."

I gave General Krueger the full story and signed my statement. The next day, Thompson was back in the Railroad Commission office. He told the inquiring press that the President had personally requested he return to Austin, that he was needed far more on the Commission than in the military.

When that statement appeared in newspapers, I received a call from President Roosevelt, asking me to Washington. He had no communication with Thompson and certainly had not made the statement Thompson had attributed to him. He was angry.

At the President's office, I learned he had acquired the papers that General Arnold had been processing for me, including my record from the Twelfth Cavalry. He was just as upset about my application for service as he was about Thompson's statements.

"Snuffy," he said strongly, "I don't want you to leave the Railroad Commission. You are the one I need on there, not that red-headed son-of-a-bitch. That red-headed son-of-a-bitch is a revolving son-of-a-bitch. Whatever direction he's facing, he's going to shoot off his mouth, and you can never be sure when he's telling the truth. If you leave the Commission, Thompson has a good chance of gaining control, and I don't want that. I know he tried to prevent you from stopping shipments of oil to Germany and Italy, and I know the many untruths he attributes to me."

He picked up the papers. "This is your application for the Air Corps," he said, and he tore them up, picked up his cigarette lighter, and burned the shreds over his wastebasket, his way of destroying something he wanted no trace of. "Now there is no file on that, and I want you to forget this."

I was angry. "Did that include my record in the Twelfth Cavalry?" I asked.

"No," Roosevelt said, "I left that intact. But if I have to, I'll destroy that too, just to keep you on the Commission."

"I can always join the army as a buck private," I threatened. "This is still a free country, and even you can't keep me from doing that."

"No," he said, grinning, "but I could try."

Although I felt he was being unfair, I couldn't stay angry at Roosevelt for long, because I understood his reasons. "Mr. President," I said, still somewhat cool, "I will agree to stay on the Commission for now. But only with the understanding that—six months after the U.S. gets into the war—I am going into the service."

FDR said we would see about that "when the time comes."

From the middle of 1941 to the middle of 1942, I traveled to Washington so often I've lost track of the different times I conferred with the President. We did discuss my military service on several occasions. I tried to reason with him, offering ways around each of his objections, but he remained obstinate about my remaining with the Commission. I told him I'd find a way of naming my successor so that no one would gain control of the Commission. He felt that was too risky. After Ickes was appointed Federal Oil Coordinator, and the National Conference of Regulatory Authorities was formed, I pointed out the Commission was no longer quite so important. If Thompson screwed things up, the federal authorities could overrule him. Roosevelt pointed out, "That's the reason I appointed you to the National Conference of Regulatory Authorities, so you would be exempt from the draft law. I need you here."

Immediately after the December 7, 1941 attack on Pearl Harbor, Culberson and I went to Washington to confer with Harold Ickes and the President, to work out the plan of operation for the duration of the war. Nothing was said about my joining the army, but it was in the back of my mind all the time I was there. Six months was what I had promised Roosevelt; that gave me until May.

In meetings of the National Conference of Regulatory Authorities, I saw a lot of Frank Phillips, of Phillips Petroleum; Judge J.C. Hunter, of Mid-Continent Oil and Gas; and Jesse Jones. Two days before I planned to return to Texas, Judge Hunter told me a group of the men wished to give a big party in my honor. They had a special 27-pound steak flown in from Texas for the occasion. I was embarrassed about the honor, but I was also touched.

It was an elaborate affair at the Shoreham Hotel, with a large number of guests. When I entered, a string band was playing "Casey Would Waltz with the Strawberry Blonde," but they replaced "Casey" with "Jerry," and as my date for the evening they produced a strawberry blonde.

The drinks must have been spiked with something, because I started slipping very fast. No sooner had I finished one than I was handed another. Judge Hunter took me on a tour of the place, showing me the bedroom suites that surrounded the dining area. All the time, the strawberry blonde was hanging onto my arm. Judge Hunter took me into one bedroom that had a beautiful four-poster bed with drop curtains on it. "This is where you and your strawberry blonde are going to sleep tonight," he said.

"Just a minute," I said. "I'm not going to take any substitutes. I won't agree to any of this until I see if this is a real strawberry blonde."

I raised her dress; sure enough, she was for real. (By this time, I was pretty near drunk.)

Judge Hunter laughed. "Now, let's go eat that 27-pound steak."

And that was the last thing I remember. The next thing I knew I was waking up in my own hotel room with the worst hangover I'd ever experienced. The reason I awoke was a ringing telephone.

"The President wants to see you right away," General Watson said.

I can't think of too many things a man with a hangover would less like to hear. I told Watson I was unwell and I wasn't sure I could make it to the White House. "I'll order a gallon of grapefruit juice sent to my room," I said. "After I've consumed most of that, maybe I'll see if I can get over there."

I was still not feeling up to snuff when I arrived at the President's office. General Watson ushered me in to President Roosevelt, who at once opened the right-hand drawer of his desk and pulled out two long-handled gourds.

"What are you doing with those?" I asked, puzzled.

He said he had called Selman Evans in Tennessee and asked him to send them by airplane.

"What the hell for?" I asked.

"I want you to show me," he said. "How does a woman take a douche with a gourd."

I wondered if my hangover had affected my brain or if the President had slipped a cog in his. "What are you talking about?" I asked.

"You don't remember?" he asked, slightly disappointed.

"I don't remember anything about douches and gourds," I said.

He said one of his men was at the dinner party. He'd returned and told Roosevelt what happened. "After they gave you a toast, you told them you wanted to make one. You made a speech, a very flowery one. When you finished, you said you were leaving because they had insulted you. They had given you a 27-pound steak, a strawberry blonde, and a four-poster bed with curtains on it, but they hadn't furnished you with douche gourds. You weren't going to bed with that strawberry blonde until she had taken a douche with a gourd." The President grinned. "Now, I have been wondering all night how a woman would take a douche with a gourd. I've heard of all sorts of things but never that."

"I've never heard of it either," I said, taking one of the gourds and examining it. "I used to drink water out of a gourd when I was a kid. I guess a woman could take a douche sort of the same way, cutting a big hole in the dipper end and a small hole in the handle end, then lying down in the bathtub and attaching it to the faucet."

The President roared with laughter. "Well, Snuffy, maybe you've invented something," he said. "But it's hard to believe you came up with it when you were drunk."

"I don't know why I said it," I told him. "I guess I was just looking for some reason to tell them to go to hell so I could get out of there."

"Well, I must admit you know how to keep your mouth shut," Roosevelt said. He told me the reason he had his man at the dinner was because he had heard they were going to get me drunk to find out any secrets I might have. "From what I hear you were about as drunk as a man can be and still stand up, and they didn't get anything out of you except your invention of douche gourds."

When Olin and I returned to Austin, we called a statewide oil meeting to announce the oil policy for the duration of the war. It was a massive meeting, with officers and representatives from all the oil companies, big and small, and with government members as well. We had to hold it in the legislative chambers. Suddenly the oilmen were the most patriotic bunch you ever saw, probably because they knew they were going to make a bundle off the war.

Some of the men I listened to that day had, only a few months before, been complaining about the fact that they could no longer sell oil to Germany and Italy. Now, listening to them talk about how they would help their country by producing more oil, I grew angry. I decided to provide a few choice comments for them.

I reminded them that many had fought me when I tried to cut off oil deliveries to the Axis powers. I reminded them that they had refused to cooperate with Oil for Britain day. I reminded them that many had not even wanted to sell their oil to the Allies. And I concluded, "Now there is one oilman here today who still prefers Hitler to his own country. He sits at the back of this chamber near the door . . . there, in a folding chair. That man is still actively working as an agent for Nazi Germany . . . Remain seated while I walk down the aisle, so that I can point him out to you . . .

I walked down the aisle of the legislative chambers. As I approached that man, he stuck out his hand to shake mine. "No," I said, "I won't shake hands with you, you Hitler-loving son-of-a-bitch." And then I walked out.

The next morning the oilman's body was found dead in a Houston hotel room. The official cause of death was "heart failure." More likely it was a case of suicide or murder by a fellow agent.

I turned over names of two other German spies to the FBI. One worked for the Railroad Commission, and the other for the Highway Commission. They were picked up by the FBI, and I never heard of them again.

I had warned the President that I intended to join the army six months after we entered the war. Though we saw much of each other during the first few months of 1942, we did not discuss my plans further. I decided that he had entirely forgotten it. I also assumed there would be no record remaining of my earlier military service. I made my plans to enlist as a buck private.

In May I announced my plans to the press and reported to San Antonio for my physical examination.

In the middle of my examination, I was standing naked on the weight scales, when a Medical Corps captain came to tell me that the President of the United States was on the telephone.

"Tell him to go to hell," I said.

"I can't do that," the Captain said. "I'm in the service, and he's my commander-in-chief."

"Then tell him I'll call him tonight," I said. "On second thought, tell him I won't call him before tonight."

"All right," the captain replied. "I can tell him that."

At first the captain was reluctant to pass me on my physical. I was overweight, and I had a plastic hip. But finally, he could see I wanted to get into the army pretty bad, so he passed me. "But you'll have to sign some waivers on your hip and promise to lose some weight." He wrote on my record, "obese but not fat."

Having passed my physical, all I had to do was wait for my call to duty. It would be difficult entering the army as a buck private at age 34, but I was determined to do it.

I called the President that night. "You thought I had forgotten," the President said, "but I hadn't. I remember you said that six months after we got into the war you were going into the service. I wasn't planning to stop you; in fact, I have something special in mind for you to do. But before you go, you've got to help me out with the Railroad Commission. You once said you could pick your successor, and I want you to do that. Can you come to Washington this week?"

As usual, I responded to his request. But first I checked with Governor Coke Stevenson to be sure he would appoint my choice as successor. Stevenson assured me that he would appoint anyone I might name; there would be no problem; it was a solemn promise. I told the Governor and also the President I wanted to appoint Jim Kilday of San Antonio, currently working with the Commission as Director of Motor Transportation. They both approved.

What Roosevelt planned for me in the Army was unexpected. "There's one very important job that has to be done," he said, "that can use your special talents. Getting the war supplies to the Russians. Until we can get a foothold on Europe, it's going to be up to Russia to hold back the Germans and keep them occupied. Right now we've got our hands full with the Japanese."

My resignation from the Railroad Commission did not go as smoothly as anticipated. The time approached, and I learned Governor Stevenson did not intend to live up to his promise. Instead, he intended—on the request of the Standard Oil Company—to appoint Beauford Jester, of Corsicana, a lawyer for Magnolia Petroleum. Roosevelt had feared something like this and expressed concern.

"Don't worry," I assured the President. "I still have a trick up my sleeve. Stevenson has been pressing me to get my resignaton in. I've told him I'm not ready, because I still have to lose some weight. The deadline for filng for office in this year's primary is June 1. I'll get Jim Kilday to file for my position that day, and I'll arrange to have my resignation turned over to the Governor late that evening."

It was a good idea, but it backfired. Governor Stevenson refused to accept my resignation and declared the office would be vacated on June

17, when my army duties were scheduled to begin. On that date, the State Democratic Committee would meet and accept applications for the post. The names they approved would appear on the June 25 primary ballot.

Immediately, I withdrew my resignation, announcing that I would continue to hold office as Railroad Commissioner until my term expired. By Texas law, this was permitted in wartime. Meanwhile, Coke Stevenson held firm in his decision that the office would be vacant as of June 17, and he stated he would appoint the winner of the primary to hold that office until the August election.

When the Texas Democratic Committee met, they accepted Beauford Jester and nine others as candidates for my office in the primary. They refused to accept Jim Kilday, the only one who had filed by the legal deadlne.

Both Kilday and I had to resort to the courts, each filing our own separate cases. We both lost. In my case, the Texas Supreme Court interpreted the law permitting officeholders to maintain their office while serving in the military to apply only to reserve officers and the National Guard. Enlisted men would be required to give up their elected offices.

Standard Oil won. Beauford Jester was elected, and shortly therefter was made Railroad Commission Chairman. The voting alignment on the Commission was now Thompson and Jester against Culberson, and decisions would return to favoring the big oil companies.

All this was no longer my problem. I was in the army, and I had an entirely new set of problems to face. When my orders came through, I was made a first-lieutenant and was instructed to report to the Port of Embarkation at New Orleans. My job was to be O.I.C., at least temporarily. Looking it up in the manual, I found O.I.C. meant "Officer in Charge of Crewing."

Like many an enlisted man, I chose to marry before going overseas. I had been seeing Laura Jones since we had met during the 1940 campaign, and had contemplated proposing marriage for some time. We were married on September 4, in a military ceremony performed at the U.S. Army chapel in New Orleans.

23

New Orleans to Bombay

The job I was handed during those first army weeks wasn't exactly what I expected from military service. As Officer in Charge of Crewing, I was responsible for hiring crews for all of the ships that embarked from the Port of New Orleans. From that description, it may sound that I was running a glorified employment service. Nothing is less accurate.

One of the first problems I dealt with involved a Belgian cargo ship that had been at sea when war began. The captain was a Belgian, the crew was Chinese. When the ship docked at New Orleans the crew had struck, staying aboard ship but performing no work.

I took some military police and went to the docks to see about the trouble, a stalemate. That ship, the largest in port at the time, was a mess; the nastiest scene I think I had ever witnessed. The uncaring Chinese crew had defecated all over the deck and even in their staterooms, and they sat or lay about in the midst of the mess. When I opened the door of one stateroom, I discovered two Chinamen in the act of sodomy. The one who was performing the act got very angry at the intrusion. He started to threaten me. To quiet him down one of the M.P.s slugged him.

We arrested the whole crew, and I went to court to see Federal Judge Borah. He said he would arrange for the Chinese to be taken care of until the end of the war.

On another occasion, I was asked to arrange for a shipment of aviation fuel from Houston through the Panama Canal to one of the Pacific islands. German U-Boats patrolled the Gulf of Mexico, so this would be an extremely difficult assignment for a merchant ship, but fuel was badly needed by our Pacific forces.

One oil tanker in port looked more like a submarine; it had sort of a rounded top, and it could carry 35,000 barrels of gasoline. Due to its odd appearance, the German U-boats might allow the tanker through shipping lanes without attacking it. One sea captain smart enough to elude them was Captain Watlers. He lived in Port Arthur, and he was then out of work, recently fired by Gulf Oil Corporation because of a disagreement with their management. His last command had been as skipper of the tanker, *Gulf Light*, which had been destroyed by submarine fire off the New Jersey coast.

I called Captain Watlers and asked him if he could come to New Orleans, with no questions asked. He agreed to arrive there the next morning.

Captain Watlers, a man in his sixties, had a temper. Anyone who crossed him would be taking a big risk. He kept a pipe in his mouth, although he hardly ever lit it. Unpredictable when angry, there was one sure sign that his ire was rising: he'd bite his pipe-stem in two, throw away the pipe end, and keep the stem between his teeth. This meant, whenever at sea, he had to have a good supply of pipes.

Watlers arrived in New Orleans, and I told him of the mission without revealing the destination. That would be given to him in sealed orders if he accepted the job. I took him to the docks and showed him the odd-looking tanker. Accompanied by the first mate, we took an inspection tour of the ship. It was clear from the outset that the first mate didn't think too highly of Captain Watlers, who said very little as various problems were pointed out.

When we reached the captain's quarters, he had not yet committed himself to the mission, and the first mate's mouth was running in high gear. He told Watlers what he would have to do and what he could not do. The mate ran on about how long he had been with the ship and how well he knew its problems. But the thing that prodded the Captain's rise in temper was the mate's repeated insistence that Watlers was too old to fool with a tub like this one.

We stood beside a little four-by-four desk in the Captain's quarters when Watler's teeth broke through the pipestem. Angrily, he threw away the pipe bowl, slammed his left foot against the desk, and reached down and pulled a leg off the desk. He had hit the mate three or four times with the desk leg before I managed to pull him off.

"Now by God we'll see who is too old!" Watlers told the mate. "I am now the Captain of this ship, and I'm going to run things! And don't think you're going to quit! You're going with me, and you're going to take orders from me . . ."

Plenty of problems needed attending to before our "submarine" tanker could set out on its mission. We hired machinists to work on it

235

and improved it enough to take it to Houston. There, other problems were taken care of. One engine was completely shot, but the engineer felt he could keep the other one running for at least three months if we could obtain 60-weight oil. Oil at that weight was hard to come by, but I went out to the Shell Laboratories and we worked out a solution, producing ten drums of oil that would meet the needs.

Captain Watlers had one special supply request. He ordered a thousand feet of cotton sash-cord, and thirty of the heaviest window sash weights we could find. He told me if he had to make Germans think the tanker was a submarine, he'd have to make it behave like one. He could not use his radio, and would travel only at night. "During the day," he said, "I'll pull in along the coast of Mexico and lay in among the rocks. To do that, I need some way of sounding for the ocean floor."

I found his sash cord and his sash weights. I also got him two dozen extra pipes, hoping that they would get him to his destination and back.

On the day of his embarkation, Naval officers arrived and handed Watlers his sealed orders. A two-by-twelve plank ran from the ship to the dock.

"When you leave this ship," he said, "you'd better hit that plank fast, because once you hit it I'm gone."

A man of his word, the moment my foot was on the dock, the two-by-twelve fell behind me. That tanker shot off down the ship-channel faster than I thought it could move.

I was not in New Orleans to meet Watlers when he returned, but he did make it to his Pacific destination and back. Shortly before I left for Ft. Dix, New Jersey, he radioed a message "mission accomplished." Upon his return, to avoid a severe storm in the Gulf, Watlers detoured to Florida rather than sailing up the coast of Mexico.

An important thing occurred while I was in New Orleans, quite by accident. Our supervising duties for the Port of New Orleans was shared by the officers stationed there. Each officer was given specific assignment as Officer of the Day, with responsibility for seeing that troop ships and supplies set sail on schedule and in compliance with all regulations. One Saturday night, a Lieutenant O'Keefe from Orange, Texas, had been assigned Officer of the Day. As it turned out, the date was his birthday, and his wife and children had arrived in New Orleans to visit and to celebrate. It might be their last chance to be together for some time, and the Lieutenant was upset.

"If the Colonel will approve, I'll serve as Officer of the Day."

Colonel Sherman approved the change of orders to appoint me Officer of the Day. Two troop ships were scheduled to sail that night, but there was a complication. German U-Boats had been patrolling about fifty miles off the Louisiana and Texas coasts, trying to sink the troop ships. For that reason there was an order that all troop ships had to be accompanied by a Naval escort. The two troop ships were ready to depart on schedule, but I found there were no Navy escorts assigned to them. I ordered the ships to remain in port, and I went in search of my commanding officer.

I found he was at the New Orleans Country Club, but I could not reach him by phone. I decided I had to stretch rules and regulations, and arranging for another officer to stand in as Officer of the Day, I went out to the Country Club.

There was a big party in progress, and both my commanding officer and the Navy Admiral were so drunk I couldn't talk to them. Angry, I went back to my duty. I decided to call the Pentagon, and when I had a General on the line, I told him the situation. He instructed me to keep the troop ships in port, and he would fly down the following morning. I didn't believe the problem sufficiently serious for him to come to handle it, especially since it was foggy in New Orleans and his plane might not be able to land. I just wanted to get the troop ships out of port on schedule.

When the General arrived, I learned the reason he insisted on coming. This was not the only incident of heavy drinking among the big brass; it was a frequent problem throughout the U.S. Command, and it was a serious threat to the war effort. The General knew me and of my relationship with the President. Immediately, he cut special orders for me to report to Washington on Monday for special duty; he asked me to take the matter to Roosevelt.

I was willing to talk to the President, but I had witnessed only one instance of the drinking problem myself. I was sure the President would want substantiation. Congressman Lyndon Johnson was only recently returned from special military duty with General MacArthur in the Pacific. In Washington, I decided to see Johnson and ask if he had witnessed similar activities.

When Lyndon was told I was in his office, he came running out to see me, all excited, telling his secretary to call Lady Bird to inform her that Jerry was in town.

"No," I said. "Don't call her. I'm here to talk about something important, and we're not going to have time for lunch. I'm on my way to see the President."

In Johnson's office I explained the situation to him, what I had witnessed in New Orleans and what the General had told me. I said, "Now, you have just returned from the Pacific, and you've spent a lot of time with MacArthur and other high brass. Did you witness a lot of drinking?"

"You have no idea how bad it was," Lyndon gushed. "It was just terrible. The officers were drunk more than they were sober, and it wasn't just junior officers. The higher the rank the worse it was."

"I'm going over to see the President about it right now," I told him. "Will you come with me and tell him what you witnessed?"

"Oh, no," he protested, saying if he got into a tangle with the high brass, it could jeopardize his career.

I lost my temper then. I cussed him from end to end, calling him every foul name I could think of, including a few other well chosen expletives not in the book. And that was the last conversation I ever had with Lyndon Johnson. When he became president, I frequently came within five or six feet of him, but I would never speak with him or shake his hand. I simply did not—and could not—respect him.

Alone at the White House, I reported everything to the President, including my conversation with Lyndon Johnson. He seemed as angry with Johnson as I, and called him on the telephone then and there and rattled off a few more names I hadn't thought of.

Within 24 hours, the White House order against excessive drinking among senior officers was issued. The threat of serious punishment for commanding officers found to be drunk in the line of duty hung heavy over the military.

This event did not make me very popular among the officers in New Orleans. One officer in particular did his best to make my life difficult. When they began to organize the Ninth Mobile Port of Embarkation, this Colonel arranged my appointment as Salvage Officer, a considerable demotion in authority and duties.

The officer in charge of training those of us assigned to the Ninth Mobile Port of Embarkation was a Colonel Hackett. He moved us to training at Camp Hanrahan in New Orleans. One of the first things he asked of the division heads was to draw up a chart for his division, indicating duties.

I made a chart, using standard squares and lines, with one square at the top, a couple of squares below it, more below them, and so on. I labeled the top square "Big Chief Thief," then "Little Thief" in the ones below it, "Littler Thief" in those in the next row, and "Little Bitty Thief" in the bottom row squares.

To my surprise, Colonel Hackett had a big laugh over my chart. Some high-ranking officers were coming down from Washington the next day, and he wanted to show it to them. I had no objection.

The officers from Washington asked to interview each officer separately in Colonel Hackett's office. When I was called, one of them, a Colonel Boothe, looked at me sternly. "I've seen your division chart, Sadler, and it's pretty funny. But you know, you ought to watch your step, because we can get you for fraudulent enlistment."

"Why is that, sir?" From his manner, I figured I was in real trouble.

"Well," he said gruffly, "on your enlistment papers, it asks for prior service record; you put 'none'. We have a record indicating that you served in the Twelfth U.S. Cavalry."

How had he managed to locate my record? I thought the President had destroyed it. "Go ahead and file your charges, sir," I said grimly. "I think I can defend myself against them."

Colonel Boothe laughed, and I realized he had been having his own fun at my expense. "No," he said, "you aren't going to have to defend yourself. We know the reason. We have orders to transfer you to the Persian Gulf Services Command. You are going to be control officer for the commanding general."

"Thank you, sir," I said. "But I don't know what a control officer is."

"Well, you'd better look it up in the manual," he said.

When I looked up "control officer" in the manual, it didn't tell me any more than Colonel Boothe had told me. The manual defined no duties for the control officer, but merely mentioned that he was attached to a general.

In November, finishing training at New Orleans, I transferred to Fort Dix, New Jersey, to await shipment to the Middle East. It was a cold, rainy November, and the troop train seemed to take forever to get there. It was constantly shunted off on sidings to allow other trains to pass. At Fort Dix, we were pushed onto a siding about two miles from the camp and were ordered to march, carrying all our belongings, through the rain, to our billets. I had an extra-long bag, because I had brought along a two-year supply of snuff. It weighed about 150 pounds.

That was a miserable march through the rain and mud, and we cussed all the way. When we arrived, we found our billet was not a barracks accommodation but a bivouac area—some old leaky tents raised about four feet off the ground with one-by-twelve flooring that had cracks big enough for snakes to crawl through.

Our ranking officer was a Major Turner. He was no happier about our billet than I was. I suggested that he stay there with the men, but not to let them settle in yet. "I want to have a look around," I said.

I discovered a two-story ell-shaped barracks building, completely empty right in the middle of Fort Dix. I returned to Major Turner and informed him I had found a better place. We led the men to the barracks and settled in. There was no heat, but there was a phone, and so I called supply and ordered some coal.

Within minutes officers arrived, demanding to know what we were doing in the barracks and who had authorized our move. I didn't answer their questions; instead I asked to see the commanding general. They asked why. "Because I want to raise a little hell," I told them.

I did raise hell with the General, and when I was through, he said we could stay in the barracks as long as we remained only in that area. He explained they kept all of the outfits going overseas separated from each other for reasons of security. He hoped we'd be very comfortable there, and if we needed anything just let him know.

The restriction to staying around the barracks was not a problem until Saturday, when there was absolutely nothing to do but walk around the area.

I had become friendly with a Major Louis Liedecker, from Houston. We were walking around the area when we noticed a big, long line of men in front of a building. "Let's get in line and see what's going on," I suggested.

"You can if you want to," he said. "I think I'll go back to my bunk and lie down."

I got into the line and asked the men in front of me what was happening inside to create such a line. "Major Hummel is in there," I was told. "He's the only man who can issue passes to leave the post."

The only Major Hummel I'd heard of was a lawyer who had been appointed defense attorney for some captured German saboteurs, taken from New Orleans to Washington for trial. He had lost the case, but he had done the best job any lawyer could do under the circumstances.

I asked more questions, and learned this was the same Major Hummel, so I stayed in line.

There wasn't a single man coming out of that building with a pass. As I got closer, I could hear the men giving reasons for needing a pass, and I could also hear Major Hummel say over and over: "No. Pass denied."

When I got up to him, I gave him the proper salute, and he asked, "What do you want?"

"Nothing, sir," I replied. "I just wanted to see the man who was given one of the dirtiest jobs anyone in the U.S. Army ever had, defending enemy saboteurs. I'm a lawyer myself, sir, and I admired the way you handled the case."

"What outfit are you with?" he asked.

"The Ninth Mobile Port of Embarkation," I said.

"I expect you need to go over to New York to see about your supplies," he said. "I'll call for a car to take you over there."

"Could I take another man with me?" I asked. "A Major Liedecker."

"Yes," he said. "But I'll have to know where to reach you in New York in case orders arrive to move out. Do you have a place to stay?"

"Yes sir," I said. "We'll be at the Hotel New Yorker."

"Do you have a reservation?" he asked. "You know, it's almost impossible to get hotel rooms now."

"I don't need reservations at the New Yorker," I told him. The president of the New Yorker was a friend of mine.

Liedecker and I went to New York that day, staying five days and having a good time. We had a little problem at the registration desk, but I made a call to Ralph Hitts, the hotel president, and we were given a beautiful suite.

When it was time for our outfit to depart, Major Hummel called us at the hotel. "Tomorrow is the day I want to see you," which was the code he used to let us know we were scheduled to ship out.

Our troop ship had been one of the finest luxury liners before the war, but its name had now been changed from the *S.S. America* to the *U.S.S. West Point,* for the duration of the war. Our destination was Basra, Iraq; our departure was total chaos. The ship had been built to accomodate 1,500 passengers. It was to transport 10,000 troups. With ten other men, I was assigned to a stateroom designed to hold three persons.

I realized what we were up against as soon as I learned who had

241

been appointed commanding officer of the troops—a member of the medical corps stationed in New Orleans at the time I was there. He held a reserve commission from World War I, and he was old, bordering on senility. Most of his adult life had been spent as a doctor on an Indian reservation, a noble calling but not one to teach a man how to organize masses of people.

In New Orleans, he did little but get in the way.

The first day out to sea, no meals were served, so there were 10,000 hungry, disgruntled troops. If things were not handled pretty quickly, I knew we would have trouble on that ship, so I went to the bridge and asked to speak to the Captain, the naval commander of the ship. I told him about the hunger situation and suggested that he ought to intervene.

An ulterior motive for getting into the act was to see that, whatever might happen, my troops got fed. Together the Captain and I worked out an organizational plan. He, Captain Kelly, replaced the commanding officer with a Colonel Fisher of the Air Corps, whose men had been doing the loudest grumbling. On my recommendation, he appointed Major Liedecker mess officer, and I was his chief of staff. After we had worked out a detailed schedule for meals, he got on the loudspeaker and announced a meeting for all officers of troops in the theater at 0400 hours, about fifteen minutes away.

I had expected Liedecker to step out and give the orders, but when the officers were assembled, he pushed me onto the stage. I saw colonels and lieutenant-colonels in the audience grumbling about taking orders from a first-lieutenant. Especially when I suggested they take out their notebooks and pencils and write down the mess schedule (eating times).

Finally, everybody got fed that night. The galley (dining area) held about 2,400 men at a time; we got the meal service running efficiently so that everybody was fed within one and a half hours.

One day one of the mess crew reported that the Air Corps was going back through the food line for seconds. I went to see, and sure enough some had squeezed into line on the second shift. I found the captain in charge of the group and told him to get his men out of the line.

"By what authority?" he demanded.

"One authority is the gun I'm wearing," I said.

"You can't use that against me or you're in trouble," he said. "I outrank you, and I say my men can come back for seconds." And he started to squeeze back into line.

I pulled my .45, and he lunged for me. I hit him on the side of the head, and he fell against the wall.

Colonel Fisher put me under arrest of quarters and told me there would be a court-martial that night. I was to be charged with assaulting an officer. One of the men with whom I shared a stateroom, Duvall West III, a West Point graduate, was appointed a member of the court. West knew the manual backward and forward, and he jumped to my defense, telling them they did not have the authority to convene a court martial.

Meanwhile, Fisher appointed one of his men, an Air Corps major, to replace me in the mess. Before the first dinner shift was half through, this major came to see me. "You've got to come back and take over. We've got the dernedest mess you ever saw."

I said, "I'm sorry, but I can't help you. Your colonel has me confined to quarters."

Later he returned. He had received approval from Colonel Fisher to have me go back to work. When I got the mess straightened out and all the men served, I was ordered to go to Captain Kelly on the bridge.

"I've heard about what's been going on here," he told me. "If Colonel Fisher presses the issue of a court-martial, I'll be glad to testify in your behalf. I have to take this ship back to the West Coast for repairs first, but then I've got to go back to Washington. I'll report what happened, and how it happened."

I thanked him. "I have a feeling it won't be necessary."

It wasn't. Right after I got back to my quarters, an airman came to tell me that Colonel Fisher wanted to see me. He was now all conciliatory. When I entered his room, he offered me a cigar.

I told him I didn't smoke cigars. I dipped snuff.

He offered me some wine.

I told him I didn't drink wine.

He said, "I want to apologize to you and ask you to forget about what happened today. You've done a good job in the mess. I don't think we could have made it without you."

"If that's all you've got to say, Colonel," I replied, "I'd like to say goodnight." And that ended the matter.

On the long voyage, we had a couple of small brushes with the enemy. When we had left New Jersey, we were in the middle of about 300 ships. A great many of them accompanied us down the coast of South America. When we got to Rio, we dropped anchor about twelve miles off the coast. The Captain called me to the bridge.

"I'd like you to take a man and go ashore," he said. "And what I'd like you to do is to buy every egg they have in Rio, all of them, and you don't have to be secret about it."

"We have plenty of rations, sir," I said. "May I ask why I'm buying all these eggs?"

"I'll tell you when you get back," he said.

I took Ruel McDaniel, a member of the crew. We bought every egg we could get our hands on. We had the supply boats filled with them, when we returned the next morning.

I went to the bridge to report to the captain. He told me why we had bought the eggs. "Did you notice I've got all the troops out on the decks? We've been creating a little diversionary tactic here. We've been trying to make the Germans think we're the main invasion force headed for North Africa. We've got about 27 German subs out there waiting for us, but I'm not afraid of subs. We can outrun them."

We crossed the Atlantic and rounded the Cape of Good Hope without incident. We had no actual contact with the Germans until we had passed the Isle of Madagascar, and then our first contact was a false alarm.

I was below in the galley, when Captain Kelly called to ask how many officers were below. "We're going to have to shut the watertight doors," he said.

"We've got 2,700 men down here eating lunch," I replied. "The only officer with me is Lieutenant Commander Mecklin. I think we can take care of it though."

"I wish you had more officers," he told me. "But there's no time. You and Mecklin get them closed."

We had barely gotten all the stainless steel doors closed before we heard—and felt—the big gun go off topside. Then moments later, he called down, "All clear."

Later he told me what had happened. He had fired the gun only as a warning. There had been a ship that was flying no flag, and it refused to identify itself until after the gun had been fired. It was a Dutch ship, and it hadn't wanted to identify itself because of a Japanese destroyer in the area.

Only a short time later, we came into contact with the Japanese destroyer. This time the naval personnel took care of the watertight doors. The guns were fired full force, sinking the destroyer.

About a day out of Bombay, we came across an Indian vessel, half tugboat and half sailing ship. Captain Kelly, to avoid attracting attention to the *West Point* before crossing the Pacific on his return trip, notified the captain of the Indian vessel what had happened. He suggested that they might like to take credit for sinking the Japanese destroyer. They accepted. When we arrived in Bombay, the news was in the headlines. "Indian Navy Sinks Jap Destroyer."

In Bombay, all troops disembarked the *West Point* to take other routes to their destinations. Captain Kelly had me issue each man rations for three days, because the travels for most men were certain to be rougher than aboard ship.

While I was in Bombay, I stopped in to see Frank Harold, a representative in India for the Texas Company and an acquaintance of mine from Port Arthur. It was from him that I learned that W.S. Farish, Chairman of the Board of Standard Oil, had died. It was strange to hear such news in such a place, so far from home. It seemed much more than a year since Farish and I had fought each other over oil quotas and monopolistic control.

.

24

The Persian Gulf Command

From Bombay, our troops were shipped to Iran by means of an antiquated British liner named the *Lancastershire.* When war had broken out, the old luxury liner had been at sea on a pleasure cruise. Its passengers had to manage finding other transportation to England, the *Lancastershire* remaining out for transporting troops in India. The entertainment unit stayed aboard, doing their bit, performing for the troops. They made a valiant effort to entertain and boost morale, but it was an uphill effort for them; they had been at sea so long their material was stale.

It was on the *Lancastershire,* while traveling through the Indian Ocean at night, that I saw one of the strangest natural phenomena I've ever seen. There was something on top of the water that glowed in the dark, like millions of lightning bugs. It was reddish gold, like fire, and it extended as far as the eye could see. The ship just plowed through it, pushing it away, leaving it parted in the wake.

We made it through the Indian Ocean and the Persian Gulf into the Shatt-al-Arab River to Khorramshahr without incident. When we landed at Khorramshar, it was raining hard. I learned the rainy season in the Persian Gulf started promptly every December 13 or 14 and continued into March. Often it rained for five days without let-up, but in some ways that was better than the rest of the year. When it wasn't raining, it was hot. Temperatures of 120 and 130 degrees Fahrenheit were not unusual. The highest I ever recorded on my ordinary weather thermometer was 177 degrees in the direct sun; in the shade it was about ten degrees cooler.

We learned quickly about the Khorramshahr mud. On top of the desert sand was a layer of very fine silt, and when it was wet it was like glue. After we landed, the British took us out to a staging area about three miles from the river. To get to this area, just an open spot in the desert, we had to march through the mud. Those three miles seemed endless; because every few steps we had to stop to remove caked mud from our boots. It was so heavy and so thick it was like walking with thirty-pound weights on our feet.

At this staging area, in the rain and mud, we set up our tents. The British set up some boards as tables to serve us our first meal ashore. Their rations had become so rotten and wormy I decided we would treat them instead. Our troops had plenty of fresh rations, issued to them before leaving the *West Point,* so we brought them out and fed the British.

That night we had uninvited guests. The jackals came in from one direction, and the hyenas from another. In the darkness and rain, the sounds they made were bloodcurdling, a mixture of howling and cackling, and when they came to within fifty yards of our camp the sound stopped, and there was an unsettling silence. The silence was worse than their cries.

It was more than one of our men could endure. He, a West Point captain, went berserk. After the third advance on our camp by the jackals and hyenas, the Captain rushed out of his tent with a rifle in one hand and a .45 pistol in the other and started shooting blindly in every direction. With great effort we managed to subdue him, and the next day turned him over to an army psychiatrist.

After that night, something had to be done about our conditions, so I requisitioned a jeep with tire chains and drove in to Khorramshahr where I could call our headquarters at Basra, Iraq. I reported our extreme conditions, and four days later we were transferred to Basra.

At Basra, I experienced a little of what is now called culture shock. Their civilization was totally different from everything I had ever experienced, but one scene struck me more vividly than any other. My first day at Basra, I passed what can only be described as a puddle of water. Three women stood in it, one washing the corpse of a dead baby, another washing some clothes, and the third filling a clay pitcher to take home for drinking water. It did not shock me later to learn that 40 percent of the mothers died in childbirth and 60 percent of the children died before age two.

Although the United States had been in the war just over a year, the Persian Gulf Services Command was something new. The British had been shipping only limited supplies to the Russians through Iran. The only means of transporting supplies was the TransIranian Railway, which had been built by the Shah's father, Shah Riza Kahn Pahlevi, at a cost of $90,000,000. It had never been intended for the purpose of shipping heavy war supplies. There were no highways in Iran, virtually no roadways. The docks at Khorramshahr were hardly adequate for what we were about to do.

The first task undertaken by our troops on arrival in Basra was the building of barracks. We were truly starting from scratch. The barracks were barely completed before General Donald H. Connolly, commanding officer of the Persian Gulf Services Command, decided to move his general headquarters to Teheran.

It was inevitable, I guess, that I would have difficulties with some of the high-ranking officers. I was General Connolly's control officer, and I got along with him most of the time, but I was grateful when he decided I would stay in the "south end" rather than go with him to what would come to be known as the "Country Club" in Teheran. Colonel Don Shingler was to be the ranking officer at the south end—which included Basra, Khorramshahr, and Abadan—and we got along very well. He had difficulties with his executive officer, Colonel John B. Luscomb, who wouldn't even come into the office, so Shingler made me his acting executive officer.

While we were still at Basra, a radiogram came through that a battalion of black troops had mutinied on the *Ile de France* and were to be tried for treason. The General was present when that message came in, and he became angry.

"The President promised me he wasn't going to send me any nigger troops," he said irately. "When we worked out the plan for this Russian supply line, I told him specifically I didn't want any niggers under my command."

Shingler and I kept trying to butt in to calm him down, both of us attempting to defend the black troops, but the General continued to rage about it. Finally, he said if he had any say in the matter, he'd see that every black soldier was court-martialed.

At that, I got angry. "Those negro troops did not ask to come over here," I told him. "And as a lawyer, I can tell you that any court-martial they hold on the *Ile de France* won't be able to stand up in an appeals court."

Connolly turned his anger on me. "By God," he said, "if you're going to take up for them, if you love niggers so much, I'll just put you in charge of them."

"That's fine with me!" I said. "I'll hold you to it!"

Before the General had time to change his mind, I ran around to the adjutant's office and had them prepare orders for me to transfer to the 380th Port Battalion, by order of General Connolly. After that, he couldn't back out. I told him, "They're docking at Khorramshahr, and I'm going there, and that's where I will set up my operations." Khorramshahr was thirty miles down the river from Basra.

The troops of the 380th Port Battalion were negros, but the high ranking officers were caucasian. The commanding officer was a Major Jordan, and I was assigned as his executive officer. Under me there were 22 second-lieutenants, who had just graduated from Officer's Training School, all white, and one thousand troops, all black.

The first night after the *Ile* docked, Major Jordan held a meeting of the officers so we could all become acquainted. I brought along a Turkish water pipe, and when we were seated in his tent, I set up the water-pipe with its long tube, filled it with tobacco, and smoked it. Of course the officers paid scant attention to what Jordan said; they were all too busy watching me with that pipe. The young officers had never seen one before, and they wanted to figure out how it worked.

A few days later, orders came through transferring Major Jordan. Since I was now the ranking officer, under Articles of War, I could assume command. I did just that. The first thing to settle was the matter of the court-martials, which had taken place aboard the *Ile de France*.

I investigated the events and causes for the "treason" of the black troops. I found most of the men had been guilty of nothing more than trying to get some fresh air.

There were white troops and black troops on board the *Ile de France*. The whites had been allowed the freedom of the ship, allowed to freely roam the decks for air and sunshine. The blacks were in the hold of the ship, and not permitted to leave their space. When they crossed the equator, all the portholes were closed, and air circulation was poor. One night, to keep from dying of suffocation, the blacks slipped up to the sun deck to sleep there. That was their "treason."

For that reason, the black "ringleaders" had been put through a court-martial.

In reviewing the records of the men, I found they had a wide assortment of backgrounds. That's why it was unfair to lump them together as "black troops," just because of the color of their skins. In that battalion, I had over a hundred ex-convicts, some of whom had been turned off a Georgia chain gang because they were willing to volunteer for military service. At the same time, I had a Sergeant Green from Baltimore, Maryland, who was an All-American basketball player, and another college graduate, a Sergeant Madison. Sergeant Hawkins had been the secretary to the president of a black-owned insurance company.

As commanding officer, I made the recommendation that the review officer disapprove the sentences of the court-martial and restore all the men to duty. This recommendation had to go first to Teheran, but then it was sent to Washington for a decision. Roosevelt had appointed the former Chief Justice of the New York Supreme Court as his review officer on this matter. Eventually, my recommendation was approved.

Meanwhile I knew I had a morale problem, and before I could even begin to deal with it I was somehow going to have to get the troops to respect and trust me.

I thought it would help to know what they thought of me already, what they were saying among themselves; so after taking command, I went for a walk in the darkness, listening at the tents. I found a tent where I was the subject of discussion.

"How did he get command?" one of them asked. "He's just a first-lieutenant."

"Oh, I hear he's got oil wells all over Texas," another replied. "He's a rich man. If you're rich, you can get anything you want."

I listened for about half and hour. What they were telling one another was so outrageous it struck me as funny. By the time I decided to step inside the tent, I was laughing. I told them I'd listened to their conversation and I'd found it most interesting.

"I think you were treated unjustly on the *Ile de France*," I also said. "If I'd been your commanding officer, you wouldn't have been confined to the hold for the entire trip, and there would have been no reason for a court-martial. As for the sentences of the court-martials, I'm in the process of appealing to Washington to try to have them overturned. And if I know President Roosevelt—and I do—every member of your outfit will be back on duty very soon."

Whether the men believed what I said or not, I knew it would be all over camp the next morning.

I followed that by promoting as many of the black troops as I could. I named Sergeant Green and Sergeant Madison warrant officers. I arranged to promote Sergeant David Edwards of New York, a master-sergeant. Sergeant Hawkins became sergeant-major of the battalion and I recommended his promotion to staff-sergeant.

I tried to give the men reason to believe that I could be a fair man although I was white and a southerner. I hoped to convince them that their show of incentive and effort would be rewarded. Men have to be allowed pride in themselves and in their accomplishments.

In short, the morale problem of black troops was no different from that of white troops, as long as they were treated with the same set of rules.

Once an inspector-general came into my office with about twelve pages of orders under the heading, "How to Handle Negro Troops." I had begun to sense some of the prejudice my troops experienced. Just seeing that heading made me angry. I took the orders and tore them up in the inspector-general's face.

"You'll be court-martialed for that," he said. "You have to sign, acknowledging that you've received it."

"I'm not signing anything that comes to me under that heading," I said. "If you had a dissertation on how to handle 'troops,' I would sign for it. There isn't any difference between negro troops and white troops. It's a morale problem no matter how you look at it, and I have my own ideas on how to raise the morale of my troops."

We had Iranian contractors build our barracks out of the native mud brick, with straw roofs; those barracks were crude, but functional. During the hot summer days, the straw allowed air in without letting in heat, and it effectively kept out the rain as well. We had been saving dunnage—scraps of boards—from the ships we had been unloading. I had the men saw the boards into pickets about two-feet high, so that we had a picket fence around the fifty-acre plot of our camp. We salvaged a lot of leftover paint from the ships, but it was all different colors, so we mixed it all together to paint the fence. I can't describe accurately that picket fence but it was sort of a violet color.

When generals came for inspection, usually they just drove by our picket fence, not bothering to come inside to inspect.

Although I was commander of the 380th Battalion, I remained General Connolly's control officer, so I had supervisory control over all of the troops who worked the docks—white and black. I set a policy that the battalions with the best work records would be the first to go home when the war was over. As a symbol of the best, I had a flag, which came to be called the "Number 1 Flag," which was to be flown over the barracks of the battalion that had proved to be the best that week.

Almost every week that flag flew over the barracks of the 380th Port Battalion. It became a symbol of pride for my troops. One day I passed a sergeant of the 380th who carried a sack of cement toward the barracks. I asked him what he intended to do with it, and he replied he was making a permanent base for the Number 1 Flag. What would he do if it had to be moved to another battalion?

"You don't have to worry about that, sir," he told me. "That's our flag, and we intend to see that it doesn't have to be moved."

I did have two men who proved to be more difficult than the rest, but they were special cases. (Two out of a thousand men is pretty good.) And those two eventually came around to cooperating.

One of these men was in the group who were court-martialed. He had received the highest sentence, 75 years in prison. Even though that sentence had been revoked, his negative attitude didn't change. The other men developed a pride in their work, and he spent most of his energy trying to figure out ways to avoid work.

When I got word that he had gone out to the hospital and checked himself in without going through the dispensary, I hopped in my Jeep and paid a call on the hospital, located three or four miles outside the town. The doctors confirmed he had been admitted, complaining of severe pain in one leg.

I asked to see the man, and he was brought to the doctor's office. I asked him where the pain was, and he told me it was in his left leg. I asked him to walk across the floor, and he did so. However, he was limping on his right leg.

When the doctor saw that the man was faking, he signed an order to release him, and I took him with me.

I always wore my pistol on my right side. But as I was driving the Jeep back to camp that day, I moved it over to the left. I could see the man watching me as I did this. Halfway back to camp, out in open desert, I pulled the Jeep off to the side of the road.

"What are you going to do?" he asked.

I said, "I'm going to make a man out of you, or I'm going to kill you." And I got out of the Jeep.

I ordered him to go about ten feet in front of the Jeep and to get down on his knees and pray. I know he thought I would draw my gun and shoot him; that's what I wanted him to think.

He began crawling to me. "I'm going to change, I promise. I'll make you the best soldier you ever had."

"All right," I said, "I'm going to take you at your word, and I'm going to hold you to it."

As far as I know, he never said anything to the other men, and he lived up to his promise. He was a nervous man, with quick hands, and he worked harder than anybody else on the docks. He didn't return home, however. He was killed one day when a big crate fell on him. The last words he spoke, as he lay dying, were, "Let's get moving. Let's get that stuff off the ship."

I used a similar approach with the other man who was a problem. He was also among those court-martialed on the *Ile de France*. The man, from Missouri, was about six feet, three inches tall, and powerfully built. He didn't shirk work; he was outright belligerent, refusing to cooperate in any way. He just seemed to want out of the army, and he didn't care if it was through a dishonorable discharge. He tried to get enough summary court martials against him to get kicked out. We had him before the summary court eleven times, and every time he was found guilty.

It was left to me whether or not to recommend a discharge, but I was determined not to give up on this man.

I called him to my office on an offense. "I'm going to try a different system on you," I told him. "I'm going to whip hell out of you." And I proceeded to pull off my shirt so I wouldn't be wearing an insignia of rank. He was a lot bigger and stronger than I was, and I was taking a big chance.

The man didn't cower, and he didn't threaten. He spoke simply. "I'm not going to fight you."

"Why?" I asked. "Are you yellow? Are you a coward?"

"No," he said. "I'm not yellow, I don't want to fight you. I've been fought and kicked all my life. My mama was a prostitute, and ever since I was a kid people have kicked me, and I've had to fight them. You're the only person ever treated me like a human beng, and I won't fight you."

"Then why have you given me a hard time?" I asked.

"I don't know," he said. "But I won't do it anymore. I'll straighten up."

He lived up to his promise, and by the time of his discharge, he was a corporal.

Those men worked hard; they were proud of their work, and I was proud of them. For a time, the Khorramshahr docks were about the busiest docks anywhere in the world. Our objective was to supply the Russians with everything they needed to keep firm the Eastern Front of the war against the Germans. The only thing that wasn't unloaded from those ships were the bombers, which were flown into Iran assembled. Fighter planes, however, arrived unassembled, as did jeeps and trucks. We established assembly plants there, managed by General Motors employees. Railway locomotives and cars came already assembled and had to be lifted off the ships, just as crates of food and arms did.

I don't know the total tonnage we unloaded, but by November of 1944, some 4,380,440 tons of war implements and goods were delivered to Russia. They were receiving supplies so fast that much of it was still sitting unused in their supply yards at war's end.

My men worked in torrential rains, and in heat that went as high as 150 degrees Fahrenheit. However, during those hot summer months, we worked an odd schedule, breaking from noon until 5:00 P.M., the hottest period of the day, working early morning and late evening hours. During those times of day, temperatures never got above 140 degrees or so.

The most difficult job the men ever had was unloading the "Jumbo Diesel." It was the largest diesel locomotive ever constructed. I had viewed it only a few years before at the 1939 New York World's Fair. When it arrived at Khorramshahr by cargo ship, I had no idea how we would ever get if off and onto the railway tracks. It was larger than our equipment could handle. I went to see the ship's captain, and asked him if his booms could lift it.

He laughed. "My booms wouldn't even be able to lift one of the wheels on that diesel."

The British had a 125,000 ton floating crane about six miles up the river, so I went up to ask if we could borrow it. They refused.

That British crane was the only thing in the Persian Gulf region large enough to get the diesel engine unloaded. I decided we would have to borrow it without their permission.

At night, I took some of my men on a tugboat, and we slipped upriver. The British had the crane secured, but not locked. I guess it had never occurred to them that someone might try to steal such a large item. We got it loose without difficulty and towed it downriver to the cargo ship at Khorramshahr.

Next morning I knew that the British would be up in arms, so I stationed military police around the docks to keep them out until after we had finished with their crane. As expected, the British arrived early, raising hell, but we just ignored them.

Even with this crane, it was not going to be an easy job. I had one man, whose name was Joe Jones, who had worked as a stevedore in Florida before the war, and he was really good at his work. He had not been able to read and write when he arrived in Iran, and as time permitted, I had been teaching him. But he taught me a few things about unloading cargo ships.

I asked Joe if he thought he could take care of this job.

"If that crane can lift it," he said. "I can set it right down on those railroad tracks on the first try."

"All right," I told him. "You're in charge."

By use of stevedore's hand signals, Joe gave directions to the men on the crane, and they set the Jumbo Diesel onto the tracks with absolute precision.

One matter of pride occurred to my men before it occurred to me. They had no objection to me as a commanding officer, but they felt slghtly insulted that they were commanded by a first-lieutenant. Other battalions were led by captains and majors. They let the command headquarters know that they wanted me to have some rank, so I was quickly promoted to captain, and soon after that, to major.

I was one of the last to know about the promotion to major. The timing on that was so quick, it took me completely by surprise. The first I heard of it was when I received a letter from my sister addressed "Major Sadler." It was a week or two before I was given the official notice, which relieved Major Jordan and made me station operation officer.

25

Allies and Other (Difficult) People

Appointed stations operation officer, I acquired a little more clout. Naturally, I used it. In some cases, I needed it. No one—whether a colonel or a brigadier-general—could tell a stations operation officer what to do, except the corps commander. The corps commander at the time was Colonel Bernard A. Johnson. Johnson had ambitions to become a brigadier-general, and that tempered everything he did or said. We didn't get along at all.

The promotion did not change my status as commanding officer of the 380th Port Battalion. It meant merely that I took on more responsibilities. And I continued to report to General Connolly on any matters concerning my troops. I was called to Teheran several times, but on one occasion I went on my own.

I arrived at the Country Club—General Connolly's headquarters—at the time of their evening meal. The generals were seated at a long table, lined up according to rank, and it was a fine meal—a lot of steak (and no spam).

When I walked in, General Connolly exclaimed, "Sadler, what brings you here? Pull up a chair and join us for dinner."

"You may want to wait on the invitation," I said. "Until you've heard why I'm here. General Graham has given an order throughout the Persian Gulf Services Command that there will be issued only two ounces of flour per day per man. I would like to make you aware of just how much two ounces of flour is. It's not even enough to make a batter to cover the damned spam we have to eat."

"How much flour do you think would be adequate?" General Connolly asked.

"We're giving enough to the Russians for them to have twelve ounces per day per man," I replied. "I think the American enlisted men should have the same amount."

Connolly turned to General Graham and ordered him to take a

command car the next morning, to go to Khorramshahr and Banda-shaphur and issue orders that our troops were to have twelve ounces of flour per day per man.

General Graham was mad, but he was even more furious when he saw the command car issued to him. It was the biggest insult he could have been given—an ancient, banged-up rattletrap with no shock absorbers.

I don't want it to seem that my troops were starving. They weren't eating the foods served at the Country Club in Teheran, but they weren't starving either. There were herds of gazelle that ran in the desert around Khorramshahr, and from time to time some of us would go out on shoots so we could have fresh meat. We had a sergeant from Decatur, Alabama, who worked the mess hall, and he became quite expert at butchering and cooking gazelle.

Though it was not like back home, the men also initiated their entertainment. They had baseball teams, football teams, and boxing matches. At times, they enjoyed touring USO shows; however, on one occasion Bob Hope arrived, discovered how hot it was, and turned right around and left, without performing. (It was only 105 degrees that day.) I recall we had Joel McCrea and Jack Benny, but for a long time there were no black entertainers. The closest my troops had gotten to a black entertainer was when Jack Benny mentioned Rochester.

I decided to try to get some black entertainers to come in. I contacted our special services director to arrange it. He secured a group, which included actresses, singers, and musicians, both male and female. Of this group four were female, and we had to provide a place for their overnight stay. I requested Colonel J.E. McDill, who was in charge of the hospital, to arrange for a room where the women would be relatively comfortable. The normal procedure was to house them with nurses. I assumed that was what he would do. It slipped my mind that McDill was from Jackson, Mississippi.

He gave the black women a room next to the hospital V.D. ward. I was furious. I drove there as fast as I could, gave him a piece of my mind, and forced him to put the women in with the nurses. I lodged a protest with command headquarters. His "punishment" was transfer to Teheran.

The Iran experience was a broadening one for me; a new opportunity to learn about the way other people live. In a short span of time, I progressed from the provincial interest of a small Texas community to concerns of my state, and then to matters involving my country. In Iran I became acquainted with other races, other nationalities, and it always surprised me when my countrymen were not interested in keeping an open mind.

I did not always like what I saw, and I never kept my mouth shut. But I learned.

Khorramshahr was, to a certain extent, an international community at the time. The Iranians themselves were made up of Persians and Arabs, and the military forces there included large numbers of Americans, British, and Russians. We were all supposed to be Allies, united to defeat a common enemy, but we did not always work smoothly together. If we did, it was often with mutual mistrust. Unexpectedly, the British were often more difficult to work with than were the Russians. It may have been we were divided by common usage of language, or it may have been some lingering resentment left over from the American Revolution.

When we had a Fourth of July celebration and invited the British and the Russians, the British refused to attend. The Independence Day celebration was our first opportunity to put on our own show. We took full advantage of it, with a reviewing stand for generals and high-ranking officers, and a parade of troops. We even had a military band, which I had inherited by an odd set of circumstances.

A troop ship, docked at Khorramshahr, had as commanding officer a Colonel Pettit. He refused to allow the troops to disembark, because he did not approve of the facilities provided the men. He made all kinds of impossible demands. He was in full command of those troops, and I was called to deal with the problem. If I could just get them off the ship, Colonel Pettit could be relieved of command.

I found the colonel had a 55-piece band out on deck, playing. As soon as I saw Colonel Pettit, I recognized the type—old southern family snob—and I knew how to deal with it. I asked him if he was one of the Virginia Pettits, and went into a routine about the Sadlers and Pettits being neighbors in the earliest settlement of Virginia. I then promised that he and his men would be given the best of everything once they disembarked.

I got them off the ship, and within a few hours, orders came from command headquarters that Colonel Pettit was relieved of command and was to be transferred. As a result I inherited his 55-piece band, and divided it into two separate units—a band and a drum-and-bugle corps.

We had both music groups for our Fourth of July celebration. All of the American generals and Russian generals from the Persian Gulf area invited to the occasion were on the reviewing stand. Most of the American generals had all gotten drunk the night before, and were suffering from hangovers. I was in charge of the review, and I fixed it so that the drum-and-bugle corps, passing the review stand first, would strike up "Roll out the Barrel." Then the marching band approached and rendered their version of the same number.

I was out on the field with the troops, observing that everything went off with precision. When both bands had passed review, a sergeant came running up to me. "General Connolly wants to see you."

I went up to the reviewing stand and found a very angry general. "Whose idea was it to have the bands play that piece of music?"

"That was my idea, sir," I replied. "Since we are supplying the Russians with barrels of oil, I thought it would be appropriate for them."

"Don't you know that's a drinking song?" General Connolly snapped.

"Yes sir," I said, "and I thought that would be appropriate for the American officers."

The Russian general, overhearing this, burst out laughing. He was a likeable man with a sense of humor. It took General Connolly awhile to appreciate the little joke, but eventually he laughed about it.

I don't say I liked the Russians I met there, but I respected several individual Russians. One, whom I truly came to consider a friend, was Lieutenant Colonel Semenchenko, who was the commander of the Soviet military garrison at Khorramshahr. A brilliant man, he had studied history and political systems thoroughly, and though he was a member of the Communist Party, he believed that communism needed to be altered to adapt to principles of democracy. He greatly admired General Robert E. Lee and discussed his tactics with detailed knowledge. At the time, I had hopes that Semenchenko might rise within the Soviet system and make the changes he espoused. He was eventually promoted to General, but he died not long after the war was over.

On one occasion, we had a supply request from the Russians that I thought the height of stupidity. They asked for ten unbroken miles of two-inch cable. I tried to persuade them to accept rolls of standard length and then splice it. It would be stronger at the splice than

With Dr. Francis J. Schott inside the compound at Khorramshahr, preparing to barbecue a gazelle.

The Duty Room of the 380th Battalion in Khorramshahr, Iran. The "X" marks Major Jerry Sadler's office.

Some of the non-coms of the 380th Port Battalion outside the headquarters at Khorramshahr. The "X" marks the window of Major Sadler's office.

With some of the other officers in Teheran. General Connolly is third from the left. Major Jerry Sadler is on the right.

anywhere else on the cable. But they insisted that would not do; it had to be unbroken cable.

With the attitude that "the customer is always right," I put through the request, fully expecting to be told it was impossible. To my surprise, the ten-mile cable arrived fairly promptly, one enormous coil which took up the entire deck of the cargo ship. To transport it from Khorramshahr by train, it was necessary to coil it onto one flat-car until it was full, then string it to the next and coil it, and so on. It took an entire train to transport that cable.

As we were shipping it, my curiosity got the best of me, and I asked the Russian officers what they intended it for, but they did not reply.

Not long after that, there was a "lapse" in Russian security, and German intelligence learned that the Russians were not protecting the Baltic Sea. Hitler sent a fleet to take advantage of this lax situation. When the German fleet moved in, however, the ships' rudders tangled up in two-inch cable and were unable to move further. They were sitting ducks when the Russians moved in on them.

I did have one rather serious altercation with the Russians. One day I was notified that two Russian soldiers' bodies were found on the highway and the Russian military were holding two members of my battalion for murder.

When it came to matters of this sort, our authority at Khorramshahr superceded that of the Russians. I hopped into my Jeep and rushed to the scene. By the time I got there my men had been taken away and were being held at the Russian camp. The bodies of the two dead Russians were still lying in the middle of the blacktop road, and there were a number of Russian soldiers standing around, waiting for our approval to take the bodies away.

One glance at the situation and I refused to grant the approval: it was clear the two Russians had been killed elsewhere and their bodies dropped here. Both had their throats cut, but there was no blood on the blacktop pavement. I informed the Russians that the bodies would be returned to them after our doctors had performed autopsies.

The autopsies revealed that the two men had not died from the knife wounds, but first, each had been shot in the neck. The bullet fragments retrieved seemed to be of Russian manufacture.

I notified our stations up the line to look out for any suspicious unauthorized vehicles, especially Russian. Quickly I got a radio message that two Russian soldiers—a captain and a sergeant—while traveling north at a high rate of speed, were stopped near Ahwaz. I requested the two be returned to Khorramshahr.

I chose some of my men and some weapons carriers and took them out to surround the Russian camp, then approached the front entrance and asked to see the commanding officer, a colonel. I confronted him with a choice. He could either give over to me my men, pending an inquest the following morning, or have us attack and take them by force. I asked him outside to show him that we had his camp surrounded.

He turned over my men.

When the Russian colonel was called before the inquest, he refused to answer my questions publicly; he was willing to answer all questions privately, but not before the court.

In private, he explained that the two victims were liquidated, a standard and routine operation for them, and it would have passed unnoticed if our two men had not happened along the road. Liquidation simplified their justice system. Elimination was usually performed by a couple of men heavily fortified with vodka; in this case, the liquidators had a little too much vodka and bungled the job.

"Liquidation is not a part of our written law," he said. "It is unwritten, therefore must be secret. If it were reported to Moscow that I talked about it, then I would be liquidated."

We did not wish that to happen to the colonel, so we dropped the matter, giving over to him the men we had captured. What mattered most was that my men, who were innocent, were free.

Toward the end of our term in Iran, the Russians held a ceremony in Teheran to honor the Americans who were responsible for getting critical supplies to their country. I was awarded the Order of the Fatherland, Second Class, the biggest medal I had seen, except for the one that Emperor Haille Selassie gave out. It was pinned on me by Mikhail A. Maximov, the Russian Ambassador to Iran, and I was honored because it was a tribute to my men for the work they had done. Some of the high-ranking officers from the Country Club were also given medals. But I considered they were honored for drinking Russian vodka.

Too, I was given a book of coupons, which represented a pension from the Russian government. I had no intention of accepting a Russian pension, so I cut the signatures off the coupons and kept the book as a souvenir.

We had relatively few problems with the Iranians themselves, considering the fact that we were a military force suddenly intruding on their territory. It may have been that the population had grown used to military rule and to foreign occupation. The ruling Shah had been in power for about two years, placed on the throne by British and Russian forces early in the war. I had no direct contact with the Shah himself, although I had a reason to call at the palace in Teheran on one occassion. What I knew of him I knew indirectly. For those materials we shipped over the TransIranian Railroad, we were required to pay a tax of one cent a pound. The Shah demanded the tax be paid in gold. We shipped that gold bullion to him in 150-pound kegs.

Once we had an especially large shipment of gold bullion to deliver to him. Word reached me that there might be an attempt to hijack the train, so I decided to ride along with the gold. The train was stopped at the town of Quom, and an attempt was made to take over the train. The raid failed, and though I had no proof of it, I had reason to believe the would-be hijackers were some of the Shah's own men.

It took me awhile to learn the customs of the Iranians and of the various Arab tribes, each with their autonomous or semi-autonomous sheiks. I was out in the desert one hot summer day, and I saw two Iranians coming toward me. One was a well-dressed man, and the other was walking along beside him carrying an umbrella over him. When they were near me, I recognized the well-dressed man as the Governor of that Iranian province. He spoke English, and he gave me a sealed document in English, protesting actions of some of our men.

"They interfered in something that was not their business," the Governor explained. "They stopped our battle."

"Your battle?" I asked. "Who were you fighting?"

He explained there was a tribe of Arabs just across the border. His provincials had quarreled with them for many years, and every so often, it was their custom to do battle with them. "Your army is in our country," he said, "and it is a matter of dishonor to us that they stopped our battle before it was over this morning."

"I've been around here all morning," I said, "and I didn't see any battle going on."

"It was right over there," he pointed, "behind those sand dunes."

I was aware that a crew of our men had been in that area on a drill. I told the Governor I would investigate the matter and report back to him within half an hour. On the other side of the dunes, I spoke to the sergeant named Pentecost, in charge of the crew. I learned that indeed there had been a battle, and he and his men had put a stop to it after some of the Arabs had started firing at them. Pentecost and his men had fired back, but aiming their fire at the sand under their feet, doing nothing more than kicking up dust and scaring them away.

I told the Governor that we would permit the battle to continue that afternoon, but only for two hours. I would sound my siren at one o'clock as a signal to begin, and I would sound it again at three as a signal that it was to stop. Our men would keep completely out of it.

It was agreed. I observed the battle from a safe distance. Right at one o'clock, the two sides were ready to charge at my signal. There were between 1,000 and 2,000 men on each side. When the signal went off, they charged at each other like the Pittsburgh Steelers and the Dallas Cowboys at kickoff. They fought mostly in hand-to-hand combat. At three, when my siren again sounded, they parted, satisfied at having gotten their dispute out of their system for the moment.

I became good friends with one young Arab who was something of an outlaw, a kind of bandit or guerilla fighter opposed to the Shah. I nicknamed him "Robin Hood." He was one of several sons of a Sheik, whose territory covered several thousand acres on Abadan Island, which included the big oil refinery there. He and the Shah were active enemies. The British had been helping the Shah in his effort to drive the Sheik and his family from Abadan.

Robin Hood was a very bright young man, educated at an English military school, so he understood the way British military operated. He also knew the area of southern Iran better than anyone, and riding an Arabian horse, he was able to elude capture and stay in hiding.

He and I made a deal. Robin Hood would supply me with any information that would be beneficial to the U.S Army, and I would do whatever I could to protect him. When he came to visit me—usually at night—he would hide his horse in a wooded area some distance from camp.

One night he told me about a German short-wave station at the edge of the mountains. He gave details of where it was located, who was operating it, and when it was used.

While he was still with me, a British lorry drove up outside, filled with armed British soldiers. I went outside my quarters to ask why they were there. The soldiers had their guns drawn; they were looking for Robin Hood.

I stormed at the officer in charge. "You goddamned Limey sons-of-bitches, how dare you come into an American military base with your weapons drawn! You put down those rifles unless you want to shoot it out with my guards!"

The officer in charge had his men lay their rifles down on the bed of the truck.

"Now," I said, "don't you ever come in here again without my permission."

After they left, I made sure that Robin Hood returned safely to the thicket by the river, where he had tethered his horse. The next day I sent some men to capture the German spy and destroy the short-wave station.

There were more than a few problems in Iran with spies and black-marketeers. We had to be always on the alert, because they appeared from the most unexpected places. One event was rather painful to me.

We had several good boxers in our athletic program, but one of the best was an undefeated Golden Gloves champion from Kansas City—a lightweight, but with the talent to be a world champion in his class. I had noticed around camp that the boxer was something of a loner, and those kind were ones you had to watch out for. He would frequently slip out of camp alone without telling anyone where he was going.

At some time, a railroad engineer informed me that the boxer had propositioned him, offering him $2,500 to stop his train halfway between Khorramshahr and Ahwaz, so that he and some Arabs could hijack it. This champion and an Arab Sheik had made a deal with German agents to steal a trainload of cloth, being shipped to Russia for making uniforms. (On the black market, at the time, a GI shirt would bring about $75.)

I told the train engineer to go along with the proposition, but to ask $5,000 for his part. On the day the cloth shipment was scheduled, we secretly unloaded the bolts of cloth from the boxcars, replacing them with troops from the 380th Battalion. Then we resealed the train cars.

The boxer-soldier arranged for the engineer to stop the train alongside a specific bar-pit, a kind of drainage ditch beside the railroad tracks. The boxer waited at the bar-pit with a crowbar and a German Luger; the Arab Sheik and his men, not far off, waited for his signal. Using the crowbar, the soldier pried open the sealed boxcar and slid the door open.

Before he could aim his German Luger, men from the 380th

Battalion opened fire on him, riddling his body with bullets. The Arabs riding up on horseback didn't realize what happened until it was too late. My men turned their fire on them, filling the bar-ditch with Arab bodies. The Sheik and about twenty men turned and fled.

We had made plans in the event a chase would be necessary. The train's flat-cars contained cranes, weapons carriers, and Jeeps. Using the cranes, we unloaded a few vehicles and set off in pursuit. Some distance away, we were able to catch the Sheik and his men. We turned the captured group over to British authorities for disciplinary action.

On another occasion, there was a spy case in Teheran, and General Connolly called upon me to look into it. A very fancy nightclub had opened up about five miles outside the city of Teheran, and it was run by a beautiful Turkish woman. The big attraction was the bevy of beautiful women who served as "hostesses," all said to be princesses, refugees from various places overrun by the Germans.

Ordinary enlisted men were not allowed in this club; only American officers were accepted. A great many of the high-ranking officers from Connolly's Country Club had been patronizing the place, and he was getting suspicious of it. He asked me to go there for an evening to see what I might learn.

I requisitioned a Cadillac and a driver, deciding my approach would be to act out being a rich Texas oilman, stuck in the Army and upset about it. I pretended to get gradually more drunk as the evening progressed. (I actually poured my drinks out unobserved.) As I became "drunker," I increasingly complained about the U.S. government.

My act worked almost too well. The Commandant of Teheran, was there that night. He objected to what I said about our government, and he got surly about the strong language I used. I finally had to let him in on my act in order to keep him from spoiling the whole plan.

I managed to attract the attention of the Turkish manager, and she and I got cosy. She let me buy her drink and let me pour them. Finally the time was ripe. I offered her $1,000 if she would let me go home and spend the night with her. She accepted, and at about two in the morning, she closed up the place, got into my Cadillac with me, and directed the driver to her apartment building, a very fancy new building, with big double doors made of teakwood.

The apartment itself was really elaborate. She allowed me to mix drinks for us at her bar, and I slipped some knock-out drops in hers. She was quickly asleep, and I was left free to examine her apartment.

I found what I was looking for in the back of a large closet filled mostly with fur coats, minks and sables. Behind the fur, a little compartment contained a shortwave radio. She used it to pass along to the Germans the information she picked up from American officers.

Apparently the Turkish woman was to periodically check in with her cohorts, because—not long after the sun arose—they were there pounding on her door to find out what had happened. I went to a window, signaled the sergeant who had been chauffeuring me, and he and the other troops stationed outside came up to arrest the group of spies.

Occasionally mistakes were made by overzealous spy-watchers. One British case of such eagerness involved Clyde Farnsworth, the celebrated Associated Press war-correspondent and his girl-friend.

I met Farnsworth when I picked him up hitchhiking. He had been in Saudi Arabia doing research for a book he wanted to write about Ibn Saud. He had very little gear with him and had just gotten into Basra, when I gave him a lift to Khorramshahr. I installed him in quarters next to mine, and he stayed at our camp for quite awhile, writing articles about the 380th Port Battalion and about me for the newspapers back home.

General Connolly and General Shingler were upset that I would trust him, both insisting that Farnsworth's indentification could be faked. When Farnsworth wrote some articles including their names, their complaints stopped.

Farnsworth told me about his girl-friend, someone he had met and fallen in love with before war had started. She was Czechoslovakian and was now trapped behind enemy lines. He had tried to find some way of getting her out to safety.

He moved on from Khorramshahr, and time passed. Over a year later, I was umpiring a softball game behind the hospital, when suddenly a Jeep screeched to a halt nearby, and a British officer got out to tell me I was needed at the concentration camp in the British post. It was extremely important. The British had captured a female spy, who had asked to see me.

I found somebody to take my place behind the plate, and I went to the British concentration camp. I was given the details of the case, and I recognized the woman's name as that of Clyde Farnsworth's girl-friend. But I said nothing about that at that time. "I'd like to talk to the woman privately," I said simply.

They let me take her out beside my Jeep, and she told me the whole story. Farnsworth had managed to get a message to her that, if she could get to Khorramshahr, he thought I would be willing to help her reach Bombay, which was where he was located. She had managed to get to Teheran, and there had hitched a ride to Khorramshahr with a Captain Menjou (the brother of film star Adolphe Menjou).

I tried to persuade the British to let me take her, very sure she was not the spy they were looking for. They refused, insisting that she was one of the most dangerous spies in the Middle East. I was given the information the British had on the woman they wanted, and I broadcast those details on our radio.

That brought results. The other woman was identified and caught. The spy proved to be a woman loosely acquainted with Farnsworth's girl-friend and had deliberately taken her name because of their close physical resemblance.

After that, the British turned Farnsworth's friend over to me. At our messhall, we gave her a good meal, and made arrangements to ship her off to Bombay to the man she loved.

26

Visiting VIPs

In Khorramshahr, we had a number of very important people travel through, observing our operations. Some were truly important, some were interesting, and some were a pain in the lower regions.

One of the interesting ones was Major George Stevens, the Hollywood film director. He was involved in making documentary films on the war effort for the special services. And he was sent to Khorramshahr to film the operations of the 380th Port Battalion. With Stevens was the same cameraman he had used for his feature films, First Lieutenant Gil Valle.

They were with us for about five months, and they filmed everything—the men working, unloading the cargo ships, assembling trucks and planes, relaxing, playing ball, eating. The men enjoyed being filmed; it gave a boost to their morale to know that a man of Stevens' importance considered what they were doing worthy of preserving on film.

Stevens set up one scene with me speaking to the troops. Loudspeakers were set up before all the assembled men. I had a large map and a pointer stick. I showed the men the Russian front, described some of the important victories, talked about the number of Germans killed, and explained how their efforts had contributed to the success of the Russian battles. I discussed how much tonnage they had unloaded and shipped by rail and truck, the major accomplishment of their work.

Then I slipped in something that hadn't been planned. "Now, I have just talked to General Connolly, and he said that the outfit with the best record over here would get to go home first when the war was over."

Of course, that was an outright lie. But I called the General up in front of the men to confirm it, putting him on the spot so he would agree to it.

That night, Major Stevens and I ate our meal together. "I have seen some things pulled on generals before," he commented, "but that was a smooth one you pulled on General Connolly today."

Stevens also told me that he would like to make a movie about my life. "But," he added, "there is only one man who can play the part of Jerry Sadler, and that's Spencer Tracy."

I thought for a moment. "I don't get the connection," I said.

He tried to explain that it was in the way I handled the men and the Generals, but I still couldn't see it.

The visit that was the biggest pain was that of a U.S. Senate Committee, which came to investigate British charges that we were not cooperating with them sufficiently. The charges were ridiculous; we were supplying them with everything they needed on an equal basis with the Russians and our own troops. Their complaints were nothing more than a sour grapes attitude stemming from the fact the British were no longer the top dog they had been before our troops arrived in Iran.

It certainly did not warrant a Senate investigation, but they sent a committee consisting of Senator Happy Chandler of Kentucky, Senator Few Brewster of Maine, with Senator Henry Cabot Lodge of Massachussetts as chairman. The hearings were to take place in Basra, Iraq, and General Connolly asked me to attend, since most of the British complaints were directed against the services under my command.

The committee heard the complaints of the British officers first. They complained that our supply services were run in a dictatorial fashion. They said we weren't letting them have everything they wanted. And they charged that other troops—American and Russian—always got their supplies before the British did. They talked at great length, taking up most of the day.

Then the committee heard from some of the American officers, none of whom wanted to say anything negative about the British. I was called on at the very end, and by that time I was angry enough to lay into the British full force.

I told the committee, "I've listened to this nonsense all day, and that's all it is—nonsense. They've complained about not getting everything they want. If we have what they ask for, they've gotten it. They are concerned about whether or not they get supplies before the Russians. They keep whining about being first. If they ask for it first, they get it first. We aren't giving anybody precedence over anybody else, and that's really what they're upset about. They want us to let them run the show, which means running roughshod over everybody else, and we're not going to do that. The fact remains that we're feeding them, we're taking care of them, and they don't like being in that position."

At the conclusion of the hearing, the committee offered no decision on their findings, but they told me privately that they could see no problem with the services command. In fact, they were very impressed with what they had witnessed of our operations. Although the workings of Khorramshahr were no secret to German intelligence, the people and the Congress of the United States were kept in the dark about the activities in the Persian Gulf.

From Basra, the committee went on to India, flying out from Abadan Island, which had the largest airfield in the area. On the drive to the airfield, Senator Chandler asked if there happened to be a soldier from Kentucky buried anywhere around there.

I thought for a moment, and then said, "If you'll settle for Paducah, Kentucky, I can take you to a soldier's grave."

He was pleased. He thought it would be good public relations for the folks back home to have his picture taken at the graveside of one of Kentucky's finest sons.

After the photograph was taken, I pulled Senator Lodge aside. "There's one thing that Senator Chandler doesn't know about this soldier," I said. "The soldier is one of Kentucky's finest, but he's a negro."

Senator Lodge started laughing, and promised to wait until their plane landed at Bombay before telling Chandler.

General Charles De Gaulle was a VIP, but he wasn't treated like one when he came to Iran. It was on Christmas Day when I met him. I had taken my 380th Battalion football team to Teheran to play against the Headquarters team.

In my Jeep, accompanied by the commandant of Teheran, we drove along a wide boulevard. We saw what looked like a riot in front of a large house set back a good distance from the boulevard. As we passed, I tried to see what was happening, but all I could make out was that there were a lot of very angry Iranians, and that some of them had managed to get inside the house.

The commandant was driving, and I asked him to turn around and go back. We pulled our guns and worked our way through the crowd to the house. The rioters had their hands on a very tall man wearing the uniform of a French general, and they were yelling and roughing him up. In a moment I realized the man was General Charles De Gaulle.

At that time, De Gaulle was commander of the free French forces, but that meant that he was in effect a refugee, an exile. The word had been passed around a day or two before that he was in Iran, trying to obtain passage to Moscow. There was also an unofficial order that he was not to be accorded a place to stay at any U.S. installation.

With our guns drawn, the commandant and I managed to get De Gaulle through the crowd of angry Iranians to our Jeep. There wasn't a lot of room in the back seat of that Jeep, and De Gaulle was an extremely tall man. The only way he was able to ride was to stick his legs around the sides of the front seat.

We didn't know what to do with the General. It was close to game time, so we decided to take him with us to the football game.

The stadium in Teheran was enormous. It had been built at great expense by the Shah's father in hopes of attracting the Olympic Games to his country. There was a large crowd for this game, with cheerleaders and bands. It was the custom of the commanding general to sit with the fans of one team on their side of the field for half the game, and then to sit on the other side for the other half.

General Connolly sat with the Teheran team's side for the first half. He had a box, and Ambassador Averill Harriman was his guest. I took General De Gaulle up to that box to join them. I don't recall seeing such silent anger in General Connolly's eyes before. And Harriman—in my opinion not the smartest diplomat in the world (that's putting it kindly)—was like a block of ice. I had placed them in a difficult position. They did not want De Gaulle to sit with them, but they could not blatantly throw him out of their box. So he stayed, but virtually nothing was said to him.

At halftime I had to escort General Connolly across the field to our team's side of the stadium. As we crossed, the General asked, "Why the hell did you bring that man here this afternoon?"

"De Gaulle may be a man without a country," I said, "but when it comes down to it, we're still on the same side in this war. You can look at his clothes and tell he hasn't had a bed to sleep in for awhile. If you can't give him a place to stay out of common courtesy, you might think about our relations with the French after this war is over."

I was unable to persuade Connolly to take the French General back to the Country Club for the night, but I did convince him to permit the Commandant to give him a bunk in Billet 8, which was less prestigious but at least comfortable.

The next morning, De Gaulle boarded a Russian plane and flew to Moscow.

After the war, when De Gaulle came to power in France, I could never blame him for disliking the United States and treating our leaders coolly.

Most historians rate Averill Harriman rather highly as an ambassador. However, from the few times I witnessed him at work, my judgment is that he has been greatly overrated. His treatment of De Gaulle was a minor matter compared to his performance at the Teheran Conference in November and December of 1943.

In November, the biggest VIPs in the world all converged on the Middle East, coming to Cairo and to Teheran for important conferences on the resolution of the war. Franklin Roosevelt, Winston Churchill, Joseph Stalin, Chiang Kai Shek, and numerous other diplomats were involved at one or both meetings. At President Roosevelt's request, I was invited to attend the conferences.

The Cairo conference was first, involving principally Roosevelt, Churchill, and Chiang Kai Shek; its objective was to settle the resolution of the war in Asia and the Pacific. I arrived in Cairo a few days before the conference was to begin, and I spent some time with Patrick J. Hurley, who was serving as a roving ambassador for Roosevelt, and who had come to Cairo accompanying Madame Chiang Kai Shek. (He was to take her from there to the United States for medical treatment.)

I was with Hurley and General Royce, when Hurley received a coded message from Secretary of War Stimson, informing him that Roosevelt had been persuaded to appoint Hurley as Ambassador to Russia, a crucial job at this stage of the war.

"It won't happen," Hurley told us. "As soon as Mrs. Cordell Hull finds out about this, she'll see that someone else gets the post." He explained that Mrs. Hull was running the Department of State, because her husband had become senile, and she had an intense dislike for Hurley. (As I saw soon after the Hulls arrived, he was right about the Secretary of State. Hull started making a speech at the airport, and he was so incoherent that Mrs. Hull had to take over and get him to sit down.)

Pat Hurley felt sure he knew who Mrs. Hull would want in the post—Averill Harriman. General Royce and I agreed that would be disastrous for U.S. relations with the Soviet Union, and we decided to try to get to Roosevelt before Mrs. Hull found out about the President's intentions and changed his mind.

However, our plan was thwarted by bad weather. Roosevelt's

arrival in Cairo was delayed by a day; and in that 24 hours, Mrs. Hull learned of the planned appointment. By the time they arrived, the decision had been made to appoint Averill Harriman.

As it turned out, I was in no condition for a serious conference with Roosevelt anyway. The night before, I attended a party at the Shepherd Hotel in Cairo. The guests were mostly Americans, and some of them got a little rowdy. There was a lot of drinking and a lot of yelling from the balcony.

At the peak of the party, there was a loud knocking at the door. I went to the door, and opened it to face a rather angry British captain, who informed me that he was in charge of British security. He demanded that we cut out the noise: it was disturbing the British so that they couldn't sleep.

His manner was surly, and my response was the same. "Well," I answered, "the British have been keeping us awake ever since we got into this war, so I guess it won't hurt them to lose a little sleep. If you're going to try to shut us up, you'll have to get someone with more rank." And I slammed the door in his face.

A short while later, I went out and joined the noisemakers on the balcony. I hadn't been out there long when a man stuck his head out of a window about two floors above, and yelled in a distinctly British voice, "Cut out that fuss down there!" There was no way of recognizing the man who was yelling.

I yelled back, "You Limey bastards, shut up and go back to bed! You're spoiling our party!"

That was the last of the complaints.

The next morning I was supposed to have breakfast with Hurley and former Governor Lehman of New York, but I was a little slow waking up, so I arrived late at the hotel dining room. There, the two men had funny little grins on their faces.

Ambassador Hurley asked, "Are you feeling bad this morning?"

"Well, I don't feel too good," I replied, "but it's not like your problem. It's not my prostate."

"Oh, I'm feeling much better this morning," he said. "I went to see a doctor last night and had my prostate looked after. What I mean is, are you in trouble?"

"Why should I be in trouble?" I asked.

Ambassador Hurley laughed. "That 'Limey' you cussed out last night on the balcony," he said, "was General Montgomery, and he's

Franklin Roosevelt arriving for the Teheran Conference in 1943.

With "King," the specially trained dog from King Farouk's kennels, a gift from a member of the King's staff.

A press photo taken of unshaven Jerry Sadler at La Guardia airport, shortly after arriving back in the United States from Iran.

fighting mad this morning. He's been storming around the hotel trying to find out who it was."

I groaned. "Does he know yet?" I asked.

"I don't know," the Ambassador replied, "but when he finds out and tries to get you court-martialed, I'll be your defense lawyer."

Montgomery did find out, but he cooled down, and nothing more was said about the incident.

I had to be at the airport that morning for the welcoming ceremonies for President Roosevelt, and all this wasn't an auspicious start for the day.

When I saw Roosevelt, I was shocked by his appearance. The strain of the war had taken its toll on him, and it was clear that he was in poor health. We did speak, but not at any length; he had to use his spare moments to rest, devoting all his energy to the strenuous meetings with other heads of state.

The most important meetings were at Teheran, where the plans were made for the invasion of Germany. General Dwight Eisenhower was made Supreme Commander of the Allied Forces, and Roosevelt wanted him to lead the army that would take Berlin. Stalin wanted that privilege for the Russians, but I had the impression early in the conference that he did not intend to stand firm on that issue.

No one can deny that Stalin and Molotov were tough and determined men, but they reminded me a bit of some Texans I've known. They're only tough toward people they don't like, and they don't like anybody until they become drinking buddies. They liked Franklin Roosevelt well enough, but they sensed that he didn't have much longer to live, and they did not like Averill Harriman.

In one late-night meeting, the Russians were warming up to the U.S. delegation. It was a long meeting, in which we toasted everything from Stalin's eyebrows to the buttons on Roosevelt's coat, and it began to appear that Stalin was very near giving in on his demand that Eisenhower's invasion force stop to permit the Russians to take Berlin.

Suddenly, at the stroke of midnight, Averill Harriman rose from the table and announced that he was going to bed. Then he turned and walked toward the door. Stalin was clearly furious, and Molotov looked grim.

Before Harriman reached the door, Stalin bellowed out a demand that the Ambassador stay until the matter concluded.

Politely but firmly, Harriman informed the Premier that midnight was his bedtime, and he never altered it for any reason. And he left the room, followed by his aide.

I caught up with his aide in the hallway outside. I pleaded with him to get Harriman to change his mind. From my experience with Russians, I felt certain that Stalin had taken this as a personal affront and that he would now become intractable. Harriman's aide tried to get the Ambassador to come back, but without success.

It was a major setback. The friendliness that had begun to develop was over. Stalin now stood firm in his demands, and the eventual partition of Germany became inevitable.

After the Teheran Conference, it was arranged that I would have thirty-days leave to return to the United States. The reason given publicly was that I was to appear on the Army Hour Radio show, and I did make that appearance with Eleanor Roosevelt. (We didn't have the opportunity to visit and speak, only to wave to each other from our glass-enclosed booths.) However, the main reason for my leave was that Roosevelt wanted me to come to Washington to confer with him under less pressing circumstances.

For at least a few of the thirty-days, I was able to rest and relax at home in Texas, seeing my wife and mother. We spent Christmas Day, 1943, at my mother's home in Anderson County, a wonderful contrast to the year I had spent in Iran, quiet and peaceful.

However, on Christmas Day, the peace and quiet was interrupted. There was a knock on the door, and my mother answered to find Orme Lively, who was from the town of Elkhart. He told her that Secretary of War Stimson was trying to reach me by telephone. There were no rural phone lines to the area where my mother lived, so Stimson had called the telephone office in Elkhart, asking me to call him back.

I called, and he wanted me to come to Washington to vvdiscuss the railroad strike.

I had a hard time getting to Washington; weather was terrible, with sleet and freezing rain. No planes were flying out of Love Field in Dallas. After waiting a long time, I managed to get the first plane to fly out of Dallas in several days. It took me to Omaha, Nebraska. From Omaha, I hopped a flight to Chicago, and from there, to Washington. The weather over most of the country was bad.

When I finally arrived in Washington, I went straight to the Secretary of War's office. His secretary told me that Stimson had not been to bed for four days; he had been in the office worrying over the problem of the nation's railroad strike. She informed Stimson I had arrived, and I was ushered in immediately. Present in Stimson's office was his legal advisor, Luke Finley.

I had never seen a man looking more worried and haggard than Stimson did at that moment. He was desperate. Travel and shipping in the United States had come to a grinding halt, a difficult situation at any time, but a critical situation in war. Neither the unions nor the management could be pressured into making the concessions necesssary to resolve the problem.

"Because of your experience on the Railroad Commission and your experience in moving supplies overseas," Stimson told me, "I thought maybe you could think of some solution that hasn't occurred to us."

"Well," I said, "there's one easy solution, but I don't know if it's one you'd want to use. You are Secretary of War. You have the authority to conscript the presidents of all the railroads and appoint them officers in the army. Then they and the railroads would be operating under your orders and those of the President."

He liked the idea, but had to talk to Finley about it, to make sure it would not be termed unconstitutional. Finley saw no conflict with the law, and they decided to try it. They drafted and appointed every railroad company's president an army colonel. Some of the presidents were already in Washington; the rest of them were contacted and ordered to report to Washington immediately.

I was present when they gathered the railroad presidents in the Pentagon and informed them of their conscription. They brought in uniforms from the Army store at the Pentagon and had them change on the spot. That was one of the funniest sights I think I've ever seen. Some of the presidents were so fat they couldn't fit even the largest of uniforms. One in particular was very upset about the situation, not that he objected to serving his country, but he didn't like having to take orders from anyone. He was scowling, and he couldn't get his shirt and coat buttoned, and I made the comment, "You look just like Sitting Bull."

The other presidents started kidding him about it, and finally he found his good humor and began to laugh as well.

The ploy worked. The railroads were placed back into operation, and the shipment of goods resumed.

On one of my trips through the airport at Cairo, I was approached by a British general who said he understood I was on my way to

Khartoum. He asked whether I intended to fly the northern or southern route."

"Why would that be any of your business?" I asked.

The general ignored my rudeness. "I've checked up on your flight," he said, "and I've learned that you are the ranking officer, and under your American system the ranking officer is in charge. I want to ask you a favor. That young lady over there needs a lift to Khartoum."

He pointed out a beautiful young woman who looked exactly like Myrna Loy, and who was wearing a British Red Cross uniform.

"She is Lord Mountbatten's daughter," the general continued. "And she is trying to get to New Delhi to her mother and father. We have a plane to fly her there from Khartoum, but we don't want to send her to Khartoum on one of ours. We've just had two of our planes shot down over the northern route this morning."

"I can't spend my time looking after her," I said. "Will she have an attendant?"

He assured me, "A lieutenant (which he pronounced "leftenant") will accompany her."

I agreed to take her to Khartoum, but I left her and her attendant to themselves, just keeping an eye on her to make sure that none of the men on the plane molested her. After we had been out about six or seven hours, she called me over to speak to her.

"I've been told that you know my father," she said.

"Yes," I said, "I've met your father."

We settled into a very friendly conversation.

There were bad sandstorms, and we were thrown way off schedule. After a while it occurred to me that she might need to relieve herself. I was a little embarrassed about it, but I asked if she needed a rest room.

"What do you mean by 'rest room'?" she asked.

I tried various way of explaining, and could not surmount the language barrier. Finally I said outright, "I thought you might need to relieve your kidneys."

She laughed.

I explained that we did not have a rest room on the plane, but that we did have a set-up behind a curtain where the men relieved themselves. It was set up for males, but we might be able to adjust it somehow.

She thanked me and said she thought she could manage until we arrived at Khartoum.

We finally landed to a huge reception. I thought all of the British brass in North Africa had collected to welcome Lord Mountbatten's daughter. They had worried because we were so late. Fearing we had crashed or been shot down, they had organized search parties.

She thanked me for helping her and invited me to visit her and her family if I should ever come through New Delhi.

Later, I did happen to pass through New Delhi when I returned from delivering a battalion to General Joseph Stillwell to aid his building of the Lido road. I decided to see if her invitation had been a serious one, so I called Lord Mountbatten's headquarters. He wasn't in, but I left my name and the name of the place where I was staying.

Within a half-hour, a limousine arrived to pick me up to take me to Mountbatten's residence. There were several war correspondents standing around the hotel lobby, some of whom I had talked to briefly right after my arrival. As I was getting into the limousine they rushed over to ask questions. They recognized Mountbatten's limousine, and wanted to know why it had been sent for me. Why was I going to see Mountbatten?

"It's top secret," I told them.

I had an enjoyable, and purely social, visit with Lord and Lady Mountbatten and their daughter. There is one thing about the British; they never let anything, even war, interfere with their social hours. They very graciously invited me to stay to dinner, and I was deeply honored.

Lord Mountbatten was one of the most sincere and one of the most brilliant men I have ever met in my life. His mind was far above Winston Churchill's or any of the British leaders I had met. That night at dinner he came closer to mentioning the fire in the English Channel than anyone had ever done. He hinted at it, telling me that Axis Sally had broadcast my arrival at Khorrmashahr, because the Germans hated me for what I had done to them.

27

War's End

The war in Europe drew to its end, and it was clear the Allies would have victory. Ranking officers became less concerned with getting the job done and paid more attention to petty details and jockeying for promotions.

Politics among the officers had become a problem by the time I went home on leave in December, 1943. While on that leave, at the Pentagon I learned there were to be some changes in the Persian Gulf command. A major change was that General Stanley Scott, who was chief of staff for General Connolly, would be returned to Washington to be chief of planning.

General Scott, one of the best officers in the Persian Gulf, would be granted another star on his collar. I would miss him. He was one of the few officers with a good sense of humor; and his duties came before his ambitions.

I recall an occasion when General Scott decided to inspect the barracks at Khorramshahr, using us as an example for other battalions. Prior to bringing officers, he came alone for a preliminary inspection.

Before a high-ranking officer entered the barracks, I would always step in first and announce, "Attention!" I did this for General Scott on that inspection. The barracks was ready for him. The men stood at attention, and everything was orderly. As he was walking through one barracks, however, the one for the 111th Engineers, a soldier came toward us from the showers, drying his head with a towel.

It didn't disturb General Scott, but after he had moved on, I spoke to the soldier. "No matter what you're doing, when you see someone with stars on, you stand at attention."

A week later we were scheduled for the big inspection. General Scott came back, bringing with him General Somerville and eight or ten brigadiers and major-generals. Now, General Somerville was one of those I definitely did not like or respect. First we went to the barracks of the black troops, and General Somerville was being arrogant and military, picking at the slightest thing that didn't match his own approach. (As an example of his nature, he never let troops stand at ease in his presence; they had to be at attention.) In the black barracks, Somerville walked over and picked up a soldier's shoe and inspected it. "Don't you ever use dubbin on your shoes?" he snapped at the soldier.

"Dubbin?" the man asked. "What's that?"

Somerville turned to me and asked, "Who told them not to use dubbin on their shoes?"

"I did, sir," I told him. "I know you ordered it, but it ruins the shoes, and I've given them something else."

Finally we got to the barracks of the 111th Engineers, where we had come across the man returning from the showers. Again, walking through the barracks, darned if this same man didn't come out of the showers, drying his hair with a towel. Suddenly he saw the generals, stopped in his tracks, and turned pale. "Stars! Stars!" He turned and ran back to the showers.

I could see that there was a slight twinkle in General Scott's eyes, but General Somerville looked at me sternly and asked, "What's wrong with that man?"

"Oh it's just that he's from Texas, sir," I said, "and he's getting homesick."

I returned to Iran from Washington, now concerned about General Scott's replacement. I knew that General Osborne, the District Commander at Ahwaz, would be bucking for the job, but I hoped he wouldn't get it. In my estimation, General Ted Osborne was worse than General Somerville. He was after General Connolly's job, and he didn't care who he had to step on to get it.

Right after I arrived I heard that General Scott had been taken to the hospital in Teheran for an emergency appendectomy. I went up to see him. I could cheer him with the news I had picked up in Washington, that he was to be named chief of planning at the Pentagon. He was very pleased.

The news spread around the Persian Gulf Command fairly quickly, and as I had expected, General Osborne started maneuvering to become Scott's replacement.

I decided to do something to prevent his getting it. I went to Teheran with Major Swank one day and we took General Connolly to Billet 8 for a few drinks. A number of officers were there that night, pouring them down. One by one, we put the other officers to bed until only Swank, General Connolly, and I were left. We had General Connolly feeling pretty good, as we walked him out to his car, and we brought up the subject of who was to be made his chief of staff.

I told him that I knew he was considering giving the job to General Osborne, and Osborne was bucking for it. "But," I said, "General Osborne isn't going to be satisfied to stop there. He's going to be trying to get something on you so he can get your job. You won't be able to trust him at all, because if he gets a chance he'll double-cross you."

"Well," he said, "who do you think it should be?"

"General Boothe," I told him.

He said nothing, but got into his car. Swank and I exchanged glances and got in the car with him. I knew that General Connolly would remember every word of our conversation the next day. He was the only man I've ever met who could do that, no matter how much he had to drink.

On the way to the Country Club, the silence was long. We had almost arrived when General Connolly spoke. "I've been thinking about what you said, and I think maybe you're right," he said.

It was about 2:30 in the morning when I got to the Green Room, where I was to sleep. I had just started taking off my clothes, when someone knocked at my door. It was General Boothe, and he wanted to know what had happened. He didn't know that he had been the subject of conversation; he was just concerned about General Connolly, and he wanted to make sure his superior was not in any trouble.

"Did anything happen?" he asked.

"No," I said coolly. "Just that General Connolly has decided to make you chief of staff."

Boothe wouldn't believe me until General Connolly told him directly.

As soon as I had gotten back to Khorramshahr, while I was signing the logbook officially "in," General Osborne came driving up and jumped out of his car. I could see him eagerly running inside to meet me.

"Well," he said hopefully, "how's everything in Teheran?"

"It was all right," I said.

"Was there any word on who is to be made chief of staff?" he asked.

"Oh, yes," I said, as if it had slipped my mind. "General Connolly is going to appoint General Boothe."

I think Osborne realized the moment I said it that I had something to do with the decision. Without saying another word, he turned like a bullet and dashed out of there. From that moment on, he did every dirty thing he could think of to get at me. On one occasion, I decided he had gone too far.

We had an area where we stored aviation fuel in twenty-gallon drums, awaiting shipment to the Russians. The area was fenced off with barbed wire. No smoking was allowed inside the fenced-off area, but I allowed the men to take breaks to go outside the fence to smoke and rest.

One day General Osborne came driving up in his big Packard. A private from the 380th Battalion, stood outside the fence smoking a cigarette, but his back was turned and he did not see Osborne drive up.

Osborne could not help knowing the private was one of my men, since he was black. He leaped out of his car, rushed over, grabbed the private and started shaking him, yelling, "By God, boy, when you see me, you get up and salute me!" he yelled. "I'm the toughest officer in the U.S. Army, and I'll whip the hell out of you if you don't!"

I was furious when I found out about the incident twenty minutes later. I didn't care what Osborne tried to do to me, but when he started picking on my men, he was going too far. I went around the base asking where Osborne was, and someone told me he was in the officer's club.

The Khorramshahr officer's club was a nice place, with an antique-looking western style bar with a brass railing, and a dance floor with two-by-fours turned edgewise, planed, and heavily polished and waxed. The enlisted men used to say: "Buy War Bonds to buy two-by-fours for the officers dance floors."

I stormed into the officer's club with my gun drawn and told Osborne that he was under arrest for assaulting an enlisted man.

He was leaning against the bar at the far end. He said I wouldn't tell him that if he had a gun.

"I happen to have an extra gun," I said, pulling it out. I slid it down the bar toward him.

Osborne just looked at the gun; he didn't pick it up. "You want to kill me, don't you?"

"Not unless I have to," I said. "Right now, I just want to put you under arrest and take you up to see General Connolly tomorrow."

He went along peacefully, and the next morning we took a plane to Teheran. General Connolly found the situation somewhat embarrassing. He asked me to leave his office so that he could talk to Osborne privately. About half and hour later, he called me back in. "We've decided to send General Osborne back to the States. You leave this matter in my hands." Connolly told me I'd better return to Khorramshahr. "I've just had a message that all sorts of rumors are spreading, and your battalion thinks something has happened to you. They're liable to mutiny if you don't show your face pretty quick. You can take my airplane to get there."

I was still hopping mad; I wanted Osborne court-martialed, but I knew that was not possible. Having him transferred to the States to a desk job was the most I could hope for. So I left the matter at that.

When, in the spring of 1945, the war in Europe was over, our troops at Khorramshahr had very little left to do. We had stockpiled far more supplies than the Russians could use. There were stockpiles in Russia and stockpiles at Khorramshahr. There was no reason to keep so many men idle; most could have been shipped home or reassigned to duty in the Pacific, where war continued.

To keep up morale, I had made promises to the men that their good and efficient work would be rewarded with early return home. Now they began to wonder why those promises were not being kept.

I wondered as well, and I decided to do some investigating. I found that the Persian Gulf Command had an excess of $52 million in its budget—all that money to spend and nothing to spend it on. They also had room in the T.O & E (the Table of Organization and Equipment) to make five more brigadier-generals and more colonels. General Somerville and some of his West Point friends were stalling for time to push through a few more promotions, and to use up some of the excess funds.

Six months passed, the troops had virtually nothing to do; and with each passing day, I sensed their morale getting lower. There was no way I could send a message to the Pentagon explaining the situation; it would not get through command headquarters.

I decided to go AWOL.

I rigged up a briefcase sealed with a State Department wax stamp on it (faked), so that in case I was stopped, I could say I was a special courier to Washington on a top-secret mission. All I had in the briefcase was old newspapers, but it looked good. I didn't know if I would ever be able to return to Iran, and I wanted to make sure I got my dog home. The dog, which I named "King," had come from King Farouk's ' kennels. It had been given to me by Farouk's trainer, and it had been trained to respond only to me. I arranged for the dog to be shipped home on a Liberty Ship, and I explained the nature of the dog to one of the men on board who was a dog-lover, asking him to take care of it and not to let it out of its crate, because it might be dangerous.

I then caught a plane out of Abadan to Cairo. There I got in touch with General Bob Smith, formerly president of American Airlines, who was in charge of the Air Transport Command. He arranged for a pilot to fly me to Tripoli. Over Tripoli we were fired on by the British, and were ordered to land. (They had not been notified of our unscheduled flight.)

We landed and got off the plane, and were immediately surrounded by British troops.

"I want to see your commanding general," I ordered the officer in charge. "I am a United States officer, and I am on a special mission." I showed him my briefcase.

It took some convincing, but the officer took me to the General, who was also suspicious. I pulled out the Meerschaum pipe that Churchill had given me, again explaining that I was on a special mission. "What in the hell were your men doing firing at us?" I demanded.

"Those were tracer bullets," the General said. "You were not supposed to be flying over this territory."

I cursed him out, threatening to complain all the way to Churchill. It worked. He let us proceed.

The trip continued to be eventful all the way home. In Casablanca, I was arrested, but I bluffed my way out of it again. After leaving the Azores, we were supposed to land in Florida, but there was a storm, and we were detoured first to Newfoundland and then to Presque Isle, Maine, where we were finally allowed to land. From there I managed to fly in to La Guardia airport in New York, and reported to Totten Field for processing. That proved more difficult than I had expected, but I had bluffed my way from Abadan to New York, and I figured I could keep on bluffing.

I was told I could not be given a billet for the night, so I asked directions to the officers quarters. I went there, wandered around the big, elegant mansion until I found a room on the second floor that was empty. I took squatter's rights, leaving my gear there while I went down to the officer's mess to get something to eat.

The first thing I got was cold stares. I knew I looked disreputable, but I didn't care. I had been traveling for days, and I was hungry and tired. An officer got up and approached me. "Major, no one is allowed in the officer's mess without a Class A uniform on," he said. "I'm afraid you'll have to leave and change."

"Like hell I will," I replied. "I've just gotten home from a war, and the welcome I get is 'You'll have to change clothes!' "

I could see that all of the men in the room were staring at my medals, trying to figure out the big gaudy Russian one. I refused to leave, and they refused to serve me, so they called in the chaplain, and he gave it a try. He made sympathetic sounds, but insisted that there was a dress code in the officers mess, and it had to be obeyed by everyone.

"Chaplain," I said. "This is Sunday night. Don't you think you ought to be in church conducting services, not in this saloon."

When I finally realized I would get nothing to eat, I went back to the room I had picked out, lay down on the bed, and went to sleep. The next morning I got up very early, well before the other officers were awake. I cleaned up and dressed, and then I made the rounds of all of the rooms, knocking on every door and commanding loudly, "I want to see every one of you downstairs in five minutes."

The officers had no idea who was waking them up and issuing such orders, but they obeyed. In five minutes there were a great many fat, flabby bellies lined up downstairs in nightshirts and half-assembled uniforms, looking bewildered. I launched into a tirade about men who sat out the war at home, making up ridiculous dress codes while other men fought. I cussed them up one side and down the other, and then I marched into the mess and ordered a big breakfast.

After I finished eating, I went to see a lieutenant who would take care of the paperwork that would permit me to leave the base. "I'm sorry," he said, "but you'll have to stay until Wednesday. Our mimeograph machine doesn't work, but we expect a repairman tomorrow. I can't cut you orders until it's fixed."

I exploded again. "I have seen plenty of typewriters around here!" I yelled. "If the mimeograph machine won't work 'till Wednesday, I'm sure you can make one of the typewriters work today!"

Finally, with effort, I got the orders cut, and after several detours— New York City and home to Austin—I arrived in Washington and went over to Arlington to the Pentagon. There, I marched straight to General George C. Marshall's office. Outside his office, I was intercepted by a WAAC captain, with a polite, "May I help you?"

"I'd like to see General Marshall," I said.

"Do you have an appointment?" she asked.

"No," I said. "Do I need one?"

"Do you know General Marshall?" she asked. "Is he a friend of yours?"

I figured this could go on forever, so I decided to give her a run for her money. "Of course he's my friend," I said. "According to what I've read in the *Stars and Stripes* and newspapers all over the world, he's the friend of every serviceman."

The WAAC captain decided I was crazy, and was beginning to suspect she would need help to get rid of me, so she called out a brigadier-general. I went through the same routine with him. While I was giving him a hard time, General Marshall stepped out of his office and recognized me.

"Jerry," he exclaimed, "what's the trouble?"

"They won't let me in to see you," I told him.

He laughed good-naturedly and escorted me into his office.

I told him the entire story of what was going on in the Persian Gulf Command. I told him of the excess of funds and the stalling for certain officers' promotions before demobilization.

General Marshall heard me out. "I want to get General Somerville in here," he said, and he instructed the WAAC captain to get him.

While we waited for Somerville, I told General Marshall that I had already worked out the plan and schedule in complete detail for returning the troops.

General Brandon B. Somerville was a typical Pentagon Fat-Cat. He headed supply services, and when the Pentagon building was constructed, all of the brick had been purchased from a company "owned" by his wife and the wife of one other general. He had been the one general who had been giving me and my "nigger troops" (as he called them) a hard time during our service in Iran.

When Somerville arrived in the office, General George Marshall told him that he had accepted my plan for returning the troops from the Persian Gulf. "Sadler has all of the details worked out, with the name of each ship and the number of troops to return in each," he said, handing him my report. "I want it to be carried out to the letter, and I want every one of those troops home within three months."

There was very little Somerville could say in the face of a command from Marshall. As he was leaving, Somerville stopped at the door and turned to me. "I'll take care of you later."

"General," I said, "I'm a shyster lawyer. I can take care of myself. And when we're through in court, we can count the bricks in the Pentagon."

After leaving General Marshall's office, I went by to see General Scott. He was very pleased to see me, and invited me to lunch with him in the general's dining room. I accepted his invitation, but said I wanted to drop in and see General Osborne first. General Scott, I think, understood, but he was the kind of man who would never interfere in another man's business.

Osborne's office turned out to be a little cubbyhole. When he saw me in his doorway, he acted as if I were a long lost friend. I exchanged a few words with him, and left to lunch with General Scott.

Scott and I were eating, and Osborne came over to us. He put his hand on my shoulder, and addressed the entire dining room loudly. "I want all you generals to listen. Right here is the best god-damned soldier that ever was in the United States Army."

General Scott had just taken a bite of food. Suddenly he guffawed, and food went all over his plate.

After Osborne walked away, General Scott said he, Osborne, was afraid I would check into his 201 file to see if a certain incident was recorded there.

"I'm not going to," I said. "I'm sure it's not there, but I don't mind letting him worry about it."

The troops came home, and I was there at Newport News, Virginia, to greet them. Every time one of those ships came in, I went out and climbed up a rope ladder to go aboard and welcome them.

I was still in command of the 380th Battalion, and I knew what was planned for us, though I could not tell them or talk to anyone about it. I had known for some time. I was looking forward to it because it meant we would be getting into the thick of the war in the Pacific. It had been one of the reasons I had been anxious to get my men home again, so they could have a rest before heading to the Far East.

I had been told about the plan while we were still in Iran. I was on orders to come to Teheran to meet with a Colonel Jones, sent to talk to me by General Joseph Stillwell (known to his men as "Vinegar Joe").

It was explained that Stillwell had returned to the United States to serve temporarily as chief of the ground forces. He would soon return to his duties in the East. "General Stillwell is planning a landing on the China coast. He would like to land his supplies along with the main force. To do that he would like to have your 380th Battalion."

Once we were stationed at Hampton Roads Port of Embarkation, Newport News, I was furnished with the plans and a map of the area of China intended for the landing. Okinawa would be the jumping off place for the massive force. About ten days later, the planes arrived at Langley Field, Virginia, to take us to Okinawa.

Then, suddenly, I began getting a series of coded messages from General Stillwell, delaying our departure. One arrived every few days. Finally, in early August, I received a coded message telling me the mission was cancelled. Two days later Japan surrendered.

It was cause for celebration. The war was over. No people had more reason to celebrate than the enlisted men, those who had given years of their lives (who had not given life itself). As long as the war was going on, the civilian population tolerated the enlisted men, but now that the soldiers were no longer wanted, the civilians dropped their tolerance.

The day the Japanese surrendered, I received a delegation of civilian authorities from Newport News and Norfolk, who asked that all the men be confined to base that night. They told me that, at the end of World War I, there had been trouble, and they did not want it repeated. Their manner annoyed me, but I agreed to keep the men on base.

I got together with the Admiral of the Navy there, and we planned about ten dances on the base, so that all of the men would have something to do. There would be WACS and nurses there, and we issued passes to the girl-friends of men who were dating locally.

We had our military police patrolling the streets of Newport News and Norfolk, and all was peaceful there and on the base. All of the men had a good time and were able to celebrate.

President Roosevelt had not lived until the day of celebration. A month before the war in Europe had ended, May, 1945, he had died, and his Vice President assumed his office. Roosevelt's powerful mind, his shrewdness in dealing with foreign heads of state, and his diplomacy would be sorely missed. Harry Truman was a brash, loudmouthed lightweight by comparison. The interests of the United States were to suffer somewhat by his involvement in international affairs.

When Harry Truman was selected in 1944 as Roosevelt's running mate for his fourth term, my Russian friends in Iran were deeply concerned about relations between our countries. As a Senator, Harry Truman had viciously attacked the United States' alliance with Russia, and he had uttered some unnecessarily harsh phrases to describe Joseph Stalin.

Russian officers had told me Stalin had clipped articles from newspapers quoting Truman. And—after Truman's election to the vice-presidency—had begun carrying the articles in his hip pocket, waiting for the opportunity to use it against the United States.

In July of 1945, just before the war in the Pacific was to be over, President Truman came secretly to Newport News, on his way to meet with Churchill and Stalin at Potsdam. I was not friendly with Truman as I had been with Roosevelt, but I did have a good relationship with Jimmy Burns, Truman's Secretary of State.

Truman's special train slipped quietly into Newport News in the middle of the night, so that they could board the destroyer, which would take them to Potsdam, in the secrecy of the early morning hours. Before leaving Washington, Jimmy Burns had called me. He was upset because there would be no dining car on the train, and breakfast would not be served on the destroyer until eight in the morning. He wanted me to arrange for him to have some grits and eggs before he boarded the ship.

I met Burns at the train about 4:00 A.M., and I gave him a choice of two places to have breakfast. I told him he could eat in the mess hall with the men, but I warned him that he would be recognized. The other choice was a little beanery outside the gates. He still might be recognized, but it would be less likely. He chose the beanery.

Thinking the information might be of use at Potsdam, I told Burns what the Russians had told me concerning the newspaper clippings in Stalin's back-pocket. Burns agreed the information might be useful, but he wasn't sure Truman would be willing to accept its importance. The new President was single-minded in his attitude that the Russians were adversaries, not friends.

The atomic bomb was dropped on Hiroshima while the President was on the destroyer returning from Potsdam. When they arrived back at Newport News, Jimmy Burns told me some of what had taken place. Throughout the conference, Stalin had been rubbing his back-pocket as if he had an itch there. His attitude toward Truman was very cool. The Russians did agree to declare war on Japan, but from everything discussed at the conference, they would expect the kind of territorial advantages they had received in Europe.

Truman, in an adversary relationship with Stalin, was not happy about that prospect. Immediately after Russia declared war on Japan, Truman decided to drop the atomic bomb to end the war before the

Russians could become actively involved.

About a week after Truman got back to Washington, there was a detailed account of what Stalin had in his back-pocket at Potsdam. Obviously Jimmy Burns decided to leak the story to the press.

While at Newport News, I had one other indirect involvement with President Truman's White House. I received a phone call one day. "This is Senator Homer Ferguson in Washington," the voice at the other end said. "I'm Chairman of the subcommittee that's checking out Tom Clark before he's appointed Attorney General. Now I understand that there is a transcript of your testimony concerning Mr. Clark before a Texas Senate Committee some years ago."

As a lawyer, I was cautious about what I said over the telephone to a man I did not know personally. I replied, "I do know Mr. Clark, but I know nothing about any transcript. I'm afraid I can't help you."

"You do understand that you are talking to a United States Senator, don't you?" the voice said strongly.

"I understand that," I said even more strongly. "I also understand that I am a U.S. citizen, and I am a member of the U.S. armed forces, and you are supposed to go through the proper military channels before you call me up and start asking questions. I can make no comments to you until you get the approval of my superiors."

That ended the conversation for the moment. A little later, General Kilpatrick, the commanding general at Newport News, called me. "You sure must have told that senator from Michigan off," he said with humor. I allowed as how I might have done that, and Kilpatrick laughed. He told me I had official permission to answer the Senator's questions.

When Senator Ferguson called back, he apologized sincerely. "We have as job to do and sure would appreciate your cooperation. We don't want to see a man appointed to an important job like Attorney General if there's some reason he shouldn't have the job. Could our subcommittee come down there to talk to you?"

We made an appointment for ten o'clock the following morning. This meeting presented me with a dilemma. Tom Clark and I had not been on a friendly basis for some years, not since the car wreck, the wreck that had almost killed me. There were things about Clark that I did not like, but I wasn't sure whether those things should be allowed to prevent him from being made Attorney General. Back before the war, I would have raised hell and high water to keep him from the job. But war had mellowed my attitude a bit. I knew that there were other men who could just as easily be appointed to that job, who had done things much worse than what Clark had done.

I knew what Senator Ferguson's subcommittee was going to ask about. It involved the Pacific-Mutual case, the recorded conversations in Asa B. Call's office, and the involvement of Tom Clark and Bill Heath. As far as I knew, those old disc recordings had long since been destroyed. I decided to answer the senators' questions honestly, without expressing an opinion on Clark one way or the other. I would tell them the bare facts as I knew them.

Senator Ferguson was not satisfied. I had done nothing more than dump the dilemma into his lap. Frustrated, he asked finally, "What would you do if you were in our shoes? Would you recommend that the Senate not confirm the appointment?"

I thought for a moment, and then answered obliquely. "Well," I said, "I'll tell you a little story. Down at Hickory Grove, where I was raised, we had a fellow who used to steal cottonseed. Now that was about the lowest a man could get, since practically everybody threw away cottonseed back then. One night there was a revival meeting under a brush arbor, and this man walked down the aisle, joined the church, and has been a good citizen ever since. Now I don't know whether or not Tom Clark has ever walked down the aisle under a brush arbor, but I want you to think about the alternative. Considering that Harry Truman is making this appointment, if you don't approve Tom Clark, you might just get a Kansas City justice of the peace."

The Senate approved the Tom Clark appointment; and, after it was over, Clark called to thank me.

"What the hell are you calling to thank me for?" I asked. "I didn't make the appointment."

Tom giggled his silly sort of giggle. "I just want you to know I appreciate your rating me higher than a Kansas City justice of the peace."

Once the war was over and the troops were on their way back from the front, I was anxious to get back to civilian life. However, my duties at Newport News continued for some time. It was one of the main processing centers for landing returning troops and arranging for their transportation to home bases all over the country, and those arrangements became a part of my responsibility. The distribution center was a big one and, for the most part, an efficient one. Generally we were able to process the troops within 24 hours. My 380th Battalion did the processing, and after the other troops had come through, I signed the orders to ship them home as well.

Troops and officers were returned to civilian life on a point system, so many points for amount of duty, so many for overseas duty, and so many for combat. That way the men who had suffered the greatest hardship were the first to be released.

When it came time for me to return, the time when I felt I should be allowed to go home, I ran into some bureaucratic red tape over points.

When they reviewed my record, they announced, "You can't be released from active duty. As an officer, you don't have enough points."

Angrily I ripped off my Russian medal and threw it down on the desk. "How many points do I get for this?" I demanded, knowing that each decoration entitled a man to so many points.

They had to admit that they didn't know. They had never seen one of them, and it wasn't included on their list.

"This medal entitles me to more points than all the rest of the medals put together," I said. "Now, I have already signed discharges for all of my men. I have no more command, and I am going home whether you like it or not."

They approved my discharge.

Going back into civilian life, I was ready to take up where I had left off in Texas politics, but much had changed since I had joined the military. While the little guys had gone off to Europe and the Pacific to fight the war, the big guys—the Fat-Cats—had stayed home increasing their power and control over the political system. All of those things I had fought against before the war had become more extreme. For the sake of the war effort, the big financial interests of Wall Street had been favored, given controls that were more monopolistic than ever. Now they were going to resist returning to normal. I knew that once power is given, it is hard to take away.

The little guys returning home were going to have a hard time adjusting to the changes that had taken place, just as the homefolks were to find it difficult to accept the changes in their war heroes. And without a doubt, those of us who had been in the war had changed. It would be hard to describe those changes, but I could recognize some of them in myself.

One of them I have already mentioned. I would be more accepting of human faults and frailties, and I would accept inherent differences among people with more understanding. I was still a fighting man. All of us who had gone to war were fighting men, but we wanted a little rest from the fighting. We wanted a few of the rewards of winning the war—the joys of home and family and friends.

The most difficult part of returning home was to realize that regaining our position in civilian life was to be a fight in itself.

Epilogue
By Mrs. Laura Sadler

I came into Jerry's life fully after the war. We were married just six weeks before he went overseas, on September 4, 1942. While he was stationed in Iran for 27 months, I, a 22 year old bride of six weeks, waited for him to return to our home in Austin, Texas. Whether he has admitted it or not, Jerry did not *have* to join the Army. By that I mean, he would never had been drafted. He was not only past the age limit, but as his records stated, he had to also waive 'obesity' and 'insufficient natural teeth' to be accepted. He was so bad about putting things off concerning his health that he probably never would have had his teeth repaired if he had not wanted to join the Army so much.

At the time, he was also Railroad Commissioner of Texas, which was considered a war-related position, and thus he would have been deferred as long as he held his office. He had three years remaining of his elected term when he resigned to join the Army. In all probability he could have been reelected to this office for many more terms.

But this was not Jerry's way. He could not wait to get into the thick of things. He never looked back and was never sorry for the decision he made—although he was 'double-crossed' by then governor Coke Stevenson, who reneged on his promise to appoint the man Jerry had selected as his replacement on the Commission. This was a bitter disappointment to Jerry. He had hoped that a man appointed to take his place on the Railroad Commission would carry out the policies he had put in place. But this was not to be.

I have always thought that everyone who knew Jerry knew him in a different light and from a different angle, and no one ever really knew every facet. Certainly, he was a good many of the things written about him in the newspapers, to one degree or another. He was difficult, he was controversial, he was truthful to the point of being brutally frank. He was strong physically, mentally, and spiritually. I have never known anyone who could cut through to the core of a matter or a situation as

Jerry could. He never had trouble making decisions. Trouble? He gloried in it! And 99 percent of the time, his decisions were right and good.

He was, most of all, a maverick. He could never be classified as this or that or even the other. But he would stand hitched. Whatever he told you on Friday would not change on Monday. He didn't mind saying 'no,' and his 'no' stood him until it could be proven to him it should be 'yes'—and that took proving. If he thought he was right, you could not change him regardless of the consequences to himself, or to whomever.

It was my everlasting good fortune to know him as well as, if not better than, anyone. I knew him first, or course, as husband and then as father to our two sons, Bill and Sam. His joy in becoming a father for the first time at age 39 was indescribable. And then when Sam came along when he was 43, the joy and pride were no less diminished but even more enhanced. He loved to tell friends that he was going to make a lawyer out of one son and a witness out of the other. And although this was a little joke, I'm sure Jerry would have liked to choose the roles for his sons and guide them where *he* wanted them to go. He learned the hard way that both sons had inherited enough of his character to choose their own way. Nonetheless, he had enormous pride in both sons.

Jerry's mind absolutely astounded me. I don't think it was ever at rest. He was constantly coming up with some new idea, sometimes it was political, sometimes business, but most of the time an idea was just pure innovation. His diversity was amazing. His business ventures were about as unrelated as they could possibly be. And after he would get some new venture started and going along pretty well, he would become bored with it and would find some impelling reason to move on to something new. We owned a sawmill at one time. Jerry practiced law, and although he made money, he never really liked the way he had to practice his profession; and he didn't have much respect for very many of his cohorts. We moved on to ranching and farming. (He had to practice law hard to afford this vocation.)

By this time we had moved back to his boyhood home in Anderson County. Jerry had made a large fee in the Murray Sells will case, and this was all he needed to get right back into politics. He ran for the legislature from Anderson County, was handily elected three times, and thoroughly enjoyed the six year tenure. Jerry wished to keep our sons on our farm just as long as we could, and I agreed.

For this reason I remained on the farm with the boys, while Jerry went to Austin. For the next sixteen years, this became a way of life for us. We purchased an airplane so that we could commute more easily, and so that the boys and I could visit with Jerry in Austin. The boys were in school, and getting them back and forth was important. But most important was Jerry's being able to come home often to his beloved East Texas and his family for rest and recreation, away from the constant pressures of an elected public office.

All the while we were raising goats, pigs, cattle, quail, catfish, and boys.

In 1960, Jerry was elected Commissioner of the General Land Office of Texas. He was elected to this office five times, and we maintained the status quo—Jerry in Austin during the week, and the boys and I at home on the farm. I went to Austin quite often. My mother and Jerry's mother lived with us, and they were great 'boy'-sitters. My mother was the younger of the two, so most of the burden fell on her to keep things going while I was away, but she never complained and performed a wonderful service for us.

Jerry was the first to raise catfish commercially in Texas. Again, he managed to garner a lot of publicity for his project. Others picked it up, improved on his methods, and the industry was born. We had built a modern and, for Palestine, Texas, a luxurious motor hotel with several dining facilities, which was very much needed in Palestine at the time. We raised catfish, cattle for beef, and goats for cabrito on the farm, to be served in our restaurants.

Jerry was a master in keeping ahead of his boys with chores. I remember one time in particular when he decided that Bill and Sam should have a peanut crop. This was the main money crop in East Texas, and Jerry was determined that the boys understand what the farmers had to endure to get from land preparation to the marketing of their produce. One day, after the boys had worked their project for many weeks, they accompanied their father to the country store. One of the local farmers asked Bill how his peanut crop was coming along, and without hesitation, Bill drawled, "Well, we're not raising many peanuts, but we're building lots of character." Jerry gulped a time or two, and so ended the peanut project.

Another of Jerry's pursuits was windpower. He had talked about it and had done much thinking and research on his own for quite a long time. We had built a new home high on a hill, and one of the first things

Jerry did was to move his mother's windmill to its new site. Thus began his grand experiment. He enlisted the help of the son-in-law of a friend of ours, and together they put together a makeshift generator which was placed on the top of the windmill. I shall never forget the day the string of light bulbs lit up. He was ecstatic! He also knew that he had to go much further than a light bulb to accomplish what he had in mind.

Through another friend he was put in touch with the President of Honda for the United States, a Mr. Kanazawa, in San Francisco. They had many long telephone conversations concerning Jerry's needs in the way of a generator. The fruition of all this 'ground work' was that Mr. Kanazawa sent three very knowledgeable engineers from Honda to Hickory Grove. One engineer was from Taiwan, one from Korea, and one from Italy. They were all bright young men. They spent a day with us, talking all the while about the generator Jerry had in mind. We understood that shortly thereafter Honda did engineer this very generator, but no one ever contacted us about it. That was okay. Jerry had accomplished his purpose. He had stirred up enough interest in windpower for someone to produce a low cost generator, one that middle class and limited-income people might be able to afford, to help them gain relief from high utility bills.

These are only a few of the ideas that flowed through Jerry's unfathomable mind. He was a constant, non-stop, inveterate thinker.

At the age of 74, he paid his filing fee to run for Commissioner of the General Land Office of Texas one more time, and was putting together a campaign—on a shoestring. Feeling it was obscene, he did not believe in the huge coffers and the PAC money that most politicians scrambled for.

He died suddenly on February 25, 1982, at our home located about a quarter mile from his ancestral home in Southeast Anderson County, Texas.

I loved Jerry, I admired him, I listened to him, I respected his character and judgment, and I believed in him. He was the most intriguing, frustrating, caring, and brilliant man I ever knew. Some thought he was a genius. I did; and I knew him better than anyone. I'm sure about one thing—there'll never be another like him.

Index